A MISSISSIPPI RIVER EXPERIENCE

MIGHTY MISS

GARY HOFFMAN

ISBN 10: 1-4392-5267-X
ISBN 13: 978-1-4392-5267-3

Library of Congress Control Number: 2009907915
Printed in the United States of America
First Printing: 2009
13   12   11   10   09   5   4   3   2   1

Cover and interior design by Ryan Scheife, Mayfly Design
Whirlpool image on cover courtesy of Nandakuman Gopalakrishnan

Box 122
Chanhassen, MN 55317

To order additional copies visit www.mightymiss.com
Reseller discounts available.

TABLE OF CONTENTS

This book is dedicated to Jacqui, whose love and support made the trip and book a fulfillment of dreams never lost. And to my son Darrin, whose knowledge, perseverance, and leadership helped make this trip successful.

A special thanks to those who read and commented on different drafts. Their insight and honesty taught me much about writing: Rod Allen, Lydia Hurd, Mary Schumacker, Glen Skoy, Jack Streed, and many others

My deepest gratitude goes to Lisa Murphy, Cynthia Rogers, and Christy Theis for their many hours of dedicated editing and support.

PREFACE

Through *Mighty Miss,* experience the excitement of a marvelous river while recapturing childhood dreams in a true life adventure.

If other truth be known about this brush with death, and I told it wrong, that was unintentional.

CHAPTER 1

DECISIONS

"Wanna run it? It's got some rapids."

Nodding agreement, Darrin instinctively digs his paddle deep on the right. Quickly and silently our canoe responds, turning toward an opening in the wing dam, a dark-water "V" some forty feet off the left bank.

Within moments the strong current grabs and pulls the canoe into more turbulence than expected. Over the water's roar I shout, "This has gotta be our last. They're getting too unpredictable."

With ambivalent agreement, Darrin nods languidly. The heat has slowed not only our energy output but also our thinking. Perhaps exhilaration from a swift current will arouse us.

The Mississippi has been broad and lazy this afternoon, wallowing in ninety-some degree heat and humidity. Riding her shipping lane forces an extra half mile paddle at each bend. The wing dams are shortcuts. Made of quarried rocks, eight to ten inches in diameter, they hold a multitude of razor-sharp edges. Hitting them with a Kevlar canoe would be disastrous. As it is still early summer, water spills over most of these manmade diversions.

"Let's move left where there's a heavier flow!" I want the current hitting against the left bank before we push downriver. As we enter the "V," I see the water rushing over the dam, redirecting waters coming off the left bank. We should get a fantastic ride.

The thrust in the narrow gap is exhilarating, both pushing and pulling us toward a calm spot. This particular one is higher and larger than any we have yet encountered. Calm spots have the look and feel of those 1940s drinking fountains called "water-bubblers."

At a wind dam, however, the water-bubbler effect is a little different. Water rushing down the front of the dam hits the river bottom with such force it wells back up, boiling over at the river's surface. It is this boiling up-and-over that causes a seemingly placid, circular area. Normally these calm spots rise one to two inches above the surrounding waters.

Earlier a bubble burst just as we were leaving it. We now paddle a bit faster when moving over them. Once the canoe hits the bubble's center, there will be an extra outward push, a real rush. Our speed quickly propels us up and onto this bubble. The rise and speed is twice as high and fast as any we have yet experienced. Something new is happening—the bubble is moving left and taking us with it. My old body tingles with excitement. Today has been tedious.

Oomph!

The bubble has burst! The calm spot has changed. For a moment we hang in mid-air, but only for a second. Dropping hard, we are immediately sucked into a vortex.

"Oh, my God," I pray silently, "save us." The smooth bubble is now a whirlpool. In one fell swoop the entire canoe has dropped two feet into a swirling mass. It has taken less than a split second. We are listing toward the whirlpool's four-foot open eye; so close I can see into its bottomless and foreboding pit. The pull on the canoe is relentless. The bow is bending downward while the rest lies flat in the whirlpool. How much stress can it take?

The sucking power is tilting us. The whirling mass is pulling the canoe inward. My pounding heart feels like it is in a vice-grip. At over forty feet in diameter, the maelstrom dwarfs us. The canoe is half its size. We are descending, out of control, out of hope…fear has silenced us.

Four years earlier
"It's your turn."

In twenty minutes I will return to St. John the Baptist Catholic church in Excelsior, Minnesota. I am the pastoral associate. A couple years after ordination in 1985, my family and I moved from St. John's to the Crookston Diocese. There I developed a Deacon Formation Program after having spent twenty years with the Minnetonka Schools. I returned to St. John's in 1995 as its faith formation/youth director. In 2001 I became its business administrator.

My lunch partner today is my lovely bride of thirty-three years. Jacqui is the mother of our five grown children. She is clearing the dishes while I set up and make the first Rummikub move. This privilege is mine since she won the last game. Today is exceptionally cold for a Minnesota November. We are glad to be settled in the kitchen's warmth. Unfortunately the peacefulness is being shattered.

"Honey, will you get that?" The phone seems to have an incessant ring at mealtimes. Neither of us wants to answer. Most noontime calls come from telemarketers who relish breaking into the last nanosecond of family peace. We divide up the responsibility for telling them: "Thanks for calling, we do that ourselves." I figure it is her turn...she is up.

After a pause and a surprised "Darrin," I know we are in for a real treat. "Are you between training exercises?"

Darrin is the middle child. He calls home often these days; he is in army boot camp. Like the rest of his siblings, he has a real zest for life, but boot camp is draining it.

After pursuing a college degree for three years, with no major in sight, he applied to Guam. The Hawaiian openings were full. His rationalization: "Studying in the warm Pacific will help me sort things out." He had done what I had only dreamt of doing while attending the frozen tundra of a Minnesota university.

When Darrin left for Guam, his second piece of luggage was a bike. For Darrin, biking a hundred or more miles is like a short break. His one-week summer vacations often consisted of rides to his grandmother's farm 300 miles south, then turning northeast to Duluth, a mere 400 miles before returning the last 300 miles to Crookston.

On Guam he began biking immediately, exploring every nook and cranny. It brought more pleasure than classes. Some professors never knew he existed. He ocean-kayaked, climbed cliffs, and spelunked sea caves. Was I envious? Sinfully so! One of my deepest unfulfilled goals in life is to bask on some south sea island, swim its lagoons, and dive from its cliffs. Swimming in turquoise waters teaming with brilliant-colored fish, spearing lobsters for dinner, and lying half naked on the warm sands is a bit of heaven. Darrin knew of my envy and often reminded me of that unfulfilled dream as he prepared for his adventure.

When the school year ended, with no graduation in sight, Darrin asked to spend a couple months at home. Quickly though, the boredom of holding down two part-time jobs and living with parents pushed him to make a major decision: the army. Now, several weeks into boot camp, it is proving a challenge. On the surface the army isn't such a bad decision for Darrin. He is unsure of what he wants out of life, but doesn't have the money to sit around waiting for enlightenment.

However, Darrin is gentle of soul, a trait hardly right for this man's army. His enlistment caught Jacqui and me off guard. We had been part of the politically correct 1970s. As we wanted nothing to do with wars, we discouraged military stints. Besides inheriting that message, Darrin is genetically gifted with a wee bit of stubbornness. Fortunately he has enough good sense to let go of stubbornness and learned political leanings. But in typical Darrin fashion, he announced he was also going to be a ranger, Special Forces. "It'll allow me to be in the out-of-doors, enjoy nature, stay physically fit, and get paid." He is now nearly three months into his hitch.

"Gary, he wants to talk to you. It sounds important."

"Hi, Darrin." I try to sound upbeat. My greatest fear is some sergeant's demand will push him to chuck the whole army experience and go AWOL.

"Hi, Dad!" His voice is excited as he jumps right to the point, both to save a nickel and blurt it out. "Do you remember your dream?"

"Which one?" I ask half jokingly, remembering the many I have shared. Dreams are hard to let go of. They are the staff of life. Room must be made for their fulfillment, and fulfilling dreams is one of my life's ambitions.

"You know, the one about canoeing the Mississippi. The one your Outward Bound friends thought too crazy and dangerous?"

I hadn't forgotten it, just repressed it. I had asked some of my fellow Minnesota Outward Bound instructors to join me on a Mississippi expedition in 1973. Knowing the experiences we were putting students through while guiding canoe trips in the Boundary Waters of northern Minnesota and southern Canada, their "no, it's too dangerous" always seemed irrational. I asked two brothers and a brother-in-law to consider it. They, too, thought it too dangerous, especially the barges. Not only would the wakes be too much for a tiny canoe, the odds of being run over were too great.

I laughed at those images. All their fears seemed crazy. I figured guiding in the Quetico and the Boundary Waters, shooting the mighty Malign and portaging the great Pooba adequately prepared me for canoeing "The River."

These and many other great canoeing memories from forty years of guiding large and small groups wash over me. My love for water activities got started at an early age. My home town has the good fortune of having three lakes and a river within its boundaries. I lived only a couple blocks from the water's edge.

"Yeo, Dad, you still there?" Darrin's voice jolts me back.

"Yes!" I sense where he is headed, but am afraid to say it. Canoeing the Miss is a special dream.

"Why yah asking?"

"I wanna make that trip!"

"You want to canoe the mighty Miss? You know how cold it is outside?"

My attempt at humor is feeble. Again I tune him out. There are a thousand things I don't dare say: "You've just signed up for a four-year hitch. How can you be so sure you'll still feel this way in 2002? I'll be fifty eight. What made you decide? How will we plan or practice?" So many questions! Don't ask them, Gary. He doesn't think your dream is a fool's fantasy. Remember, his commitments are better than cash in the bank. He never folds on a promise.

The adult in me wants to squelch his offer. Instead I hear myself saying, "Darrin, if you're serious, I'd love to make that trip with you."

While my enthusiastic response delights me, the lull that follows puts an uneasy feeling in the pit of my stomach. More probing questions begin to haunt me: Darrin, what about you and me? We might just be the most stubborn father/son combination walking the face of the earth. How do you dare chance going with me? Have you forgotten how foolish I was just a few years back when we were putting on a new roof?"

I say nothing. Even though there is a strong urge to blurt out, "Darrin, we both always know we're right. How can we ever compromise enough to make such a trip?" I can't say it. My heart tells me this is a redemption chance for all my parenting errors.

But then, just as quickly, new red flags enter my consciousness. Maybe he is just feeling down because the army's not what he expected.

Maybe he needs the comfort of a dream to put up with the drudgery of army life. Yes, this would be a great goal to keep him going while he works through the challenges of being a ranger.

As I wonder, Darrin begins planning, "So, how yah gonna get in shape?" I hear a chuckle. It is a warning. He knows he will be ready after four years in the military.

I sidestep the question. "My summer canoe trips with the youth group should help. I purchased new camping equipment. We could use it." One thing about preparations, both Darrin and I like to fly by the seat of our pants, I more than him. Somehow we know things will work out if we just stay focused.

After getting off the phone, I turn to Jacqui. "How will I ever keep up with a twenty-seven year old at the peak of his physical fitness? He'll be my age when I was guiding in the Boundary Waters. I'll be my father's age four years before he retired." She just smiles and gives me a warm, supportive hug.

CHAPTER 2

NEARLY DERAILED

The four years of planning and preparation passed all too quickly. We are now three weeks out. In those intervening years more than one significant event happened. The most important: Darrin's marriage to Schalleen Nelson. They began dating two years ago and were married two months ago. Although Schalleen is a marvelous companion for Darrin, she is not supportive of his Mississippi adventure. More than one conversation has gone something like this: "If you loved me, you wouldn't leave me for two months."

"You know I love you, but I promised my dad."

"You're not married to your dad. You promised me."

"Keeping my promise to him is a good example of how faithful I'll be in marriage."

"But I'm asking you not to go."

Her unhappiness has left me with final preparations. Fortunately food requirements are simple: lightweight and easy to fix. Cooking utensils are also simple: a coffeepot, two saucepans, two soup bowls, spoons, and cups. These utensils prepare everything from oatmeal, soup, rice, barley and beans, to pasta, pasta, and more pasta; enough "boiling water dinner" for a different meal every day.

For breakfast we will eat something hot and healthy, not lightweight, sugarcoated fluff that is going to burn off fifteen minutes into paddling. To the half dozen varieties of hot cereals will be added chocolate and raisins. Fresh fruit, vegetables, cheese, Wasa bread, prunes, and one-pound, stuffed, unrefrigerated sausage meats round out our daily needs. Carrying only a few days' supply of fresh fruit, vegetables, and meats means replenishing when stopping for water. With the menu and food list complete, I am awaiting Darrin's honeymoon return.

It is now three days since he has returned from Australia, two days before the Mississippi trip. He has yet to call or come over. Even though I am the eternal optimist, doubts are creeping in. Why hasn't he been around to help? Has Schalleen talked him out of it? So far I have dismissed those thoughts with the old adage, "no news is good news." Still I know I should stick to my gut feeling: call and ask.

Darrin and I were forewarned by experienced trip suppliers like Ken Kettering, "There will be an emotional toll." There are books and articles about seemingly perfect father/son, brother/brother, and friend/friend relationships when Mississippi trips began…perfect until tensions from close living and split-second decisions miserably tore them apart. Some of those broken relationships never mended.

Even though communications is the name of success, I am already hesitating…and we haven't even started paddling. This lack of communications is ridiculous. I know he is staying at her folks' house. We are less than thirty-six hours from starting, and the shopping isn't completed. I have got to call.

"Gary, Darrin's here!" Jacqui's voice is surprised and cautious. It is definitely not her usual singing excitement when children show up. "He's not getting out."

I head out. As I round the driver's side, he rolls down the window. "Good to see you," I call out.

He offers me a limp handshake and, "Jump in." There is no, "It's good to be back," or "I am excited about the trip." We just head off.

Hesitantly I ask, "How was Australia?"

"It was good. We did a lot of hiking. Stayed a couple days with a family Schalleen knows."

Again hesitantly, "Where we headed?"

"The grocery store. Got your message we needed to shop."

"Yeah," I bite my lip. At the store we head for the soup and pasta aisles. I gingerly inquire, "Got any preferences?"

"No!"

After several more stabs, I tire of being dissed. "Okay, what do you want?" I am trying desperately to control my frustration. Everything is not okay and my dream feels unhinged. I am tiptoeing around, afraid of a confrontation, afraid of losing the trip. He knows I'm uneasy. Still, he will not share his concerns.

Instead he grabs two boxes of soup and throws them into the cart, "I really don't care what we choose. Let's get outa here."

Okay, that's honest. Now I know I can wait this one out until we are on the trip. I don't want to lose my dream. I pray my silence is not a mistake. Quickly we throw several other dehydrated foods into the cart and head for the checkout lane. Once home he leaves the truck running while I get out and gather up the groceries.

"I'll see you when we take off," is all I hear as he backs out.

"What the hell is going on?" I want to shout back, but don't. I know this is not the Darrin who was looking forward to canoeing the Mississippi. I must be feeling Schalleen's transplanted frustrations.

Watching him drive away as I walk up the steps causes me to wonder if our minimalist preparations and lack of communications bode anything but failure. It will take a miracle for this dream to come to fruition. He won't communicate. I am no better. Yet we are planning on going…I think. Some people describe Darrin and me as being stubborn like Pit Bulls—never letting go until the final outcome is known. We call it determination, a character strength. However, it now appears to be a weakness.

CHAPTER 3

COMPLICATIONS

It is 8 AM. Old Blue, Darrin's truck, is pulling up. Jacqui and I head out. This will be our first visit with Shalleen since the honeymoon.

"Hi, good to see you guys!" Jacqui calls out.

Schalleen's hello is polite but reserved. It is followed with, "Honey, I need to get back." A quick kiss and she is backing out.

"Everything is in the van except for your personal pack. Wanna check?"

"No, I trust you." Darrin opens the side door and throws in his pack. "Whata we waitin' for?"

"John Mugford, the Excelsior Bay reporter." Although anxious to jump into the van and make the mad dash up north, avoiding the traditional Memorial Day weekend rush, we cannot. "Let's go inside and wait, get some coffee. John should be here any minute."

When John pulls up, Darrin says, "I'm anxious to get going."

"So am I…this should be quick. Let's greet him."

"I want nothing to do with the interview."

"Okay." I look over at Jacqui. She gives a slight nod, my indication to stay relaxed. By the time we get to the car, John is out, camera in hand.

"Thanks for coming! This is my wife, Jacqui. Darrin is the other half of the adventure."

"Jacqui…Darrin…glad to meet you."

"Let's go in," I encourage, "we can talk over coffee."

As John and I sit down, Darrin moves to the other side of the breakfast counter. From there he can listen without being in the middle. Soon I make my first mistake. "Yeah, Darrin was in the 102nd." He is around the counter. "No, it's the 101st." So much for wanting nothing to do with the press. My mistake opens the floodgates. He takes over. I suspect he hung around because we often see things so differently. I tend to be optimistic, always viewing life through rose-colored glasses. He sees life more black and white. As often as not, he believes anything written down actually happened. I am more of the mind that all stories are true, some parts actually happened.

John's questioning brings me back into the conversation. "How much did the canoe cost?"

"Sixteen-hundred," I respond.

"You said you wanted a Cadillac of canoes. Sixteen doesn't sound that bad."

"It isn't. I hate paying full price when used is just as good. About the time I was ready to buy a new Wenonah, Ken Kettering of Kettering Kanoes offered me another piece of candy. He began talking graphite paddles. I ended up wanting them as badly as I wanted the Wenonah. By going used I got the canoe half price and the graphite paddles were within reach."

While coming up to speed on my particular choice, John asks, "But why the Minn III?"

"Its design. It's Kevlar…lightweight and fast. I'm told it can take a beating."

After several more questions, we go outside for pictures. Darrin and I pose like people going on safari, but holding black paddles not rifles. The Duluth packs bulge in front and the canoe is nestled atop the van. We appear ready to take on the mighty Mississippi.

As John pulls out of the driveway, we throw the Duluth packs in back. The three of us, Jacqui, Darrin, and I, head for the Red Lake Indian Reservation, nearly a hundred miles beyond Lake Itasca, the source of the Mississippi.

The previous summer, while helping put a new roof on the mission rectory, Father Pat asked me to use the canoe trip as a way to draw attention to the mission school's endowment campaign. It began this way: "So, whata yer plans next summer? I got another roof that needs repairing."

"I'm fairly certain the youth will be glad to return. I can't. I'll be canoeing the Mississippi, a long-held dream."

At that moment I could see a gleam come into Pat's eyes. "Hey... yah ever think of using yer trip for a social need?"

My senses immediately went to red alert. "No. I'm not even sure my partner would like it. He likes things simple."

"I can envision the excitement your trip will generate. I'm trying to find a way to promote the campaign."

Father Pat is the consummate salesperson. I couldn't disagree with the obvious. "I'm sure it's a worthy cause, but I'll need to think about it. I can't make that commitment alone, and my partner doesn't like mixing business with pleasure. I'll get back to you." I love using those last six words. They buy time, allowing decisions to be put off while gathering data and detecting pitfalls, or just allowing a selfish request to pass into oblivion.

I did think about it, and prayed about it. I called Darrin a few days after returning home. He had several misgivings, but reluctantly said he would consider it. As is usual with Darrin, he is careful. When he calls back, he indicates "no" but realizes my interest in helping out. "You make the decision." Although it was not an endorsement, I decided to go ahead. Now, as we travel north, I am not even sure if a press release has been written. When I called Pat last night, he seemed fuzzy on details.

As we pull up to the mission rectory, Pat is there to greet us. "Good to see you guys." Warm hugs follow. After a bit of small-talk, but before our feet are firmly planted, Father Pat blurts out, "I've sold some canoe advertising."

His heart is in the right place; it's just not the right way to raise a couple million. Our canoe is big, but not that big. Twenty feet by six-or-so inches of above-waterline space will not support six-inch block letters for eighteen advertisers.

Before the discussion can go further, Pat sees concern on Darrin's face. He excuses himself as Darrin grabs my arm and says, "The canoe's going to look like a stock car." Darrin is plenty unhappy. Jacqui moves away. "Put advertising on it and I'm outa here." The more he talks, the more frustrated he becomes. I need a quick resolution and head off to find where Pat has taken refuge.

"We need to talk."

"No, problem. Got any ideas?" he asks.

"Yeah. How about St. Mary's Mission School Endowment, Mission@paulbunyon.net on the canoe? Put your sponsors on the website and I'll call in updates." He likes the solution and quickly consummates the deal so as to avoid an abrupt and untimely ending.

As I step back outside, a car is pulling up. Pat is right behind me. He grabs my arm and leads me toward the car. "I want you to meet Deacon Mick and his daughter, Therese. They're launching a tandem bike ride around the old boundaries of the Rez. They want to draw attention to a history project…figure it'll take 'em four days."

While my mind immediately wants to ask, Why are you telling me this? Father Pat says, "We're doing a joint send off of the trips." Pat's pace quickens as he rounds the car to greet Mick and Therese.

He leaves me standing beside Darrin whose eyes show new concern. I answer, "I swear, I don't know a thing!"

Before we can discuss it, Father Pat motions. "Guys, come over here…meet Mick and Therese." They are good people. "Mick's been assisting the Red Lake History Committee with research."

After learning of the injustices to the Indians, Mick wanted to call attention to it. "To make sure people never forget," he says.

Never forget? Why? Is there a good reason to hold on to old wounds? I bite my tongue. This new revelation brings to the fore Darrin's, "I told you so," and his stare says it all, "Get us outa this one."

As if on cue, Father Pat turns and says, "The local PBS station is coming out…doing a story…should be here any minute." Now I am nervous. Unfortunately there is no time to consider it. Their van is just now coming down the long drive. Immediately the PBS crew sets up and begins rolling the cameras. I have no time to collect my thoughts; they have a ten o'clock deadline. It may not be met. Darrin is dragging me away.

"We need to talk!" As Jacqui has already retreated, Darrin heads in her direction. "I didn't come for this, and I want nothing to do with it. I'm outa here. Mom, will you go with me?" I can't blame him. After taking two steps, he stops and returns. "You are neither Lewis nor Clark, and I'm not some flunky military personnel sent along to do menial tasks! We are fifty/fifty. If you take the glory, leave me behind!" He turns and marches away. He means business.

My heart is heavy. Darrin's feelings are clear: he is done foot soldiering and wants no more injustices heaped upon him. His statement mirrors both his days as a soldier and his love of reading. He read about the Lewis and Clark expedition in preparation for our trip. As I have never served as a foot soldier nor read *Undaunted Courage,* I cannot argue his empathy or identification with Clark's foot soldiers. Plus, his comparisons are beyond any discussions I want.

As I watch him hurry away, I am reminded of our thirty-year difference and the great physical shape he is in. He has already expressed concern over whether I will be able to pull my weight. Now his misgivings in connecting the canoe trip to an endowment campaign are in the forefront.

After walking back, I listen to Mick's interview. I am hopeful each trip will be emphasized for what it is. Ours is an endowment campaign. His is a call to heal past injustices. How will PBS handle these two different stories? Another car is pulling up. Pat introduces me to the local history committee's chairperson. She is the last to be interviewed.

The rest of the late afternoon and early evening pass without incident. At 10 PM, Darrin, Jacqui, and I sit down in front of the rectory's living room TV. We listen as the Red Lake's history spokesperson weaves a tangled web. It is now apparent: Ninety percent of the endowment campaign sound bites were cut. The trips appear as two prongs of a demonstration against injustices to the Indian people. I am a bit unnerved. Darrin smiles and begins laughing.

With a healing voice Jacqui says, "It's good to know you see this isn't your dad's doing."

As we head back across the mission grounds to the convent guestrooms, Darrin touches my arm and eyes me intently, "This memory will provide some good laughs, right?" I say nothing. Once inside the convent he stops me again, "I hope the great supper the sisters fixed wasn't the last." He smiles at his clever play on words while shutting his bedroom door. He gives no opportunity for a reply.

As I sink into the soft mattress next to Jacqui, I find it inviting to leave the day's mishaps behind. My mind recalls the dinner of freshly caught crappies fried in potato flakes and hot peppers. My mouth waters anew. The peacefulness of the countryside now envelops me.

Lake Itasca

Leaving Jacqui

Stumpage

A Cold Beginning

CHAPTER 4

ITASCA TO IOWA VIGNETTES

MAP ONE, 764 MILES

Red Lake

Mission

Lake Bemidji

Cass Lake

Lake Winnibigoshish (Winni)

Stumpage

Hanging Dog

Grand Rapids

Lake Itasca

Big Sandy Lake

Aitkin

Brainerd

Camp Ripley

Little Falls

WISCONSIN

Monticello

MINNESOTA

Minneapolis

St. Paul

Minnesota River

Red Wing

Wabasha

Mt. Trempaleau

Bikini Yacht Club

LaCrosse

Bad Axe Landing

IOWA

SEND OFFS

The morning sky is clear and bright. Although sunshine floods the convent dining room, it is no match for the cold northwester. During the night the temperature dropped thirty-one degrees. At the moment it is forty-four! Old Man Winter is keeping spring at bay, a harbinger of the coming week.

While piling on the pancakes and sausages I comment, "This'll be a cold beginning."

Jacqui is more optimistic. "It's a peaceful morning."

"Yeah, a far cry from the drone of Highway Five," Darrin jokes as he stokes his furnace with an extra large portion of sausages and eggs.

"It feels more like the sound of silence," Jacqui says.

I look at her. "I like that. All I heard last night was the lone howl of a dog." Right now the birds are chirping endlessly. Their chorus seems to match the peacefulness of the night.

"I hope all your mornings are this peaceful." I look over to see Sr. Marina regarding us. Perhaps she is wondering how we will fare in this colder weather.

Breakfast is quick as we need to head to the south shore of Lower Red Lake. A drumming and smudging service is planned for the send offs. Darrin, Jacqui, and I are quiet as we get out of the van and approach Mick, Therese, and the others. Darrin is anxious, "How long's this gonna take?"

"We should be out of here shortly," I reply. As the daylight hours are still short, and tackling shallow waters with downed trees will be today's experience, luck will be needed to cover the planned distance.

Quickly the drumbeat creates a meditative, prayerful mood. Tobacco is offered and sweet-grass lit. The sweet smelling smoke is wafted over us via an eagle's feather. Smudged in blessing, my mind wanders back to another Saturday, a decade earlier on the Red Lake Reservation. It, too, was a smudging, healing service—one I had helped to organize. It was an opportunity for Christian leaders in northwest Minnesota to acknowledge their church's transgressions against Indian peoples. Now here I am, a decade later, entering into another drumming and healing ceremony. This one also orchestrated by a deacon.

After learning of the wrongs committed against the Indian people, Mick's new knowledge brought pain and a call to action, the same rationale I had applied to the healing service ten years earlier. But Mick has no knowledge of that healing service nor does the young Indian woman leading our prayer.

It is déjà vu. I see again how a strong social conscience tries to fix things. The drumming and smudging are akin to communal confession. We recognize the sin, seek healing, and promise to keep from repeating the sins.

How many generations will it take to realize we do not have to forgive ourselves for the sins of our parents, just prevent those sins from happening again. How many generations will it take for the children of parents who were hurt, to be able to forgive? As we cannot escape our past, perhaps it is helpful for each generation to do reconciliation. Certainly the action is a reminder to touch others in loving and caring ways. The not forgetting also allows new leaders to step up as healers.

A blast of cold air draws me out of my rambling thoughts. The stiff, north wind, swirling smoke about my face, is stinging. It feels like red ants biting. However, my attention is drawn downward. The cold is penetrating my tennies. My toes sting like frostbite is about to enter. Across the circle is Sister Stephen bundled in a long, black winter coat with a bright, red woolen scarf tucked neatly into the front. She is snuggling herself deeper into it. Her hands, secure in over-sized woolen mittens, are pulling a dark stocking hat lower. She shudders, as if to ward off the cold.

This is a typical Minnesota spring, temperatures dropping from seventy-five to thirty-five in a matter of hours. I am glad Darrin and I weren't taken in by last week's warmth. We are prepared for Minnesota cold and bone-chilling temperatures. However, this cold is a fearful reminder of the hazard in early spring canoeing: capsizing and dying from hypothermia.

Although beautiful and prayerful, the drumming is a delay. We will need to re-think our plans. Fortunately we have Jacqui following our progress and meeting us these first two evenings. If necessary, she and the van can assist. Should Darrin and I need a third party to bounce off the day's events, she will be there.

Darrin is getting fidgety. He is now moving around the circle to join Jacqui and me. The drumming and smudging were not in our plans, and the cold northerly chill is not helping matters. I hope he doesn't push too hard once he joins us.

"Let's get outa here…we're supposed to be on the river by now."
He is right. However, we are on Indian time, running two hours late. I
look at Jacqui. Even though she knows we are trapped because our send-
off crew is a part of the bike's send-off crew, she nods agreement.

As soon as the prayer ends, we head out, but not fast enough. Father
Pat grabs my arm. "They want you guys in the picture…waving good-
bye to Mick and Therese."

Minutes later, while climbing into the van, Darrin's tone says it all,
"That was too long! We never agreed to it!" I know if I don't acknowledge his frustration, it will carry over into today's paddling.

"Look, Darrin, I'm sorry…Believe me, I didn't know about any
of this."

"I know. I'm just happy it didn't last longer. I mighta said something…." He pauses. I listen. Nothing more is said.

The silence is short-lived. Soon a sign indicating the mileage to
Lake Itasca State Park appears. The exhilaration is instantaneous. A
four-year dream is meeting us head on. I can taste it. There is a tingling under my skin. "Thirty minutes and we'll be there!"

Broad smiles match inner feelings. We begin singing the old stand-
by: "In 1814 we took a little trip, along with Colonel Jackson down
the mighty Miss-a-sip. We took a little bacon and we took a little bean,
and we met the bloody British in the town of New Orleans. Oh we…."
On our first trip to New Orleans, we taught the children that song.

Soon the Laughing Waters, the Mighty Miss, will treat us to endless days of idyllic paddling. Abruptly my thoughts are sabotaged by
the adult in me. Save some jubilation for the drudgery and boredom
that will come when crossing Lake Pepin, a twenty-seven-plus mile
paddle. Save it for the heat, humidity, and dead calm of the lower
Miss' pools, and the dreaded southern headwinds that will bring your
canoe to a halt.

"Go away," I blurt out. "I want the kid."

"What are you talking about?"

Before I can answer Jacqui, Darrin responds, "There it is!"

The "it" is Itasca's entrance. The dream ends, reality begins. The
effects of the cold are immediately evident. No cars are lined up at the
registration building. While here the previous August there were easily
ten to fifteen cars backed up, and fifty to seventy-five people were in

the background of every picture. Today, one of the biggest tourist days of the season, we will be lucky to find half a dozen.

Upon entering the registration building I am given the once over and then, "Your photographer arrived…asked if you'd come through." The ranger's greeting throws me off. I find myself in the middle of a conversation.

"Anyone else start a trip?"

"Only three…an older guy last week, two younger guys a week and half ago. They (the two younger guys) were maybe nineteen, from Monticello (Minnesota)."

The ranger's emphasis on younger is noticeable, again reminding me that I am in the middle of a conversation and being scrutinized. Why? Do I look that old? Perhaps he knows something I don't. Maybe he believes I wouldn't be so enthusiastic if I knew what lay ahead. No! I won't change my feelings or plans at this moment. I look him straight in the eye and smile. I won't be turned back every time someone has a premonition. It will alter my history.

Before I can respond, he continues with some unknown insight. "I don't think the younger guys are actually planning to go all the way. They thought it might be too much." He smiles, "They have only two weeks. The older guy is recently retired, doing the whole thing. You'll probably catch him in a week or so."

Finally, a hopeful note, an old guy doing it, an adventurer who appreciates the finer things in life: a relaxing 2,500-mile canoe trip. After purchasing the day permit, we drive to the lot nearest the headwaters.

While unloading, people approach. "You guys planning to canoe the Mississippi?"

"Yup!" The floodgates open.

"How long will it take?"

"We've set aside two months," I reply.

"How far can you paddle in a day?"

"Thirty-five to sixty miles."

"Wow!" It is either a sneer or jealousy. I can't tell which.

Someone else asks, "What kinda job you guys got tah take two months off?" A question I hadn't expected.

What does he really want? I have often struck up conversations like this, holding back, dancing around. I bite my tongue, "Darrin is recently outa the army…I saved up two years' vacation."

"Army man, huh! Must be the power." Okay, enough with the snide comments. Darrin just smiles. I again turn my attention to repacking.

"Will it actually take you guys two months?"

"We'd like to complete it in less," I say.

"Why don't yah start when it's warmer?"

"Cooler's easier. The river grasses are barely up and won't slow us down. The marshes are easier to navigate when you can see through them. There are canoeists who have spent an extra day or two of paddling in the tall summer grasses. We'd like to avoid that."

Living in northern climates gives some instinctive knowledge. The winter snows mat down the previous summer's grasses and add depth to the marsh waters. The freeze kills the thick, river grasses, breaking them loose to wash downstream and decay in deep pools. For us the higher spring water means less bottom scraping. All of these factors are important. Right now the Mighty Miss is just a babe, a mere rivulet of what she will be.

Most people think of the Mississippi as a half-mile or more wide, forgetting her humble beginnings while she is working her way up. The original explorers must have had it hard. There were no dams on the upper Mississippi then. Today's dams form huge lakes, miles long, taking much of the zigs and zags out of the river, both above and below Minneapolis. However, once the Minnesota and St. Croix rivers pour into the Mississippi, she will never again be a babe. Until then, however, hitting bottom where the Mississippi is unencumbered by dams is likely.

"Say, what about food? I don't see no ice chests."

"It's in the Duluth Packs, two weeks worth." All of this time Darrin is keeping himself busy, checking items, staying out of the conversations.

"Yer pulling my leg…Fourteen days food? It's half full."

"We'll buy meat and fruit whenever we stop for water."

Early French voyageurs made Duluth packs out of stiff, sailing canvas. They were heavy and bulky. Today's packs are made of lightweight, flexible canvas, with several outside storage pockets for first aid kits, maps, etc. Because these packs are about two-foot square and frameless, they often resemble dirty bags of laundry when lying low and flat in a canoe. Being frameless allows the weight to be spread out evenly from gunwale to gunwale.

Besides the normal shoulder straps for backpacks, Duluth packs have an additional three-inch wide strap call a tumpline. Each end of it is attached to one side of the pack. During portages, the tumpline is placed over the packer's forehead. It is used to relieve backpressure while carrying 100 to 150 plus pounds on a half-mile or more portage. The backpacker moves his head forward any time he wishes to temporarily pull weight off his back.

"Hey, you're lucky to have such a tall partner when it comes to marshes."

"You're right," I say with a grin. "When he stands up, he's tall enough to see over the dead grasses." Darrin smiles appreciatively.

The kid's dad asks, "Can a guy your age really do fifty miles a day?" From the tone I know where he is going.

"I believe I can." I hoist my pack up and turn to Darrin, "Let's carry the gear to the interpretive center and get some pictures." The small group of onlookers begins to disperse. We thank them for their interest and kind wishes.

The Itasca Interpretative Center stands about one hundred yards from the actual beginning of the Mighty Miss. Its courtyard centerpiece is a magnificent, sculpted, metal globe.

Beneath planet earth, imbedded in the stone, are plaques with all of the appropriate acknowledgements. Surrounding the globe are the traditional waist high informational signs containing pertinent geologic, scientific, and factual data on the Mississippi. The courtyard itself is bounded by an interpretive center and two other mainstays in state and national parks: restrooms and gift shops.

As Darrin fills a five-gallon jug from the headwater's aquifer, I pile packs in front of the globe. Jacqui takes our picture. We pose as world travelers, but only for a moment. We are anxious to head down to the river's edge. The short walk is a stark reminder that the good old days are no more.

When I was a young boy, this path was dirt. It is now asphalt most of the way. Shortly before the river, the asphalt gives way to pea rock. Someday I suspect a ranger will come along and realize all good paths should be paved to the river's edge. Perhaps he or she will be able to visualize a nice cement shoreline of pre-molded landscaping blocks on each side of the river.

When I first came here there was no interpretive center, gift shop, modern restrooms, or paved adjacent parking lot. Yet, amazingly, it was still a great place to visit. It was and is a place where a child can safely wade across the Mississippi and live to tell it.

My friends who had never experienced it always found my stories a little hard to believe. As a youngster I loved to dramatically explain how I stepped (in one fell swoop) across the Mississippi. Most of my friends couldn't conceive of it. The truth is I couldn't do it then nor can I today. A couple running giant steps might get me across. The Mississippi's source now seems a little wider than when I was a child. Today it seems to flow more naturally out of Lake Itasca. Planners have been hard at work over the years. They have given tourists a riverbed that looks ancient, as though it was here since the dawn of time.

One thing humans are absolutely convinced of is their ability to improve upon Mother Nature. Right now that makes little difference, for this is the spot where the waters of Lake Itasca give birth to a mighty river. The descent begins by water gently caressing stones appearing to hold back the lake. The scripted look gives a feeling that if the rocks were taken away, the lake would gush forth in one final exhale.

Itasca is one of those "magical moment places." Here adults as well as children can be exuberant. I sure am. Will I feel this way when our trip is over? What will my answer be to the inevitable, "Would you do it again?"

I pray it will be, with all the emotion and honesty of a cherished memory, "At the drop of a hat!" Right now I wouldn't trade this vacation for any other experience in my life. Darrin's offer is allowing me to feel young again. This dream is beyond anything my fifty-eight years have recently imagined.

I am hoping to be twenty pounds lighter in forty-five days. Although I have never really considered myself flabby, I truly am out of shape for this adventure. Even though I had four years to get in shape, I didn't. Now, leaning against a twelve-foot high tree stump created as a signpost for the beginning of the Mississippi, Jacqui takes my picture.

This manmade tree stump reads, "Here 1,475 ft. above the ocean the mighty Mississippi begins to flow on its winding way 2,552 miles to the Gulf of Mexico." These are magic words. With a little effort and a few days I will be able to say, "Hey, I canoed 2,552 miles, the entire length of the Mississippi."

The overnight chill is hanging on tenaciously. Although the sun slips in and out, momentarily warming the day, the northwest breezes, old man winter's dying breaths, immediately cool it back down.

Some younger boys, boys my age when I first came here, are eyeing Darrin and me with envy. They know a big boy's dream, his adventure, is afoot. They know we are going canoeing and camping on the big river. After visiting with his parents, one has come over and put his hand on the canoe and the other on his hip, very similar to the way I am standing while touching the tree stump.

It is a proud moment for both of us. The canoe and its lettering, St. Mary's Mission School Endowment, Red Lake, Mission@ PaulBunyan.net, are background for his beaming smile. Before leaving, Father Pat printed out two new sets of those decals, replacing the sponsor decals. Darrin graciously helped put them on. We were also given bright red, white, and blue decals depicting the Red Lake Nation. These are boldly emblazoned on the bow and the stern, both sides. I am proud of that. Will others feel that way, or will it cause the prejudices some hold against Indians to come out sideways? Maybe having the Red Lake Tribal decals emblazoned on the canoe will be a good social experiment.

We are ready to launch. Where is the send off crew? Ah, yes, they are still on Indian time. Chomping at the bit, the racehorse in me says the gates are open. Patience, however, continues to be the order of the day. God's time is always the right time. Ah, here they come.

With everyone assembled, we place the canoe into Lake Itasca, wading the first twenty feet to where the rock dam allows the waters to gently begin a trip down the Mississippi. Inquiring minds will want to know that it takes a drop of water about ninety days, traveling day and night, to reach the mouth of the Mississippi, the Gulf of Mexico. Extrapolated in terms of normal canoeing speed, which is five to ten miles per hour, New Orleans should be ours in forty-five days.

Ceremoniously, like the Jews of old would have lifted the Ark of the Covenant, we lift and carry the canoe on our shoulders. It is our protection in the battles ahead. Once over the river's rocky mouth, we gently place it down and float it to shore where two half full Duluth packs, weighing perhaps fifty pounds each, are ritually placed before and aft the midsection. The final placement of personal packs behind our canoeing seats is like a christening. I laugh. Darrin looks up. "What gives?"

"Just remembering a young canoeist who disregarded my personal pack rule." To aid young canoeists I always give them a packing list and say, "Take only clothing and gear you can fit into a small, personal, day pack." It helps them determine what is important for a five to ten-day canoe trip.

"It was a warm August morning when we were preparing to leave at 6 AM. All had assembled at the 5:30 start time save one. With the trailer packed, he showed up at 6:05. In tow was a Duluth voyageur pack posing as a personal pack. Clearly it didn't fit the guidelines. Neither his timing nor his pack were good omens. When I asked about the pack, he matter-of-factly said, 'It's all important stuff.'

"With the group ready to move out, it wasn't the time to ask him to re-pack. I decided to deal with it at day's end. The others listening in that morning and the next day gleaned years of experience. Unfortunately, he didn't. His cavalier attitude forced me to take extra precautions. His canoe mates were unhappy. They nearly capsized twice the first day, taking on small amounts of water. He was oblivious to it all. Later his mother informed me that I had treated her son unfairly. My final response was, 'I'm never happy when someone's actions endanger other people's lives.' Do you know her response?"

"No, you haven't told me this one."

"She informed me her son's older brother and sister had spent months in Europe using that pack. Go figure!"

We now float the canoe back to mid-stream and walk it a hundred feet downriver. No bands are playing or crowds cheering. Most tourists barely take notice. A couple people are curious and follow along the bank, calling out questions and fondly giving words of encouragement.

Ahead is a single log laid across the river: a tourist footbridge. It gives bragging-rights. It is an opportunity to tell your friends how you balanced on a huge beam that traversed the entire width of the Mississippi.

Slowly the bow is pushed down to slide under the log. Now on the other side, we climb in for a short stint as Tom Sawyer and

Huck Finn. Should we succeed, we, too, will feel a great sense of accomplishment.

The riverbanks are well groomed here, thanks to the experts who developed a Disneyland beginning. The water's depth floats our canoe along without a bump. Once this area was a wetlands and the water flowed through unevenly. Now it is a tranquil river with banks, a sandy bottom and knee-deep waters for wading. During the next couple days it won't be so. After this short paddle through the park, the river will return to its natural state: marshes, sandbars, and downed trees, all of which love to grab and hold unsuspecting canoeists.

Ahead is a small wooden bridge, arched in the middle. Lined up atop are Jacqui, Father Pat, and Sisters Marina, Stephan, and Philip. This will be their last hurrah in our send off. As the canoe emerges on the other side, they are holding their hands out in blessing. Their words of love echo in our ears: "May the blessings of the Lord be upon you. We bless you in the name of the Lord." It is a sweet refrain sung from caring, loving friendship. It quiets me as tears well up in Jacqui's eyes.

"Dad!"

Quickly I turn back. A green, ranger pickup is stopped atop the next underpass. Two rangers are merging and heading down the bank. The underpass is newly constructed. Its entrance has wide flanges that quickly narrow the water into a three-foot opening. There is extra headroom to allow canoeists to sit upright while passing through. "Hi, guys…see yah on the other side," the younger one calls out.

Upon entering the underpass, the channeled water lifts the canoe and gives it an extra forward thrust. Quickly the swift water controls the canoe. There is no room to paddle or steer. Grabbing the cement walls will not do. Valuable skin would be rubbed off.

"We gotta stop!" Darrin pleads. Looking over his shoulder, I see the concern. Churning waters after the exit mean we are about to hit something. As we cannot get out and walk it or back-paddle, we lift our legs, jamming boots against the concrete walls. They do the trick. We stop just short of the outlet, allowing Darrin to step over the bow and guide the canoe around some recently placed, jagged rocks.

The rangers are excitedly waiting. "Hey, what'd yah think of it… the culvert?"

After the canoe is fully exited, we lift it over the manmade barrier. I look up at the rangers but hesitate. The rocks are spread out nicely in a semi-circle radiating out from one side of the culvert to the other. The rangers seem jubilant, anticipating rave reviews. I look to Darrin. I want his take. Seeing his expression, I turn back. "The flow is perfect. But the rocks are a hazard." The rangers' smiles begin to fade. "The rocks are too high. We'd have hit 'em pretty hard if we hadn't used our boots."

Darrin quickly adds, "The aesthetics are great though. I like the gurgling sound."

I turn to look. Was I that direct? Did my voice sound irritated? Perhaps it was challenging. I had thought the rangers were going to stop us for a license check. I should have sounded thankful. The underpass was carefully planned, given just the right amount of fall to rush a canoe through, but it isn't perfect yet. I am sorry to burst their bubble.

"Sorry to hear your disappointment. Got any suggestions?" the older one asks.

"Sure, put the rocks lower...spread them out more. Use only smooth ones." The rangers seem pleased with Darrin's reply.

It will be interesting to come back and see if they have taken any of our advice. Too often we humans are so proud of our handiwork that criticisms seem negative. This is not the case. The park service did a superb job with the underpass just as their predecessors did in the early 1930s when they began to work on the park's riverbanks. Those early preservationists developed a Mississippi Headwater's State Park that will always be accessible and amenable to visitors, while at the same time preventing serious destruction to the surrounding environment.

Our Minnesota forefathers and mothers knew they would have to improve upon Mother Nature's Field of Dreams if it was going to be accessible to large numbers. By cleaning the messy, marshiness from Lake Itasca's outlet and replacing its first hundred yards with a sand bottom and rock shoreline, a picturesque beginning was created.

Unwittingly, though, they created a tongue-like extension. It is curiously similar to the exits of old amusement park funhouses. The ones where the area surrounding the exit is painted with a laughing, wide-open clown's mouth whose huge red tongue sticks out onto the deck where visitors exit. The Mississippi's tongue, however, is more like that of a thirsty dog whose tongue is hanging out on a blistering day.

After these source rocks are fifty yards of riverbed that is kept about twenty feet apart. By adding a sandy bottom, the river is a marvelous place for milling crowds to wade. The effect for tourists is a picture perfect place for posing in knee-deep water. All of this causes tourists to imagine an easy paddle to the gulf.

It is somewhat akin to what Sydney Pollack maintained when he said, "You think not getting caught in a lie is the same thing as telling the truth." I say this because once outside of the park's boundaries, where Mother Nature is still in control, downed trees and muddy, swampy areas challenge canoeists. But the sights, sounds, and smells will match any Boundary Water experience. The water is pure and nothing like the severe warnings of polluted, foul, smelly waters between Baton Rouge and New Orleans. It is not that Mother Nature hasn't done her best to keep the Miss clean; it is that human nature's worst has accumulated there.

The information we gleaned from various sources leaves few illusions about the river. Some things sound mythical, however, like the claim that there are no sandy shorelines or camping areas below Cairo, Illinois. Maybe this trip will give some definitive answers to that and other observations made by previous canoeists. Also, what about the current? How much will it aid our trip? There must be unique channels and fast-moving areas, but will they make the downstream paddle a piece of cake?

Reality begins at the park's border. The river is now arched with tangled, fallen trees, intertwined and held in place with bended saplings. The first mile discloses two barricades of downed trees: forced portages. As the floodplain plants have yet to leaf out, finding a way around the barricades is easy. Seeing deep into the woods is awesome.

Our first two hours produce several enchanted areas where mature trees formed high, cathedral-like arches over the river. It is primeval. I expected elves and dwarfs to greet us at any moment. Were we not bound by a schedule, we would have waited for them. The forest has a lure. It beckons like a safe refuge. Hansel and Gretel must have felt it when coming upon the gingerbread house. The peace and quiet here dispels the pains of everyday life. Even the sounds of dipping paddles are muffled.

The cares of daily living are being easily forgotten. Right now my relationship with Darrin feels more like a brother and close friend. We are glad to have each other, to be sharing the moment. Now at the top of the Mississippi, we feel like we are on top of the world. Glad to be here. Glad to be together. Darrin is proud to have given me this moment. I am grateful for his willingness to share a once-in-a-lifetime trip. Huck and Tom must have felt this way when they said, "…Away we went, a-sliding down the river, and it did seem so good to be free again and all by ourselves on the big river and nobody to bother us."

Having spent about $2,500 ($1,600 for a canoe, $440 for paddles, $300 for food, and $200 for miscellaneous) and packing plenty of Endowment Campaign fliers, the preparations are behind us. What could go wrong?

"Schalleen didn't want me to leave…said it's too soon after the wedding." There is sadness in Darrin's voice. "She's concerned about a two-month separation. Her preoccupation has been exhausting." His words are a testimony to one of life's pre-eminent ironies: Our greatest happiness often causes our greatest pain. What I can say? Nothing! It is best to change the subject and re-visit his pain at a later date.

"Your going means a lot to me. I doubt I will ever be able to adequately express my appreciation."

"Thanks." Silence follows. "You do know we're canoeing the longest river in North America?"

"Yes," I respond.

"We'll pass through one fifth of the states. It is the fourth largest river in the world. Only the Nile, Amazon, and Yangtze are longer."

"Perhaps the Amazon should be our next," I say with a smile.

"Let's get through this one."

He is right. Enjoy the next forty-some days. This trip is a first-hand introduction to Mes-Sipi, The Great Father of Waters. It feeds our country both physically and spiritually. The amounts of coal, oil, and natural gas traveling this river is staggering. We will only see a small portion of what the economy eats up. Besides energy, there is a constant stream of grain barges passing downstream. Each year, more than 400 million tons of cargo passes along this river corridor. Forty-six percent of all the grains exported from the United States float down the Mississippi.

Over twelve million people live in the 125 counties and parishes that border her. They provide goods and services amounting to over $35 billion a year. This trip should show firsthand how the river, with its tributaries and dams, allows commerce to take place. I am looking forward to experiencing the rich, delta flood-plain used to raise some of the world's finest beef.

Two point three million cubic feet of water, on average, move downstream every second. Living means avoiding mishaps while riding it. Imagine a wall of water fifteen to thirty-five feet high and anywhere from a half-mile to two miles wide, moving at a speed of three to five miles per hour, everything in front being swept away. Nobody wants to be a part of the 400 million cubic yards of mud, sand, gravel, and debris washed into the Gulf each year. But understanding that raw power a little better is another story.

"The wind's still pretty cool!" Darrin's comment is meant as thankfulness. We are canoeing in ideal weather. It is the low fifties and partly cloudy, work hard and sweat little. The waters are pure, cool, and drinkable, a far cry from St. Louis and points beyond. We passed Wanagan's Landing five miles after Lake Itasca. Camping was permitted, but five miles is not nearly enough for a day's journey when trying to reach New Orleans before summer's end.

"Vekin's Dam is coming up. We might need to portage." Darrin's concern is for naught. There may have been a dam here in logging days but not now. All traces are gone. The riverbed is a narrow valley and it is easy to imagine where the dam stood. The DNR map cautioned Class-One rapids. Not today, just a peaceful river with outstanding scenery.

These first few miles seem to be a warning that no matter what has been written or read, very little is known. The Mighty Miss is always a mystery. Seductive, like a beautiful woman, she refuses to give away all her secrets. It is now apparent that some of the "River Experts" claims are only good for the day they passed through. Monday's experience may be here on Tuesday, but it could just as easily be gone forever. The only truth sinking in right now is the river is unique and mighty, even in her humble beginnings, and adding "a grain of salt" to the book learning will be essential. The map has already shown rapids and dams that aren't. It has got to be an inkling of what is to come.

As we finish a quick break at a beaver dam, Darrin does a map check. "Coffee Pot's (landing) coming up." Coffee Pot is where Jacqui agreed to meet us. The beaver dams are the reason our canoe is not hitting bottom even after sparse winter snows. "Says here (a DNR map, Department of Natural Resources) we'll hit a major bog at the junction of LaSalle Creek and the Mississippi. Get this: 'Finding and staying on the main channel will be a challenge.'"

Shortly after leaving the beaver dam we find Jacqui waiting on one of the many bridges crossing the Mississippi as it snakes north to Bemidji. Yes, the first sixty-five miles of the Mississippi flow north. Just outside Bemidji, the Mighty Miss turns south forever. "We're making good time. What say we go beyond Coffee Pot?"

"Where to?" I reply.

"Stumpage Rapids seems doable."

"That's fine with me. Show Mom." Jacqui comes off the bridge and joins us at the river's edge.

Shortly after leaving her, the Mississippi again vanishes into a large bog, totally disappearing, causing us to make several wrong turns. To quickly get back on track, we drag the canoe over fifteen-to-twenty-foot-wide bog sections. These are encrusted with thick, dead grasses, bent over and matted down. The freezing winter temperatures and snows did their job. The brittle grasses are slippery and match the wet, floating earth which heaves and sinks as we traverse it.

These disintegrating grasses are providing more nutrients to an already rich bog. It is a good reminder of Mother Nature's exponential swiftness in transforming shallow waters into dry lands, lands that will support small willowy trees. Eventually, long after our lifetimes, there will be no bog water filtering through, just a river channel like the rest of the Mississippi.

One memorable moment of Boundary Waters' "crashing" (portaging through woods where there are no trails) was traversing a former bog. Long ago dried up and now carpeted with six to twelve inches of trembling sod, young saplings two to three inches in diameter held on precariously. The thin layer of earth, no longer suspended on water but stretched between rock formations, trembled and sent ripples shooting across the hollow land. Our diversion on that hot, humid summer day, where deep woods mosquitoes were on a feeding frenzy, was pushing down thirty- to forty-foot trees with one finger.

The downside of transition land is breaking through with one foot, a common occurrence. The real danger is breaking through waist deep or more. The hollow areas are ideal nesting places for ground hornets. Young campers are always amazed when taught the best defense: "Stay calm! Step out of the hole. Take one step away. Stop." It confuses the hornets. They are looking for a moving target. With nothing to chase, they go back and begin repairs and the hiker can safely walk away. Run, and along with the stings, twisted ankles, and broken legs await you.

Our greatest concern today is cold. Slipping off the slimy banks will mean a drenching in hip-deep, cold, spring waters. These northern Mississippi bogs are some of the slipperiest, slimiest, dirtiest bogs around. Short cuts are only exchanges for mud and wet. Backtracking is not effective. The maze of waterways causes greater frustration. Ken Kettering advised using a fourteen-footer (canoe) for this part of the trip. "The twenty footers are harder to maneuver in the narrow channels," he said. He is right.

The upside to bog paddling is the variety of ducks and songbirds. So many species of ducks: Redheads, Wood Ducks, Teals, Mallards, and a sough of mystery ducks. All of these provide beauty to an otherwise barren landscape. Adding to this is the sweetness of marsh song birds. The chorus of Meadow larks, yellow and redwing blackbirds, marsh wrens, sparrows, and killdeer is definitely in stark contrast to the dark brown, decaying, and crumbling topside of plants exposed to winter's kill. There are only a few sparse tips, less than an inch, of new, green marsh grasses. The underwater grasses are no more than a half inch. All of this, combined with raccoon, fox, and other animal tracks in the black earth helps diminish the bleakness of early spring. The Mississippi Headwaters River Trail map says there are "242 kinds of birds, 23 species of reptiles and amphibians, and 57 species of mammals" in this area.

After leaving Bemidji and heading south, every day will show longer water grasses. In the Twin Cities the early summer water grasses will be in full bloom, several feet long and swaying gently in the warmer current. After scraping the river bottom a number of times this afternoon, and dragging our canoe over slimy land, it is clear how great the marshland challenge would be in late summer with its low waters and thick grasses.

"I wonder what it would be like if we'd taken the ranger's advice."

"What advice?" Darrin ask.

"Oh, that's right, you weren't there. He asked if we wanted to rent a beaver for the sloughs…fifteen dollars. Turned him down, said we were purists."

"That sounds like part of the DNR's program to offset budget cuts. The state fish hatcheries are doing something similar."

"How's that?" I ask.

"Renting walleyes. The biggest challenge is harnessing them. But ten dollars a day isn't bad."

"Muskrats go for that amount, but beavers have more tail power and can claw through the bogs," I add.

The late afternoon rendezvous point is just ahead and Jacqui is waiting on a high spot overlooking the marshlands. The view is terrific in both directions. The bummer is we see there is still a long marsh paddle ahead.

After a short break we leave Jacqui sitting on the hillside, in the comfort of full sun, reading and watching our progress. For nearly an hour she can see us zigzagging. Thankfully there is a cooling breeze out of the Northwest for the sun is now unhampered by clouds.

After a few more hours, the deepening sunset causes darkness to close in. "Is that a campfire?" I ask.

"It should be Stumpage," Darrin replies.

Jacqui's cooking fire is a guiding light. Mingled with the smoke is the welcomed smell of a hot meal, beef stew if my nose is accurate.

Seven hours of paddling brings excited exchanges on what we saw and enjoyed. Jacqui's reading in the warm sun and out of the wind, with nature speaking around her, proved very relaxing. I note tiredness but satisfaction with twenty-five miles—no real soreness. Darrin speaks of the challenges provided by early spring canoeing. Tomorrow we will see ten to twelve hours of paddling but probably no more than thirty-five miles of travel. The swamps and bog lands will demand additional time and effort.

Two things are already clear. Canoeing the Miss allows one to become part of a unique history. Less than five people do the whole river each year. Secondly, it is easy to quit a Mississippi expedition at any time. There are bridges and pullouts every few miles.

Our first point of interest today was Gusvig Landing, named for a family who donated land to create the public access. It was only two miles from Itasca. A half-mile past Gusvig was the first of the thousands of rivulets, creeks, streams, and rivers dumping into the Mighty Miss. It is called Sucker Brook. Darrin noted this and asked, "Do you think it is meant as a warning?"

STUMPAGE'S KILLING FIELDS

I am eager to leave. The first rush of adrenaline is still pumping. The thrill of a lifetime does not wear off easily. It is a half hour before dawn. No alarm clock lifted me from the sandman's grip; it was Mother Nature. Right now she is cradling us in her arms.

Accepting her embrace, going with her flow, living within her boundaries, always allows awesome experiences and keeps me alive. Too many have been chewed up, squashed, and spit out, thinking they could conquer her. Going with the flow also means an endless array of treats beyond the imagination: sunsets too glorious to explain and gray days that give a whole new meaning to black-and-white landscapes.

Yesterday there were shades of green water grasses so brilliant and varying that we wondered how we had missed them in earlier river trips. Some water grasses were so tightly packed and plump, they appeared to be wiggling green caterpillars all trying to occupy or chew food from the same spot. Other water grass varieties flowed more freely, like silky, green ribbons sown with thin, white-laced edges.

During the next two weeks Mother Nature will chill us in the early morning, warm us by midmorning, and cause us to sweat by mid-afternoon. Her wind and sun will do their best to dehydrate us. She is not about to be doctor mom. As intruders, we are called to abide by her rules. Doing so will give us the privileges of walking, swimming, and paddling beside animals and birds going about their daily routine, giving little notice to the outsiders.

Right now the blackbirds, marsh wrens, and others are providing an early morning serenade, cheering us on with lusty mating calls. If these were human love songs, our penchant might be turned from paddling. As I sip tea and listen, I wonder, Do birds always begin singing a half hour before sunrise? What about us? How long will it take us to get up and dressed as the weeks progress? How long will it take to get the water boiling, food set, dishes washed, and utensils repacked?

The sun is beginning to burn off the chill. There is a need to get moving while the coolest part of the day is with us, more bogs await. Although we didn't rent a beaver or muskrat yesterday, today our canoe weevil is unpacked and ready. Previous trips have shown its usefulness. Sold in hardware stores throughout northern Minnesota, it was invented by the same person who invented smoke-shifters.

A single canoe weevil can cut though bogs and marshes like a welding torch does soft metal. These devices cut out miles of looping river-bends as well as doing away with dragging canoes over slimy bogs. Such a feat is accomplished by cutting a deep furrow, a new water path through the narrowest part of an oxbow.

Normally people forget about a river's humble beginnings, where its waters often seep through sloughs and marshes, draining, seeking to regroup in a deeper riverbed. These marshes are often a quarter mile or more wide and one to five miles long. Always in low-lying valleys, they are sandwiched between thickly forested hills that hold the humidity and provide ideal breeding ground for mosquitoes. Today's map readings show several, five-mile bogs. But five miles by way of the crow is fifteen zigzagging canoe miles.

Each time the river dumped into a bog yesterday, the challenge was to discover which of the five-fingers (channels) was actually the main channel. Seeing the direction channel grasses bend does little good, all bog grasses bend in the direction the water is flowing. This enigma, however, pales in comparison to oxbows. When the river turns right or left in a marsh, it will go straight for a quarter to half mile before bending around a narrow corner and heading back in the direction from which it came. Bogs love to snake back and forth, often leaving less than five feet and usually no more than twenty feet of semi-dry land. Knowing this makes canoeists either go crazy or get creative. Yesterday we went crazy. Today we will use the canoe weevil.

The first lesson in using canoe weevils is to become familiar with the narrowest point of land in an oxbow. This is determined by standing in the canoe and overlooking both sides. Once a spot is determined, back up and paddle hell-bent toward it. It is a little like hitting the weakest link in a chain and blasting your way through.

Think of a canoe weevil in terms of a garden weevil. Canoe weevils function by tearing away the thickly matted roots of marsh plants. To be most effective, it is attached to the bow three inches below the waterline. A small but powerful turbine is activated by water rushing through a bell-shaped funnel, similar in design to a trombone bell. The funneled waters turn a tiny turbine. A full head of steam is necessary to spin the canoe weevil's claws at a high RPM.

The claws, situated just in front of the bell-shaped funnel, allow it to spew debris to the sides, preventing muck from getting sucked into the turbine. Canoe weevils carve a neat channel from one side of an oxbow to the other, preventing a lot of zigzagging.

In those few instances where the canoe weevil might get clogged or break on a fallen log, we will cross by dragging the canoe fully loaded. Unloading a canoe is both laborious and dangerous. Laborious because of the re-packing; dangerous because fully loaded packs left lying on soft mud have a tendency to slide in the water and sink into oblivion. There is one advantage to dragging canoes: playtime in knee-deep mud and waist-deep water, a way to relieve some of the day's drudgery.

"Hey, Dad, daydreaming? It's time to shove off."

The river and Mother Nature are again a festival of sights and sounds. Already we have spotted seven species of ducks, numerous finches, cranes, and Kingfishers. The Redwing Blackbirds are a dime a dozen. All these birds continue their serenading. It is neither a cacophony nor a true chorus. It is more like a symphony with many instrumental solos. Sometimes the orchestra has only a combo or sextet. Other times twenty to thirty pieces are sectioned off on each side of the river, very stereophonic.

As there are so many different voices producing such marvelous sounds, listening is a pleasure, even with a mechanical ear. The sheer art of so many voices in harmony enhances the magnificent sights. Each section of birds seems to come in at exactly the right moment as the wind sways trees and grasses. It is akin to listening to a Berlioz opera, where color and passion are expressed vivaciously. Here there is no need to close one's eyes and visualize created images. They dance before us.

"These sounds and fresh smells are what I'd hoped would greet us. I imagine Jacqui must be in seventh heaven," I muse.

Darrin is a bit more insightful. "I remember how you two always talked about your days in Outward Bound. I was hoping I might experience some of what it was like."

"You are!"

"We're approaching Bears Den Landing," he calls out.

"I don't see no bears." We laugh. Thankfully there were no traps at Fox Trap. If there had been, we would have set them off. Something in the heart of us all wants magnificent animals to roam free. Ahead is Pine Point Landing. It does have numerous pines.

"What's that?" Darrin calls out.

"It's a river dragon." Like others I have seen, this one slowly lowers its head in the shallow waters before quickly shooting it up. The jerking is meant to warn us away. At Disney Orlando one could experience this on a boat ride around a castle moat, but it wouldn't feel so scary.

This dragon is ready to grab our canoe and chew a hole in it. It has been trapped at this bend for many years, a holdover from the logging days of a century ago. Its fate was sealed after the spring thaw when the loggers floated the winter's cut to the mill.

During those floats, lead logs often got jammed into soft sand or silt at a bend. Stuck, it would be driven deeper and deeper by succeeding logs, hammering away like pile-drivers, pounding the hapless log for having nosedived into the soft bottom. Once down, the log is doomed to a lifetime of bobbing and weaving with the ebb and flow of subsequent currents.

Actually, surrounded by the beautiful scenery here, this log is far more fortunate than the hundreds of hidden two-by-fours in the walls of lonely South Minneapolis tenements. On this day, the current is just right. The attraction will last for years.

We are again passing through a sea of tall, land grasses, bowed and bent low by the winter snows. In more than one museum in northwest Minnesota, North Dakota, and the Province of Manitoba, there are two-story displays dedicated to the prairie grasses that were once so prevalent on the plains of the Red River Valley of the North.

The roots of these plants were ten to fourteen feet deep and the stalks were ten to fourteen feet high. Encased in glass, these gigantic roots and stalks are a magnificent sight. Just as marsh grasses are both a dream and a nightmare for canoeists, so were those prairie grasses for early pioneers. It provided plenty of hay or straw for the cattle, but watch out for prairie fires.

These six-foot-plus Mississippi bog grasses are a quick reminder of previous canoeists who have gotten lost and roamed a half-day or more before finding a route out. Old-timers tell of races from Itasca to Bemidji won and lost in these bogs. A couple times we wondered if we were lost.

"We're going to need to pull through." Darrin is referring to a ten-foot stretch of bog land. "We made a wrong turn again."

After traversing it and paddling a few strokes he announces, "It's another dead-end pool."

Sometimes I wish we had started with a fourteen-footer. Can't say Ken Kettering didn't warn us. No, we were going to do the entire experience in the Wenonah Minn III. No canoe switching for us. This longer canoe has, however, forced a learning curve for a modified draw stroke. Our turns have gotten quicker.

"I do like seeing the beaver and muskrats in these inner sanctums. They never seem too concerned with our being here."

I agree with Darrin and add, "Perhaps they know we aren't trappers."

Last night, with a campfire burning, the smoke masked a foul odor. This morning, with no fire, its potency was tasted: rotting beaver carcasses. Trappers use Stumpage for skinning their winter's take. After noticing the skeletons, I began counting. I quit at sixty. It was a vexation to my spirit. The policy of this trapper was to skin and toss the carcasses into the tall weeds surrounding the camp. It was obvious that scavengers were feasting upon them. In the big city we call it recycling.

The bogs are gone now. The river bottom is golden. The sands are gently tumbling in the current. There are no rocks nor debris. Its two-foot depth is crystal clear. In a few places the sand is mottled by shades of new, green grasses, perhaps an inch high. They shimmer and wave delicately like hula skirts in slow motion. The vegetation and cool day are making for a great experience. If this were late summer, those grasses would be long and woven together by the ever-shifting currents. It is the summer grasses that love to grab and hold onto paddles, intent on pulling them out of canoeists' hands.

Like the river grasses, the trees are just beginning to bud in the Bemidji area. It is an odd sensation to experience spring twice. Nearly a month ago spring happened in the Twin Cities. Those trees are now near full bloom.

Several times today the canoe entered and exited darkened for-
ests. It happened where the river narrowed and towering arched trees
interlock fingers to block out sunlight. Below, where no groundcover
had emerged, was a clear sightline, an unobstructed view akin to looking down the rows of empty church pews on week days. The lack of
ground cover is a reason we saw so few animals in those areas.

As darkness nears, Bemidji is eight miles away. Lake Bemidji is
where Eddy Harris of Mississippi Solo fame got side tracked. Harris,
from Kirkwood, Missouri, soloed the Mighty Miss in the early 1980s.
It is hard to imagine anyone wanting to leave in the fall as Eddy did.
Not only are the bog grasses tall, the river waters are low and clogged
with tightly woven algae. To top it off, Minnesota's fall weather is more
unpredictable than her spring. Eddy's rationale, however, was great. He
would canoe the northern part of the Mississippi in the cool of a Minnesota fall, hitting the southern states when the summer heat was spent.

Harris' faux pas was allowing a miscalculation and chance meeting
to dissuade him from canoeing one of the most exquisite portions of
the Mighty Miss: the Bemidji to Brainerd section. When Eddy landed
his canoe on the western shore of Lake Bemidji, he failed to properly
secure it before leaving to get food and water. Upon returning, his
canoe was gone. What seemed at first maliciousness, turned out to be
carelessness. A seasoned canoeist never leaves a canoe half in the water
on the upside of a windy lake. That is what our colleague of an earlier
era did. The waves rocked his canoe off the land and sent it drifting.

From Garrison Keilor's Prairie Home Companion, the world
knows Minnesota men are all good looking and her women are strong.
Perhaps it was Eddy's fate to meet such a woman. She spotted him
looking bleakly out across the lake. Sensing something amiss, she came
to his rescue—a beacon of hope on that gray, gloomy, forlorn fall day.
One can almost hear their conversation.

"Hey! What's the problem?"

"My canoe's missing."

"Did you pull it up and tie it?"

"I dragged it halfway onto shore."

"Well it's not unusual for wave action to pull it off. Tell yah well...
get in my truck...I'll help yah find it."

If his canoe had not been stolen, she knew where the wind would
take it. Stealing canoes anywhere along the Northern Mississippi is

quite unlikely. Minnesotans know losing water transportation endangers lives. Survival items are left alone, especially in canoe country.

In the Boundary Waters summer canoeists often come across trapper lean-tos. Except for dust and spider webs, these shelters are left completely undisturbed. In the bitter cold of winter, when the trapper returns, he finds his survival items intact. Eddy hoped his new companion would help him find his canoe intact.

Their search was not futile. She was dead-on accurate. After driving around the southern edge of Lake Bemidji and up the eastern, they spotted his canoe being driven against the shore. Had it ended there, Eddy would have had the trip of a lifetime. As it turned out, between his inexperience and both their concerns for his safety, he decided to drop the paddle between Lake Bemidji and Brainerd. Accepting her offer, he loaded everything into the back of her pickup and portaged to Brainerd. My heart goes out to Eddy as I have already canoed a portion of it. He missed a magnificent stretch. Despite their misgivings, we will paddle it.

As this day ends, my lightweight paddle has again proven to be a back saver. For an experienced canoeist, paddling is like walking: normal. Replace a sixteen to twenty-ounce wooden paddle with a few ounces of graphite, and it is like putting on a pair of lightweight walking shoes for the first time. The lightness brings an instant realization on how much easier the workout will be.

The same is true for featherweight paddles. It is a whole lot easier to lift four to six ounces 25,000 times a day than sixteen to twenty-two ounces. The 25,000 comes from averaging what a good canoeist can do on the open water: forty to fifty strokes per minute. Paddling ten hours a day translates into 50 strokes times 60 minutes times 10 hours equals 30,000 strokes. Take away 5,000 for rests and stops and 25,000 is close to accurate. My present canoeing pains actually come from sitting. I forgot my seat cushion. Avoiding fatigue during prolonged canoe trips is important. Fatigue causes poor canoeing posture which in turn leads to back pains.

Having a crew chief these first two days is good. Not only is someone there to listen to our excitement and concerns, we only needed to carry a day's supply of food and water. After breakfast tomorrow that will change.

CASS' LOONS

Realizing so much unknown lies ahead, Jacqui's hug is firm, "Call me when you can?"

"I will. Won't know our Twin Cities (layover) plans til Monticello," I offer.

She turns to Darrin, "Take care of Dad."

"I will," he says seriously while flashing me a smile.

Jacqui's music responsibilities will keep her busy during my absence. She won't have much time to worry. I wished I could say the same for Schalleen. Darrin spent over an hour on the phone with her last night. She would like to see him return.

Even though the hard work of tackling marshes for two days diminished our enthusiasm, the miles to Lake Bemidji prove effortless. Before heading across the lake, we conjecture as to where Eddy Harris landed. Once satisfied, we head out.

Soon we are approaching a young man, perhaps seventeen, piloting a green, fiberglass canoe. His clean, white t-shirt is in stark contrast. Leisurely, smooth strokes give him the appearance of doing a yoga exercise. He is definitely enjoying the moment, like a young otter's easy strokes while floating the current. I am fixated on his peaceful demeanor and looking forward to meeting him.

"If we don't change course, we'll miss the outlet." Darrin's interruption warns me the desire to intersect is bringing us too far north. Veering right, never to meet our young confrere, I wonder who he is and what his goals in life are. He looks like someone worth meeting.

The paddle across Lake Bemidji is just over two miles. From the middle of the lake, Bemidji is disappointing. Not because it isn't a great place to visit, it is. But out here there is no feeling of the bustling, summer resort city, the laughing, happy people that make up the summer clientele. Viewed from the lake, at this early morning hour, the city feels abandoned.

Two white pleasure crafts are crossing a half mile ahead. Each carries a businessman dressed in a suit, apparently headed to the office. "Why do you suppose pleasure boats are usually white?" Darrin turns and gives me the "what's with the question" look. I am about to answer when it hits me. These boats reflect a sixties' truism. Someone turned it into a song, the title of which eludes me. The key phrase is, "little boxes, pretty boxes, and they all went to the university."

White boats are a status symbol for Minnesota's middle class, college-educated, and upper-blue-collar workers. Parked in a driveway or beside a double-attached garage, they are standouts. They get the occasional weekend use, but little else.

Forgetting my question, Darrin continues looking for the elusive gap. "We need to find the outlet."

"Perhaps there."

"No." Darrin is right. As we close in, the shoreline opening turns out to be a street.

"How far do you think we've traveled?" I ask. We both speculate the distance from Lake Bemidji's western shore before choosing another "V" shaped shoreline opening. Our next guess also turns out to be a road. Staying about 100 yards from shore, we hazard one guess after another until we finally find the outlet further north than expected. Our leisurely Memorial Day paddle now takes us back into the narrow confines of the Miss.

No longer needing to meet Jacqui at a prearranged place, we continue moving at a relaxed pace, enjoying being lowered and nestled between banks thick with trees and the wind blowing well overhead. There is peace. The short, lush green bank grasses, intermingled with sticks of straw, only add to the serenity.

"Nature is calling."

That is fine with me. My morning tea and food also need releasing. Besides trees, the river is now lined with cabins. It would not do to use someone's yard. As there are no owners moving about, and approaching a vacant cabin might garner a 911 call, we stay the course. "Where are the friendly Minnesotans when you really need them?" I ask.

"No one's up yet."

I point with my paddle, "There's a kid a couple hundred yards downriver…to the left"

Quickly we head toward him. Seeing us coming, he runs up the hillside yelling, "Dad, Dad." He is going to wake up the whole neighborhood. Near the top he stops and turns to watch our landing at their dock. He then renews his pleas.

Within moments, a friendly family of four is greeting us: Mom, Dad, and two boys from Warroad, Minnesota. Before much can be said, I point to the outhouse, "Could we use it?"

As Darrin is needier, he goes first. During my turn at paying respects to this venerable institution of the backwoods, Darrin finds out more about the family. They are laughing and talking in earnest when I return. As Father Pat was once a pastor in Warroad, I ask, "Does his name rings a bell?"

The mother answers affirmatively. "A friend introduced us at a local restaurant. I remember his warm smile and handshake."

Changing the subject, her husband says, "This land once belonged to her dad. She has been coming here since day one." Pointing to an old Oak near the river, he announces, "Her dad was proud of this spot, hung a sign there."

Noticing quizzical looks, she quickly adds, "The sign's gone. Someone stole it…must've thought it'd make a great souvenir." These last words are said both sadly and with what I perceive to be tongue-in-cheek. Silently I ask myself, How does a stolen item bring fond memories?

Darrin asks, "What'd it say?"

Closing her eyes for a moment, her face begins to glow, "Here lies the most northerly point on the Mississippi as it winds its way to the Gulf."

It sounds better than Kilroy was here! Or, you're 2,579 miles from Wall Drug. Her tone and the inflections leave a feeling of standing atop the Mississippi and seeing clear to the Gulf. Although it is a missed picture-taking opportunity, her image makes up for our loss.

After shoving off, I make a vow to Darrin, "If I ever do this trip again, it'll have no deadlines." To be able to touch the people and the land, not just the water, to soak up every detail as well as the sights, sounds, and smells is a must. Finishing the journey should be secondary to the people and the companionship along the way. Hang onto that thought, Gary. Maybe the frustrations Ken Kettering talked about won't come about.

Already a unique history is shaping up through the fascinating stories and thoughts people share. A few are paranoid about river mishaps. We are ignoring their fears as being unhealthy. We do, however, take their thoughts as prophetic reminders to keep our guard up, avoiding mishaps at bridges, locks, and campgrounds.

Cutting into my thoughts, Darrin says, "We should make the Ottertail Dam around noon. The map shows good fishing."

It is indeed. After portaging, there is a festival of walleyes in a pool near the downstream bridge. We make a second and third pass back over them. Some thirty walleyes, in the one to three pound category, are enjoying the warm sun and cool waters. "This is what it's about!" The pleasure on Darrin's face and in his voice cause me to be thankful. I never wanted this trip to be just about my dream.

Floating slowly downstream we come upon several more pools of walleyes. Any fisherman would go crazy here. A fever would set in. Perhaps he'd think he'd died and gone to fisherman's heaven. My brother Bob would. His love of fishing goes way back.

"Hey, did I ever tell you Uncle Bob talked me into skipping school when I was in third grade."

"Get outa here! Third grade. I think not...where'd you go?"

"Fishing. I did catch hell for it. Funny, I don't remember Bob being caught."

The afternoon scenery continues to mesmerize. The river is now flowing into Wolf Lake. "Dang, we misread the map. We're going too far south." Darrin's disappointment comes from knowing we'll arrive at Cass Lake an hour later than expected.

At 5 PM, Cass comes into sight. It will be dark before we can set up camp on the other side. It is a stroke of bad luck to enter such a large lake (eight plus miles) with only a couple hours of canoeing light. The Wolf Lake delay, and now the headwinds coming across Cass, will prevent a crossing in the remaining light. Our leisurely pace this afternoon, protected by Mother Nature's tree-lined banks, did not prepare us for the crashing white caps ahead. This could be a major paddle.

Fifteen minutes after entering the fray, Darrin asks, "What's happening?"

"Good question." The whitecaps and waves are dying. The headwinds have ceased. The lake is becoming eerily calm. The sky is mostly clear, a few clouds. We cannot see a front, and the birds aren't chattering wildly as though something is about to happen. Then it dawns on me. This is an evening calm, an opportunity, a window. Without a word, our paddling becomes frenetic. Our crossing is straight through the middle of Cass. We may be tired, but we are not stupid.

Quickly picking up speed, the canoe knifes over the surface. A soft hushing comes from our charging through still air. Exhilaration replaces dejection as our canoe sails into deep waters. The placid surface becomes a huge mirror, reflecting every aspect of the surrounding landscape. The trees and cabins are captured, reproduced on the water's surface. Our movement is the last brush stroke to a perfect painting. There is a gentle canoe wake, some two hundred yards long, fading into the western horizon where the darkening sky has shades from pink to deep red. The sun balances atop mature pines. A cooldown is settling in.

From fear to excitement! An opportunity to paddle wide open on a huge, deep lake! Cass' winds could easily whip up three to four-foot waves. We both feel giddiness in beating the odds. The energy of the first day is again driving us.

Our good fortune is pushing the speed envelope. The ability to slice through the water is both comforting and dizzying. The calmness, the speed, the nearness with which the gunwales are to the water's surface brings a new sensation: the canoe will, at any moment, nose-dive into the murky waters, exactly as loons do, headfirst. The sensation is hypnotic. The calm, the speed, the dark waters, they are messing with my depth perception.

Shaking my head does no good. I refuse to quit staring into the dark waters. The effortlessness combined with speed, twilight, and being only a few inches from full emersion is creating a real high. The illusion also says our fast skimming cannot last. It will end in stumbling. The canoe will be engulfed. The faster we go, the more the adrenaline pumps, the greater is the intensity of belief we are about to plunge straight down like a submarine making an emergency dive! It is like vertigo except the impression is that we can dive and run under water.

How long will it take to become fully hypnotized? I won't look away and lose this feeling. It is intoxicating, heady! Faster! Faster! In unison we are driven by a desire for speed. Fatigue has long since passed.

Then it happens! We hit the center of the lake! Without speaking, paddling ceases. We turn to take in the western sky, now spreading soft pinks against a dark green landscape. After an hour of hard paddling, the 360-degree shoreline view and beginning of twilight bring a hush. Moments ago the dark abyss, the twilight waters, seemed ready to pull the canoe under. Now the tranquility and gathering darkness create an intense silence, gliding the canoe to a total halt. The sensation is a newer, purer form of floating.

Normally I would rather be nearing camp or cooking dinner. Not so now. The beauty embracing the moment is guiding us to a taste of heaven. It has been a while since we spoke. There is no need; the beauty speaks for us. There are no regrets at not paddling, only reverence. Neither dares comment and spoil the perfection. It is one of those bonuses we had hoped for. Then softly, intensely, Darrin says, "Can you believe this?"

He has hardly gotten the words out of his mouth when a male loon pops up portside. It is less than six feet from my body. From my first days in the Boundary Waters, loons have fascinated me, especially mother loons. They always seem to gather their broods in large numbers at early evening. Although I have never been to Central Park in New York City, I have always imagined the loon's evening paddle to be like mothers strolling their babies through that park, meeting and greeting other moms. Those early trips brought leisurely paddles for the loons and me.

Often in those paddles the game was to draw as close as possible to the mother loon, knowing her instinct would be to save the children. Sensing danger, she quickly moved them away. The young would paddle like crazy to keep up. Sometimes babies popped up on mom's back and watch as we paddled by. The last thing they wanted, adults and babies, was to be near us. They eschewed us with pride. The real young, those who could not fly nor dive, often ran pell-mell atop the water when frightened. Single adults dove into the depths, wanting miles between themselves and us. That is not happening now!

As we are quietly leaning back, dead in the water, soaking in a peaceful evening, the loon seems unsure of what to do. A stare-down begins. He has floated so close that I can reach out and touch him with my paddle. I am astounded. Neither Darrin nor I dare speak or move. Even our breathing is without a sound. The loon's stare feels like he's trying to read my mind. It is so intense. I have never felt that from a bird. In a way it appears we are being given a dirty, questioning look, "What are you doing in my territory? Get out!"

The stare is definitely a challenge, not a put down. Neither of us moves. Neither wants to lose the moment. What are we waiting for? Without a sound, his mate rises in majestic splendor to his right. The two loons now look at each other and then back at us. We aren't moving; neither are they. After eyeing us long minutes, they look away. Then, just as quickly, turn back to stare. They do this several times. It is as though they are trying to determine if it is safe or not. Are we a threat? We are not! They begin what they came for.

The male goes first, bursting forth with a long, low call. She replies with a perfect echo. A third loon, somewhere on the western shore, returns her echo. As that echo begins to fade, the male goes again and so does his mate. This time we hear not only the third loon on the western shore, but a fourth on the eastern shore. Each time the male calls, the mate echoes. Each of her echoes is re-echoed by more and more loons joining the chorus. The re-echoing is coming from a multitude of places. How much is actually a true echo off the water and how much is other loons, I can no longer say. All I know is at this moment we are sitting in the middle, the starting point, of a loon chorus bouncing back and forth across the lake.

Is this an evening newscast or hello to the whole gang? Does it even matter? The experience is beginning to overload both the right and left brain. It is a lifetime experience to be so very close to the leaders of such spectacular, plaintive sunset calls. Even if the trip ends this evening, it will be worth this special moment!

Many are the evenings I have sat on the shore of some northern lake at sunset, listening to a loon's call, and the echoed, re-echoing responses. They are hypnotic, enchanting, and haunting because of the wail-like quality. Now here I sit, privileged to meet the leaders. After fifteen minutes, without notice or warning, they stop, quickly departing. Without so much as a wave, they dive. It is ended.

"Don't go," I want to shout! "Stay, linger!" It cannot be. I offer a quiet prayer of thanks. Already a meditative tape, similar to the peace found on warm, sunset beaches, has wrapped this memory for summoning at a moment's notice.

Although we could sit here all night philosophizing, we need to make the Cass Lake Dam Park, set up, and eat dinner. Reinvigorated for the final leap across Cass, the second half goes as quickly as the first. However, more serenity is in our speed.

As the dam comes into sight, there are docks and what appears to be a canal on the right. Old-timers must have dug the channel to fish Cass and Winni without having to portage. Much has been written about this stretch of the river. Its backwaters, and those two huge lakes, offer some of the finest fishing in Minnesota.

There is a young Indian girl standing on the end of the dock, staring intently into the twilight. She seems to have noticed the Red Lake Nation emblems on our canoe and wants to make contact, but she is being careful. Her family is getting ready to leave. Except for the father, they are all wearing sweaters and sweatshirts to ward off the coolness. He is wearing a red and black checkered, long-sleeve woolen shirt. It is a typical, Paul Bunyan, macho, Northwood's look.

The mother and this girl are wearing matching light blue skirts trimmed in three, colorful half-inch, contrasting braids. They highlight what are surely dancing dresses: very festive looking. Perhaps they are returning from a powwow. The waist is done in tucks so that when dancing the skirt will flow out.

The girl is in the sixth or seventh grade, the oldest of the children. Her demeanor speaks both shyness and coyness. Is she flirting? Her arms are wrapped around the end dock-post, hugging it lightly with her head leaning tenderly on the rounded top, as though it were someone's shoulder. As we close in, her stare is wistful and questioning. Something is keeping her from speaking. She glances in the direction of her father.

He has the boat ready and is assisting her mother in. After her siblings tumble in, he gives full attention to his daughter. She is ignoring him, refusing to acknowledge his stare. She knows she must, all have gone quiet. They are holding their breath. The silence is getting more intense as the pause lengthens. The family is careful not to look at us, yet they know we are involved. She is not moving. Dad and family watch her for movement, while she watches our every move.

What does she want? She will need to decide quickly, the family wants her in the boat. The silence is deafening. Still, she can't quite bring herself to break away, even though it means she will catch someone's wrath. Dad is growing impatient. He stands. Mom and the siblings brace for the worst. Finally, in the quiet, she releases her hold on the pillar. There is a sigh of relief in the family as she reluctantly turns her attention to the boat, quickly walking the ten feet.

Once aboard, the other children look at Dad. When he says nothing, their exuberance begins anew, laughing excitedly about the day's events. As we pull alongside, the father throws out a challenging greeting. His tone speaks volumes. Once again his actions enforce a rule of silence and heads bow appropriately. Although he smiles, he is holding back. Perhaps it is the lettering and logos on our canoe. Maybe it is the fact we are white. Whatever the reason, his trust is faint and reluctant.

"Are you boys fools? Don't you boys know better than to be out this late? Where yah headed anyway?" The emphasis on boys is surprising. I am older than him. The tone is definitely a put-down. Yes, we boys really do know the consequences of paddling in the twilight and crossing such a large body of water in near dark. We would prefer to be setting up camp without mosquitoes feasting on our sweat, grime infested bodies. There is really very little he or anyone can say that we aren't already well aware of.

I bite my tongue and answer less than enthusiastically, "We're headed to New Orleans."

He laughs mockingly. Perhaps it is a show in front of the children. Then he adds, "A lot of men better than you boys started out with the same intentions. They didn't make it and neither will you."

That is one too many mistakes. Both Darrin and I love a challenge, especially a feisty one. My reply: "It is indeed our intention to go all the way, and we'll do it no matter what you think!"

He just laughs again and sarcastically wishes us good luck. As his ten-horse Johnson roars to life and sputters down the short outlet, the family is discussing our dream. Fortunately they don't all agree with Dad. That is satisfying. The young girl, who first met us with a reserved smile, now waves courageously. Soon they are out of sight.

The campground is adjacent to what is left of the channel. Its log wall makes for easy docking and unloading. Quickly setting up camp, we lessen our tensions over the lateness of the hour by joking about the father's prognosis on our success. We'll show him, prove him wrong!

In truth, people seem evenly divided on our chances of success. The ones who encourage us, tell us of their dreams. Those who discourage us seem to have lost their innocence. Now they find it hard to dream dreams that carry risks, risks necessary to making dreams happen.

While setting up camp and fixing the meal, there is a last hurrah in the western sky. Even Dick Hansen's canoe country paintings could not do justice to this sunset. It is spectacular. I stop fixing the meal. "I'm going for the camera." Magnificent sunset moments pass all too quickly. After retrieval and aiming, I catch the sun sliding into oblivion behind Cass and between two, tall white pines. "Got it!" The sun hung just a moment above the waterline before dropping totally under and allowing darkness to envelope everything. "I'll be anxious to see that one." Darrin nods agreement.

After a quick meal and before the mosquitoes get too much blood, we are in the tent trying to relax. "Can you believe that guy?" Darrin asks. "What the heck was going on?"

My response is filled with sarcasm, "Maybe it's our inexperience."

Darrin is about to twist the thought more but pauses. He is soft and reflective, "We did let our guard down on Wolf Lake."

"Yeah, we did." I say no more, hoping our days ahead will never lose the relaxed feelings of this afternoon and evening. Yet I know we need to remain more alert while soaking up every passing moment.

"How much time do you think it'll take Mother Nature to bring us back to our senses?" Darrin laughs.

Today has been what dreams are made of. Not only were the skies that deep blue of summer, but the river was so clean. Its current leisurely moved the light-brown, sandy granules to sparkle like tumbling diamonds. The overall cool, partly cloudiness of the past three days has been ideal for canoeing. In between each front we get plenty of sunshine and serenading from feathered friends. Canoeing in coolness and plenty of sunshine, while listening to happy birds, is truly pleasurable.

This portion of the river is unspoiled environment, a true sanctuary for loons, eagles, ducks, and a multitude of smaller birds. Eddy Harris missed one of the all-time great places on the upper Mississippi, every bit as gorgeous as any Boundary Water lake but with a greater multitude of birds and walleyes.

While doing the dishes we donated several pints of blood to the local mosquito patrol and I commented, "I'll give them credit for one thing..."

"Who?"

"The mosquitoes"

"What are you talking about?"

"They keep the human population down."

DEATH ELUDED

The demands of canoeing caught up; we overslept. We are excited to get going as we have read much about this area. Its land formations alternate between swamps and sandy shores with towering pines. Gliding silently from below the Cass Lake Dam and with no more than twenty strokes, we are immediately rewarded. The water boils near a reedy patch. Intrigued, we glide into the feeding frenzy.

Walleyes surround us. If I had a landing net, I would be tempted to break the law and dip them. Oh, I wouldn't keep' em! I'd just do it to garner bragging rights for having landed so many at one time. I have never encountered Walleyes so close together and near the surface. It is what I would expect from carp.

"Are they spawning or feeding?"

I shrug, "I don't know."

Turning back to the main current, bald eagles seize our attention. Two take flight. Several more are perched in towering pines and facing downriver, ready to leap at a moment's notice. Each time we get within fifty yards, they take flight. We are disturbing their morning hunt. I want to shout, "Turn around, head upstream…near the marsh." Perhaps the challenge of a hunt is more to their liking. Straight ahead is the largest gathering of bald eagles I have ever seen. There are fifteen in one, tall, white pine near the river's edge.

For over an hour the number of eagles does not diminish. If it is their feeding time, it is lasting a long time. Will they guide us all the way to Lake Winnibigoshish? Their presence is surely a testament to the great fishing between Cass and Winni and to the health of the environment. Although perched and ready to pounce on any fish that dares break surface, we have yet to see an eagle swoop and make a catch. But watching their head movements, scanning the waters for prey, is enough.

We have seen bald eagles every day now. At the Rez we were told their presence is a good omen. If true, how long will they guide our trip: Iowa, Missouri? Then what?

"Hey Dad, remember how we flew across Cass last night? We should name our canoe Golden Wings."

As the canoe has a golden hue, I like his idea. "Fine with me."

As noon approaches, so does the outlet to Winni. Traveling in a protective windbreak all morning, flanked by huge pines, has again left us feeling snug and secure. A half mile or so ahead, beyond the outlet to Winni, is some real wave action. As it poses no immediate danger, Darrin wants to head out into the waves and take advantage of the wind. "It'll be at our backs!" he says.

True, the waves are headed in a northerly direction. But due to some spectacular scenery, 65-degree weather, and a great windbreak, we have been lulled into a peaceful, almost lazy paddling experience. We are too relaxed. We are not ready for the change and serious cold-water conditions. "It's too choppy."

"But the wind's outa the South."

"Yeah, but there's a collision going on. Look up," I say.

"It won't blow rain 'til tonight. I listened to the marine radio."

Well the good weather can't last forever, and we have had a great paddle from Cass to Winni. Perhaps the wind doesn't have a clear claim on her. No, the winds from the two fronts are butting heads and forcing the trees to do the same. "I don't want to get in the middle of that kind of action." I point to the tree tops.

Darrin looks up but says nothing. He believes the southern winds are dominant and will give us a great assist, a quick cross. Hugging Winni's western and southern shore, to avoid the choppy waters, will add over seven miles to the paddle. The weather feels like it could go either direction, warm or cold.

As we pull around the last point of land, before heading directly onto the lake, we see that the southern winds are winning the battle. However, the two winds are arguing fiercely. The northern is demanding winter remain; the younger, stronger, southern wind is saying, "No way!" The mixing is not a good sign.

"What say we pull over, eat…discuss it?"

Darrin's "Fine!" has a negative ring to it.

Passing out of the river's mouth shows us for the first time how protected we have been. Huge whitecaps are forming at the end of the calm waters. The tall pines lining the western shore have created a windbreak for the first hundred yards or so. Although large, the waves don't seem insurmountable from this vantage point. However, I clearly remember two occasions of sitting on protected shorelines when waves didn't seem insurmountable. Later, when I'd gotten myself into the middle of the action, I wished I had stayed ashore.

Lunch is our chance to discuss strategy. Any assault on Lake Winnibogoshish will need a plan. Winni, as the locals call it, is a stretch of water at least fourteen miles wide from where we are now located to where we want to be.

Protected from the wind, we bask on sun-warmed rocks. It feels good. Although our bodies are relaxed, our eyes are glued on the lake. Sausage on rye crisp, smothered with peanut butter and jelly, assuages appetites and minds trying to determine whether the waves are too high, too unsafe.

Darrin believes the challenge is not too great. I believe it is too risky. Darrin is younger and stronger. Post army, he still believes himself invincible. He is the reason Outward Bound was started. Youth and strength always seem to want to conquer Mother Nature, rather than find a way to live with her. Learning to live safely with challenges is what Outward Bound is all about.

Darrin bolsters his arguments: "Those waves can't be more dangerous than being shot at in Kosovo! Besides, a little wave action will be exhilarating after Cass."

I want to say I have never been shot at, but it is not a time for comebacks. Instead I find myself saying, "You're talking like a twenty year old. I want what's safe."

Immediately sarcasm comes out. "Hey, the great Outward Bound man isn't afraid of a little wind is he?"

"I don't want a decision based on a challenge."

"You're afraid!"

"Yes I am. I've done dumb things before." Red flags pop up as the conversation turns away from weighing pros and cons. I have lost some of my zest for challenges. My fear factor now kicks in earlier. I won't tell Darrin this for a sneer has already formed on his upper lip. It centers on my unwillingness to cross the open water.

Perhaps it's not too rough. No, that's an illusion. I need to find a way to rationally explain the dangers we will encounter. The lake is a huge expanse. We can barely see the tops of seventy-plus-foot trees on the opposite shore, and we need to go miles north of that. The truth is we can't see where we want to land. It is on the other side of the horizon. We can only see a point of land eleven miles away.

I, too, don't want to paddle the extra miles, the southern route. Perhaps we can take advantage of the wind. If only I could find some reassurance. It would be a real coup to use the wind in such a major paddle.

After additional quiet time, Darrin picks up the discussion. "If we take the compass reading, the wind will be directly at our backs, cutting paddling time. The southern route will take too long. It's out of the way!"

"Yeah, but is the shortcut worth the risk?"

With a grin Darrin adds, "Look at the map. It's not that far."

"It is, and the waves are…."

Too late! His little joke has taken me off guard. He has gotten the opening he wanted. He begins anew, but with greater emphasis, "You're afraid…aren't you?"

"I told you I was…I've been in similar situations. I remember being a young, naïve college freshman doing the Boundary Waters. My roommate said he'd get us a good deal on canoe rental as his grandfather owned the last resort on Moose Lake. If needed, we could pick up extra supplies there."

"So what happened?"

"Before leaving I phoned. There was a last-minute hitch. He couldn't join us. But a younger brother wanted to go. I asked, 'Is he an experienced canoeist?' For Danny and me there was no turning back, our vacations were etched in stone. Steve's response, 'Well, not exactly. He enjoys canoeing, but doesn't always make the greatest choices.'

"Ignoring the words 'greatest choices,' I blundered ahead in the wrong direction. 'Can he pay his way?'" I now pause and look directly at Darrin, "Don't ever let money be a motivating factor." It is more of a plea than preaching. "Steve's reply was, 'sure, he's got a part-time job.'

"'Well, then he's welcome.'"

"The first day out Mike talked us into shooting Basswood Falls… claimed he'd done it before. Needless to say we capsized. Although we salvaged everything, we spent the next day drying out. That experience proved to be the easier part of the trip.

"Two days later we decided to cross Lac La Croix. Lac La Croix is a lake like Winni, ten miles or more wide. It was a warm summer day, thank God for that. Paddling was unremarkable when we started. Shortly after we hit the middle of the lake, the sky became overcast, thoroughly dark. Heavy winds and rain started. Within moments we were paddling parallel to our waist as waves rolled over the sides. The only thing in our favor was we were headed into the wind. We wouldn't capsize even though the canoe was engulfed.

"Out of stupidity we didn't panic in the warm waters. As we couldn't turn the submerged canoe around and float back in with the waves, we decided to paddle forward…got nowhere. Then God sent an angel. Lac La Croix is quite literally a boundary water lake between Canada and the United States. Motorized boats are allowed on it. Our angel captained a large boat. It had two sleeping cabins below deck and could safely ply those waves.

"While Mike and Danny steadied the canoe, I stood up, frantically waving my paddle. The captain noticed and came to our rescue, or so we thought. He greeted us with, 'What the hell do you dumb #%*ing kids think you're doing out in the middle of this #%* &%# #%*& ing lake? You dumb —s! I'll help you get the water out and then you're on your own.'

"Once aboard we were greeted with, 'Make it quick…I got a poker party I don't intend to miss.' As we struggled to get our waterlogged packs aboard, I knew getting back on the water would put us back under. Before he could say more, I offered to pay him. He reluctantly agreed to take us to shore. That experience taught me to stay off stormy lakes."

Darrin's chiding smile lets me know he hasn't heard a thing I have said…or doesn't want to. I wish I could have passed along my history with his genes. It would have saved a lot of wasted words during his teen years and now. My story goes over his head like the southerly gusts. He reiterates, "You're afraid!"

"Yes, I am."

Additional exchanges do not dissuade. Foolishly I offer a compromise, "All right. I'm willing to venture near the wave action. If it's too dangerous, we turn back." Immediately I know it is dumb, really dumb! There are no good compromises in dangerous situations!

"Sure!" he replies.

Rested, we move out, but with one key factor overlooked. The canoe sits four to six inches above the water. We sit another three feet above that. The wind catches us twenty yards before the wave action. Quickly and efficiently, we are thrust into the mix and begin riding a five-foot-plus wave. Pushed straight up, we teeter on the top before crashing down the other side. Any attempt to turn will result in capsizing. We are caught! The burst of southwest wind that caught us acted like an Alberta Clipper and sent us sailing. Even the skies seem to have darkened. Immediately upon hitting the wave bottom, another is rushing under us, lifting us up and thrusting us forward.

A decision must be made: capsize purposely and swim back without the canoe, or run with the wind. Neither of us wants to abandon ship and end the trip. Quickly and foolishly we decide to run with the waves. Gear is more important than lives. Traveling at a fast clip, with little power over the direction, we are in God's hands.

The only factor in our favor is the direction. Each wave rolling in lifts us up and sends us scuttling northeasterly down the other side. It is very similar to small ocean rollers only much closer together. Our advantages are three: we have both surfed with boogie boards, Darrin has ocean kayaked, and the waves are large enough and far enough apart that they don't come crashing over the stern. The downside is being pushed lickety-split, much like a boogie board when it first catches a wave. However, there is no room for error.

The wind and wave action quickly lower Golden Winds into a third trough. She is bottoming out a split second longer. Why? The answer is immediate and to our left. Bearing down is a set of two waves. The northwest wind is now going to take its turn at sinking us. The broadside blast will sink us without adjustments.

Only now, after being driven into the rough waters, is the second set of colliding waves evident. These two sets of waves are in a fisticuffs match. It is unnerving. When watching the wave action on shore, to judge its pattern, only the southwestern punches were noticeable. Now, too late, a left uppercut is about to land.

The first set of three waves was frightening as each picked up our twenty-footer and shoved it forward like a toothpick. Now it appears we were toyed with, setup for the knockout punch. "Paddle left… hard," I scream!

It is not quick enough, water sloshes over the side. Darrin is now experiencing my worst nightmare. His new-found anxiety comes out in anger, "What the hell yah doing back there?"

If I shout back, it will do no good. I need to save my breath for instructions. At this moment we would both be jumping for joy to be taking the protected western and southern shoreline, the long way. The sense of danger in this cold water has both figuratively and literally invaded us. If we don't react quicker, water will continue to wash over the sides.

"Why'd you get me into this?" he shouts. He sounds like a son wanting to know why his dad let him down. When the wind had been riding high over our heads, and we didn't felt its fury, it was safe. Now, in the open, the raw power is quickly bringing us to our knees. This is the fall that comes from thinking you can control Mother Nature. I screwed up. I knew better. I had more experience.

In the late summer and early fall, when these waters are warm like Lac La Croix was, a Winni bath would have no harmful effect. But here, in these cold waters, where the ice just melted a few weeks ago, human bodies don't stand a chance without wetsuits. These are winter waters, comparable to the early spring runoff of the Rockies. That cold sucks the air out and holds it out. A fifty-eight year old will not last long in this water; neither will a twenty-eight year old! How many have died on Winni from hypothermia?

Why did I ever consider the open lake? No! I can't think about those things. I've got to concentrate. I've lived in Mother Nature 24/7. I was lazy. Now there's no turning back. What was I thinking? Concentrate Gary! Even staying with a swamped canoe will mean certain death. How could I do such a dumb thing? You don't have time for these discussions. Don't blame yourself, stay afloat. Your decision was a joint decision, equal blame. Don't accept his anger. No one forced him even if you should've used better judgment.

Yes, concentrate, there is little time to assess what is happening. React or go down. It is a long way across. Even small amounts of water will eventually sink us. The southwest waves are again lifting and catapulting the canoe northeast. The swells, however, have intensified. They are now well over six feet. Here comes the second set from the northeast. We need better timing.

"Paddle left, harder!" I scream again, and I do the same. This time it is not broadsided nearly so much, only a light spray and a few drops. The scariness, however, is not lessened. We have turned too far east and must adjust back.

The suddenness with which these two sets of waves come crashing, from different directions, always leaves the illusion we are about to be capsized. It is this sensation that is keeping us from remaining calm. Even though it appears we may remain afloat, the suddenness is unnerving and demands full attention. We can't let up.

"Paddle right!" I shout. There is no time to think. The next set of waves is always upon us. Timing is everything. Again and again I yell to switch and paddle hard, first right then left.

My personal situation with Darrin is now tenuous. Although relaxing a bit, he is demanding rationale for every command. As there is no time to waste, I continue in a quick, staccato fashion.

He also continues, "Why yah ordering me around?"

This is dumb. I don't have sufficient time to explain. I go silent. It does no good. He keeps contending with remarks like, "That'll get us broadsided…we're turning too fast…it'll capsize us."

Finally I shout back, "We haven't yet!"

The weight of that statement gets through. He quits speaking and obeys even though he is going against his vow, "Never again will I listen to a commanding officer bark orders." When he left the army, he no longer wanted to listen to anyone's bark. Although I find relief, there is sadness in his capitulation. I call out, "I promise. I'll explain later…trust me!" He nods.

For the moment it is all that matters. He is digging in with all of his strength and allowing us to make every maneuver. We are now changing directions quickly. I wouldn't trade him for any other canoeist. Paddle hard on port, avoid being broadsided. Paddle hard on starboard, ride out the next set of waves: a definite pattern. But each maneuver takes enormous energy.

We cannot continue to expend so much. We need to relax if we are to persevere. This pattern will be confronting us for the next few hours. Although knowing the pattern lessens fears, the energy being burned is severe and a test of endurance.

The die is cast. The first set of three waves pushes us farther north; the second set of two pushes us farther east: three one way, two the other. The advantage appears to be ours if we can hit the eastern shore. The momentary lull after the set of three waves gives me a chance to think. But we can't let our guard down, even for a moment. We must continue to grapple.

Nearly two hours into the endurance and over halfway, we are beginning to realize we may not have enough easterly push. We could miss the last point on the eastern shore and end up in the North Bay, another three plus miles of exerting vast amounts of energy. That possibility is creating a new tension.

To ward off hunger and thirst, we learned to grab our water bottle after one set, open it after the next and drink from it after the third. The same is true for energy bars. Our bodies are brutalized by the energy being burnt. In spite of the cold, we are drenched in sweat. The crossing has become a monumental task neither of us is willing to give up.

It is nearing three hours. Tired and paddling on sheer adrenaline, we are finally close enough to know we can make land without being blown into the North Bay. Still, corrections need to be made. The canoe must go a little less East on the set of two waves and a little more North on the set of three waves, as the wind and waves presently are poised to smash us on a rocky shore. The question is: How do we land the canoe without capsizing or crashing?

Once, as a member of an adult Outward Bound brigade, we lashed seven canoes together. The plan was to harness a southerly wind by rigging the kitchen tarp into a square mast and sail a chain of seven lakes. However, before beginning the sail, all the possible consequences were not considered. Once out and moving, it took the power of two steersmen to keep a straight course. Secondly, all the other adults and gear had to be moved into the bows. Even though this decision helped keep the canoes lower in the water, the wind in our sail still lifted the entire front half of all seven canoes, its gear and people, off the water's surface, riding half in and half out at break-neck speed.

Approaching the northern shore of the seventh lake brought a final realization: stopping. There was no way to take the wind out of the sail as there wasn't time to cut it down. Fortunately a twenty-foot wide sandy shore lay to our right. The canoes were traveling at such speed they leapt out of the water, crossed a forty foot sandy shore and came to rest atop a thicket.

In the silence that followed someone remarked, "I'm grateful those bushes weren't trees."

Another said, "Or those rocks to our left." That scenario is now running through my mind. Darrin, too, realizes the options are few. Shooting beyond the point may take us to the north shore of North Bay. We have no idea what that is like.

Darrin calls out, "If we can't land before the point, maybe we can maneuver around to its downwind side."

"Could we be that lucky?" My sarcasm comes from discouragement. After spending three hours crossing, there seems to be no safe landing in the wind and waves. If we don't land in the next mile, turning the corner is the only hope, and it is not without peril. The crosswinds are strong.

We are now adjusting our paddling to move closer in while continuing north. We soon find ourselves within a hundred yards of shore, searching for a landing spot. Something isn't right! The compensation to prevent hitting the eastern shore, while running parallel and inching in, is working too easily. Even the waters appear calmer.

Oh, my God, not again! Pummeling has begun anew. This time it is on starboard. The blows are quick and successive, like a bloodied boxer being hit but no knockout blow coming. The colliding winds out of the northwest and southwest, after pounding the eastern shoreline, are rebounding off the trees and turning into straight-line winds. Straight north that is, buffeting us as they skip back out just above the water's surface.

Caught between the western wind and the funneled north winds, with no rhyme or reason to their buffeting, we are rocketing north. Failing to take into account the impact of winds interacting with other masses now has us charging up a narrow, thirty-yard wide alley.

Quickly regaining control leads to a new decision: Do we try to inch in closer and land our Kevlar canoe on those rocks? Do we have any hope in this wind tunnel of making a right-hand turn at the point? How will the funneling winds behave when they collide with the westerlies blowing across the point?

Hugging the shoreline closer in seems to be our best bet. Another miscalculation! The tunneling winds take a new grip on the canoe. They are pulling it in while pushing it north. The rocky shoreline is about to have us. "Do you want to capsize and fight it in the water?" I shout!

"No!" Although close enough to jump and save both ourselves and the canoe, we are arguing.

"We're drawing in too quickly…we're going to hit the rocks no matter what," I say.

"That's because you're moving us in too fast."

"I'm not doing that!"

"Okay, let's jump then."

"No, wait…something's happening," I shout.

"Are you crazy? Make up your mind!"

God has got to be with us. The wave action is changing again. It is hitting the rocks so hard, the reverb is causing a northerly current, an identical action to what happened when the wind hit the shoreline trees. Not only are we now well below the radar of the strong winds, we are being pulled by a mild northerly current. How strange it is! Heavy wind and waves are all about us as we sit in mostly tranquil waters, five feet wide and moving north. It just doesn't seem possible.

"Somebody's got strong prayers! The water's finally on our side! Let's ride it to the point." Darrin agrees. A few moments ago all I could think of was Ulysses' voyage and the sirens wanting to draw his crew onto the rocky cliffs and certain death. Surely it was experiences like ours that gave way to sailors spinning yarns about how the wind and waves seduce ships.

Feeling some of my muscles relax, I admit, "I've been praying pretty hard."

"Me too!"

For the most part we were never in control and were forced to go with the flow by not panicking too much. Some sailing knowledge and white water experiences also helped. "My heart is still pounding," I shout. "How many years have I taken off?"

"Why yah shouting?" Darrin asks. Yes, why am I shouting? The noise is above us. "I now understand what you were trying to tell me on the other side."

His comment makes me want to shout, "Yes!" but I don't. The open water crossing was dumb. How many more times will I say, "Never again?" Panic and stupid decisions are why people lose their lives in the wilderness. We just won a 50/50 coin toss. Next time we may not be so lucky.

I am about to pursue that thought when Darrin cuts in, "How much water in the back?" He knows it is normal for water to collect in the stern.

"About an inch or two. My personal pack is soaked"

As I look back up, I get a vacant stare. It is how I feel inside. Does he even remember what he asked me? It must have just hit him how lucky we are to be alive. There is only silence and lily-dipping now, dawdling, happy to be alive. Then it begins, just a few drops at first.

"We've got to get moving." Over my shoulder black clouds are descending. Heavy rain is imminent. The old axiom proves true: When it rains, it pours! Within fifteen minutes we take on more water than the previous three hours.

"There's a dock ahead. Let's empty the canoe." After doing so, we stay on deck, waiting out the rest of the downpour. Once back on the water, we double time it to Tamarack Point Campground, pulling up just before the skies open up a second time. Quickly stowing gear in the nearest campsite and flipping the canoe over it, I breathe a sigh of relief. It is truly over.

My eyes well up. "I'd get on my knees and kiss the ground if it weren't so muddy." Darrin nods as pent up emotions begin to flow. Not even being soaked and shivering concerns us as we hug for comfort.

When the heavy rains end, we pitch the tent. While changing into dry clothes and rain gear, Darrin brings up dinner. My reply, "After all those energy bars, I'm too full. What say we head up to the ranger station?"

While exiting the tent, Darrin grabs my arm. "Let's get a picture before Winni calms." Quickly he retrieves a camera. The gray, windy weather continues to show the lake somewhat as it was during the crossing. He wants a concrete memory of its power. I can't say I blame him.

My suggestion: "Let's get a picture in the morning if she's calm. It'll make a great comparison."

The ranger station turns out to be a large camper-trailer. Tamarack uses a host ranger. This is not uncommon for the smaller parks in

Minnesota. Basically host couples collect camping fees and ensure the grounds are well maintained. In exchange, they receive free camping and a small stipend.

The lights are on. A gentle knock brings a younger looking, retired couple: the Coxes. He is dressed in a warm woolen shirt. She has on a puffy pullover sweater. Both are wearing working pants. We are soon sitting around a dining table, exchanging histories.

"In the summers we host Tamarack," she says. "In the winter we live on a boat, docking either in Florida or Missouri."

Within moments we have a personal connection. "We lived most of our married years in Tonka Bay (Minnesota). Ever hear of it?" he asks.

Darrin and I laugh. "We lived there twenty years," I answer. Even though we lived within a half mile of each other, we had never met.

"We're returning tomorrow," she adds.

"Really?"

"Yeah, we're headed for the Dunn funeral at St. John's in Excelsior. Familiar with it?"

We laugh again. "I'm the associate there. My wife will be singing in the funeral schola. Will you take our greetings...let her know we crossed Winni safely?"

"Absolutely."

After filling out the necessary paperwork and paying the site fee, I decide to turn in. Darrin heads to Birch's, the nearest resort. He wants to call Schalleen.

Back at the tent I marvel at how this trip is turning out. Indian smudging and drumming, bird choruses, a beaver graveyard, more bald eagles in one day than I have seen in a lifetime, loons popping up, and good luck on a stormy sea. I rip out a sheet of the diary: oranges, cotton swabs, vitamin C, meat, cheese, postcards, call Jacqui, and St. Mary's Mission. "Thank you, God. Goodnight!"

HANGING DOG

The morning is calm and cool as we bathe in the waters that nearly took our lives. Steam is rising off the lake like an incense offering. The world feels quiet and peaceful. We are still so very grateful to be alive. Our morning prayers noted this. It is almost surreal to sit here and look at the tranquility, the peacefulness that has descended upon Lake Winni. Less than twenty-four hours ago she raged against us. Now, while brushing my teeth, I'm all smiles. I am still alive!

The lake's present calmness is like the beauty of Cass. Although anxious to begin paddling again, something holds us back. It is a bit like getting back into the saddle after being thrown. Winni is such a powerful animal. I have fear mixed with respect and caution. As Darrin is not making a move or hinting at getting back on the water, I suggest, "Let's get supplies." My real motive is a heart-to-heart talk with Jacqui.

"First," Darrin says, "let's get pictures with Winni…she's calm." He smiles and goes for the camera.

As he takes my picture, I feel like Jack when he snuck up on the sleeping giant. I am posing for bragging rights. For all intent and purposes, yesterday should have been my last. So, why am I still alive?

"What part do you suppose Golden Wings played in the crossing?" Darrin's question causes me to reach back in time, remembering what led up to purchasing her. It was a prairie canoe trip on the Cheyenne River in the Badlands of South Dakota. I laugh out loud. Prairie canoeing, now there is an oxymoron. But truly, it was like nothing I had experienced in forty years of canoeing.

There were no insects, black flies or mosquitoes. The sunsets and sunrises were eye-dazzling. Sleeping under the stars, blanketed only by summer's warm air, atop sleeping bags, was an experience I had never done on any previous canoe trip. Certainly I will never do it on this Mississippi trip.

Imagine the size of mosquitoes on the humid flood plains and sloughs of the lower Miss. Sleeping under the stars there would mean an obituary: "Two bodies were found, caved in. All the blood had been drained." Not even in the marshy depths of the Boundary Waters are there hordes of muscle bound mosquitoes like those patrolling and controlling the southern portions of the Miss.

But the three days on the Cheyenne were different. We struggled in serpentine shallows while experiencing the best the prairie had to offer. I have done a lot of river canoeing, encountering Bull Moose, deer, lynx, and more. But pulling the canoe to a halt thirty yards upstream from over three hundred head of Hereford was outstanding.

The power exhibited in their stampeding down one embankment, across the shallow river and pounding up the other, was exhilarating. Standing guard were two magnificent bulls, one on each side of the river, pawing the ground and kicking up yellow clouds: a direct warning to us. Their angry stares and snorting came straight out of an old Western, menacing and challenging, thrilling and unbelievable. Had it been a high water, we would never have experienced this or the dead carcasses downstream.

Ah, yes, the sweet smell of rotting cattle, a breathtaking sight. It happened the second day. We had broken camp shortly after sunrise and were rounding a bend. My partner immediately piped up, "Geez, Gary, what are those birds?"

"Turkey Vultures. Let's stop paddling."

Over a dozen vultures were poised neatly on wooden fence posts, wings outstretched, appearing to stand on tiptoes, balancing awkwardly as though drying dew off their wings, or doing a morning stretch prior to flying. Behind them, circling in the distant skies, were two more groups of five or six, slowly descending in ever-tightening circles, desirous of feasting upon rotting carcasses exposed by the receding waters: juicy morsels, breakfast tidbits.

Later, as we passed one of those maggot's delight, my bowman excitedly said, "Hey, Deacon, the meat's rotted off the head...the horns are still attached." Admittedly 99.9% of the flesh was rotted. But he gave little thought to the remaining one-tenth of one percent, "Can I take it home?"

Not even two plastic bags kept the odor in check. By the time the trip was over, summer's heat had baked the skull in our enclosed trailer. The gear and clothing were rank. The following Sunday my bowman's mother stopped to say she had ordered her son to, "Take that thing to the farthest corner of the backyard! Get it outa the house!" She then looked me straight in the eye, "By the way, who encouraged him to bring it home?" Feigning innocence was to no avail.

After the Cheyenne, while the youth were busy painting walls at the Indian mission, an opportunity to visit downtown Rapid City arose. It is not New York City, but it does have a draw: a Cabela's Sporting Goods. I had heard much about these outlets and was anxious to visit one. On this morning the youth were in the capable hands of adult volunteers who had slipped out earlier for a decent breakfast while I ate cold cereal and drank orange Kool-Aid with the youth.

At Cabela's I explored the latest in camping equipment, but found the canoe selection sparse. However, it whetted my appetite. Back in the Twin Cities, I began a canoe search in earnest. Connecting via telephone with Ken Kettering of Kettering Kanoes, I was introduced to a man with a keen interest and understanding of my desire to canoe the Mississippi. I was never sure, but I think I felt a smile over the phone as I related my long history with aluminum canoes and my lack of knowledge as to how the canoeing world had leapt ahead while I was hibernating.

"Come over. I'll show you some great canoes."

An hour later a forested stretch of Mississippi shoreline, converted to a canoe/kayak business, greeted me. After introductions, I got Ken's background. "I grew up on the river…inherited my love of canoeing from my mother. She used to run the business." He was a child of the river. Through the years he had helped outfit several Mississippi expeditions.

He introduced me to the Wenonah Voyager, Minn III. It seemed perfect in every detail. Growing up on the mighty Miss near Winona, Minnesota, the designer realized the burden of paddling an aluminum canoe upstream. He did something about it. After successfully building racing canoes, he designed a lightweight wilderness canoe to sit low in the water, hold lots of gear and move fast. Research has shown that longer canoes, up to twenty two feet, move faster in the water. This made the Minn III's twenty feet an immediate attraction. Prior to the Minn III, every canoe I had paddled was seventeen feet or less.

This canoe's main attraction is how it lies low and flat on the water—stem to stern. The old, conventional aluminum canoes are curved up at the bow and stern, causing them to ride high, keeping a vast majority of their surface above water. A narrow, one-inch keel is required to keep it from being blown sideways across the water, like a beach ball in the slightest breeze. Also, because aluminum canoes ride high, a longer, heavier paddle is required for stroking. Finally, research has shown canoes curved up at both ends cause a greater drag, more paddling.

As Ken Kettering spoke, my mind turned over these facts. "The Kevlar rides low in the water, hugs it from stem to stern, side-to-side. It acts as its own keel. Rather than having drag from riding high, it knifes through the water. Riding low, close to the water, also means shorter, lighter paddles," he said. It was as though he was reading my mind. "Ever use a graphite paddle? They weigh only a few ounces. This bend allows them to pull more water. Here, lift this wooden paddle…now this graphite." After lifting the black, graphite paddle, I was sure I had died and gone to canoe heaven. The longer, wooden paddle weighed in at over sixteen to twenty-four ounces. The graphite: only a couple. Here were two major improvements to make a trip easier.

Purchasing a used Wenonah saved enough money to buy the graphite paddles. In the early 1970s I paid $100 for a new, fairly heavy, fiberglass canoe. Now, thirty years later, I was listening to Ken Kettering tell me that the cost of one, shiny new graphite paddle was $220. I would have to do some fast-talking to convince Jacqui I had done the right thing. As I am no spring chicken and she wants me to come back rested, I will tell her, "Honey, this paddle is what an old man needs to survive a Mississippi ordeal. The Kevlar canoe is needed for its many safety features on the treacherous Miss."

I turn to Darrin, "It was the canoe that led us safely across Winni."

"I believe it."

As we approach Birch's driveway Darrin muses, "The walk seems shorter."

"It is," I smile, "You're more relaxed. We're happy to be alive."

Birch's store is very small: no oranges, vitamin C, lunchmeat, cotton swabs, or cheese. They do have postcards, a telephone, and short order meals. While Darrin calls, I sit down and order breakfast. The missus is fixing meals. Her husband is sitting kiddy-corner on the L-shaped counter, eating his breakfast. It is a typical small resort bar that doubles as a breakfast counter.

While the bacon fires, she turns and eyes me directly. "Last night your son told us you crossed Winni in the afternoon." Her husband stops eating and looks over, a fork full of scrambled eggs hanging in midair. He nods his unshaven face in agreement. He wants in on this conversation. I am a bit sheepish admitting to such stupidity. I pause, looking for an intelligent answer. There is none.

"Yes, we did."

In the silence that follows, he looks to the missus for more direction. She begins with a slight edge of sadness. "A year ago this May, almost to the day, two young guys did the same thing." She is not pushing her story in any way. She is very calm about it, wanting to watch my reactions as she punctuates each statement. "They followed the same route you did...hit the same bad weather...weren't so lucky... they capsized." After capsized, there is a longer pause. "If I understood where your son said you came out, it's exactly where we found their bodies washed ashore...life jackets still on...died of hypothermia." She stops and waits for a reply. She has made her point.

My heart is saddened at the loss their families must have felt: two, young, healthy, active guys, gone forever. I realize more profoundly our good fortune. In the silence that remains, I try to comprehend how my family would feel if it had happened to us. There is really nothing I can say. Coffee is served. After bacon and eggs, I call Jacqui. "Hi, honey...."

Minus supplies, but full of understandings, Darrin and I head back to the canoe. The paddle begins with a heart-to-heart talk about risks, decision-making, spouses, and family. "We forgot our priorities."

"Yeah."

Even though our mood is upbeat, we are quiet and reflective for over an hour. The beauty of this day is washing away emotional pain but not the lesson learned. The wind is at our backs with a partly cloudy sky alternately warming and cooling us. As the rains passed during the night, we are enjoying perfect canoeing weather.

Darrin is studying the map as we canoe. "Hey, that's Crazy James Point. Wanna give him a holler?" I do, and we do. There is no answer.

"Isn't James the name of that soloist who left Itasca the week before us? I doubt he did the open water. He wouldn't be that crazy." Darrin nods agreement.

Soon we find ourselves sliding under a bridge. "This is Highway Two," Darrin calls out.

Highway Two is a benchmark. We often traveled it while going from Crookston to Bemidji or Duluth. It is the east-west connection between North Dakota and the shores of Lake Superior.

After passing under the bridge, a fisherman dressed in worn bib-overalls, threadbare at the right knee, comes into sight. His flannel shirt is tucked in. A winter hat, earflaps pulled down, warms his head. He is sitting on an overturned, five-gallon, plastic bucket. The label indicates it once held McDonald's pickles. Taciturn answers, mostly grunts, greet our hellos and questions. He wants to be left alone.

Ahead is a small, wooden railroad trestle. We are near Ball Club, passing between layers of silt that once formed the bottom of Lake Agassi. These rich, black riverbanks are narrow, steep, and muddy, making the Miss look more like a farmer's drainage ditch.

"Whata yah think?" Darrin points up. I shrug my shoulders. However, his question peaks my curiosity. The frayed end of a rope is swinging and rubbing against a steel plate attached to the underside of the trestle. Whatever was hanging from it must have been there awhile. The rope is new and an inch thick. Needless to say it leads to much speculation.

"I find a lynching hard to believe. This isn't the Temperance!" We laugh and allow our imaginations to continue working overtime.

Two hundred yards downriver of the bridge and rounding a bend, I quit paddling. "That's odd. I coulda sworn the mud on the riverbank moved. Stop a minute. Yes, something is moving!" I point to a floating tree branch snagged on the outer bend.

"I don't see anything. Maybe it was just loose mud."

"No, stop…mud doesn't move like…see…it's moving again!"

"I can't see what you're talking about."

"We're goin' back." Immediately I begin back-paddling. Reluctantly Darrin follows suit.

"It's a puppy." I say.

"Yeah, but what's holding it?"

As we move in closer, claw marks show a long struggle on the slick, black silt of the bank. Several times the pup was halfway up before sliding back.

"There's a rope around his waist and twisted around a branch." He lies exhausted, half in and half out of the water. I lift both the puppy and branch into the canoe. The rope is looped just behind his front legs and just in front of the rear. His chubby little belly protrudes between the two. The loose end of the rope is frayed from rubbing; it is the other end of the bridge rope.

"How long do you think?" Darrin asks.

"Your guess is as good as mine. It must have been a while. The rope has left deep indentations." As of yet the pup has made no sound, not even a whimper. Though sad, his eyes shine that love only puppies can give. His soft, furry body, caked in mud, is a perfect camouflage on the bank. He can't stop trembling, probably from exhaustion and cold water.

"He's a golden lab. Can't be that old…a couple months," Darrin declares.

Although the dog makes no sounds while I place him on the life jacket, his expression is gratitude. "Hand me that sponge." His tiny body writhes as I try washing the mud off. I stop. The canoe, drifting and changing angles, is now allowing sunshine to flood just beyond his head. He attempts to pull his body into it, but in vain; he doesn't have the strength. I push him and the lifejacket into full sun. The soundless heave and relaxing sigh bring a look of contentment to his face.

We speculate on who the miscreant was, perhaps an ornery child. We hope no adult would do such a cruel thing. "Whoever did it needs some serious help."

"Let's name him Goldie, after the canoe." I like Darrin's suggestion.

"He can be our official mascot," I say. "He is young and will easily adapt to canoeing. We can pick up bedding and food. He will be a great watchdog." I have to talk fast. Darrin is not big on spur-of-the-minute changes.

"No, way! I'm willing to keep him to the Cities. Schalleen'll find him a good home. She can handle this." He is right. Schalleen is a true animal lover, particularly dogs. She has rescued several. It would be a natural for her to take Goldie, give him the love he needs, and then find him a good home.

"Perhaps Pepper would like a companion," I smile while thinking of my little black and white Shih Tzu.

Darrin doesn't appreciate this comment either. "I am not taking a dog to New Orleans."

He knows me too well. His tone is reminiscent of the trouble we encountered hooking up with the fundraiser. Silently I respond, "Okay, Dad!" Besides, a week or so is time enough to decide. Goldie is not going anywhere. It is too hard for him to move. Unfortunately he will not accept water or food.

"We need to get him to a vet," I say.

When evening arrives we make camp atop a bank, in the middle of nowhere. Goldie is laid under the overturned canoe. This protects him from the light rain. As he is still not interested in food, Darrin mixes dry milk with warm water. Goldie laps it up but turns his head at seconds. While we eat supper, sounds begin emanating from Goldie. He is heaving. The action is very hard and yet he doesn't whimper. There must be internal injuries.

We turn in early and sleep comes quickly. As so often happens when one is dead tired, the sleep is abruptly cut off. Goldie is barking, perhaps scaring off an intruder. These are the first voluntary sounds he has made. It must have taken a great deal of effort and come from a deep, inbred instinct. I quickly check the area and return to Morpheus' arms. A heavy downpour begins. As Goldie is snug and dry far under the backside of the canoe, I roll over, hoping for another hour or so of sleep.

Goldie is spending the morning on the bottom of the canoe, basking in the sun's warmth. Although there are no clouds, there is a slight headwind. Just before noon we arrive at Schoolcraft State Park. Goldie is left in the canoe while we eat. It is not helpful to move him.

"That's Goldie. He's whimpering. I'll take a look." I find Goldie convulsing and bleeding from the mouth and rear. It is what we feared. His end is imminent. "Darrin, forget lunch…come here."

After climbing into the canoe, we both place warm, comforting hands upon him. It is such a small gesture, but holding him would cause too much pain. He is responding. His sad eyes are brightening, as if to say, "Thanks." His sighing and breathing are heavy. Darrin gently strokes his fur. The bleeding will not stop. In spite of his pain, he appears peaceful before his breathing ceases. We did what little we could. In less than forty-eight hours we have gone from near death to witnessing it. For the second time in forty-eight hours, we cry like babies.

After regaining composure, Darrin asks, "Do you mind if I bury him?" He is able to hand-dig in the soft peat adjacent to the dock. We gently lay Goldie to rest, as though he were a great hero. He faced death so peacefully. We offer prayers of thanks for his brave spirit and prayers of healing for whoever harmed him.

After eating in silence, we pause again at his gravesite, finding it hard to just get in and paddle away. Darrin smiles, "It's good to know he'll have visitors." Darrin is right. Goldie is buried less than ten feet from the Schoolcraft landing.

On the river, a map check makes it apparent things are not going as planned. For two days we have not met minimum miles, yet it is of little consequence. We are thankful to be alive. Goldie's troubles and pains were far greater than ours.

Remaining quiet and paddling hard makes the time pass quickly, but it is tiring. I am not in the shape Darrin is. Rather than risk another confrontation over whether I am "carrying my weight," I keep my mouth shut. My aches are similar to those coming from doing snow or sand shoveling. As if on the same wavelength, Darrin shatters my thoughts. "This trip isn't worth it. I'm paddling less."

Stunned, I want to shout, "Get outa here!" Again he must be figuring he is making up for "the slacker." As neutrally as possible I say, "Okay. What gives?"

I would have been better off keeping my mouth shut. Darrin has launched into a lecture on his latest thinking. Actually it is more like he is discussing the issue with himself. The more he talks, the more his attitude becomes a source of irritation—both for him and me. I admit paddling is easy for me; I enjoy it. "If you weren't slacking off, you'd be in more pain."

So my lack of talking about my pain means I am slacking off. He believes there should be some consequence. I button my lips tighter. With plenty of time to think and stew, I count the number of strokes each of us does. I do six for every five of his. Changing my pace will only worsen the situation. The trip is worth more than a fight over who is doing the most paddling. He must be feeling some other pain. Perhaps it is both Goldie's death and Schaleen. He has not said anything about last night's telephone conversation with her.

The afternoon's silence stinks. Too much time is passing without resolution. We can talk about Goldie, but all other conversations fail.

Periodically one of us brings him up, allowing some release of personal frustrations. The only salve on Goldie's pain, now our pain, is that his last hours were somewhat happy. He did not die cold and forsaken on a damp, muddy riverbank. Then irritation at the bugger who did it turns to anger as we imagine how long it took the new rope to fray and break.

The good news is the wind. It has been strong and at our backs all afternoon. Eventually, though, our frustrations come out in another mistake. We paddled an extra half-mile south on Blackwater Lake. We are now approaching Grand Rapids.

WHAT BLONDIE FORGOT

It is a couple hours before dark. Pokegama Lake Regional Park, the Corps campground in Grand Rapids, is insight. The campground sits along the west side of the Corps' dam. It appears quiet and peaceful in the late afternoon sun. Everything is warm and green. However, because no resolution on the minimum number of daily miles has been reached, we are both unhappy and refusing to get out of the canoe. Of particular concern to Darrin is his back.

"I want to make New Orleans," He begins amicable. "I looked at the maps. We can make it by doing thirty-five a day."

Thank God, I pray silently, while nodding agreement and saying, "Okay."

We leave the gear in the canoe and beach it just above the dam while heading to the ranger's office. The office is manned by a good-looking blonde, perhaps a senior in high school. "Hi!" she calls out.

"Got anything out-of-the-way…quiet?" I ask.

"I'm not familiar with the sites. Here's the map." Her smile is dismissive.

"How far is this toilet area?"

She looks at the map and shrugs. "Can't say."

"How far from the office?" I ask, wondering if this is going to be twenty questions.

"Dunno."

Feigning little interest, Darrin takes his smirk and stares at the pamphlet rack. But being impulsive and not wanting to be left out of such an intriguing conversation, he turns back to test the waters. "How far to a grocery store?" As Grand Rapids is not big, he must figure this is an easy question.

"I couldn't tell yah. You guys want to tent?" She is now getting a bit testy.

"Yes."

"We have only one area for tenting."

After showing us the place on the map and pointing it out from the office window, Darrin, still amused, continues. "How about a regular site, downriver of the dam, away from the highway." On getting out of the canoe, we noticed Highway Two was less than a half mile away.

"Not possible!"

Darrin's head jerks back. Amusement leaves his face, "Why?"

"They're for campers." She means trailers.

Skepticism enters Darrin's voice, "Even if we're willing to pay?"

"Yeah…some sort of rule."

Laughing would do no good; she is serious. Fortunately tiredness has precedence over irritation. While pointing to the shower symbol on the map, I say, "I don't understand where the showers are located."

"They're right here, but we're closing shortly. You'll need to be quick." Quick is the operative word. She has begun filling out our camping permit. "You guys will be in the tenting site," is her less than reassuring statement. With the fee paid, we head out to unload and return for a shower.

The park's rural character gives a relaxed feeling. On this warm, early evening, people, particularly the young, are hanging out around the dam. Some are strolling hand in hand on the walkways; others are sitting on the grassy knoll next to the dam. A few youngsters are enjoying jumping off the fishing pier located just below the dam. The current is swift. I cock my head. "Does that sound like sirens?" No response is needed. A fire rescue truck is headed this way. Dropping our packs, we head toward the crowd gathering below the dam.

"What happened?"

"Some kid hit a piece of glass while jumping off the pier." The wooden pier is located over the deep rapids just below the dam.

Although its intended use is for fishing, it is an ideal jumping spot. The rapids can be caught for a quick downstream trip. The wooden railing is easy to climb and the flat top makes an ideal jumping platform.

Within moments the bleeding is stopped and the excitement dies down. As it does, I murmur, "Next there'll be a large sign forbidding jumping off the pier." Darrin is not listening. A couple has shown interest in our trip. Not wanting to be bombarded, I head back to the tent for a towel.

After showering, I thank the ranger for her hospitality. Her cheery response, "We'll open again at seven or eight," takes me aback. Which is it? Are they really that laid back around here?

After dinner I call Jacqui and tell her about Goldie's life and death. It is as sad for her as it was for us. I change the subject. "The usual is happening. We are choosing nicknames for each other. Zeek, Rosco, Fink, Skeeter and Enis, all with an appropriate Minn-a-sotan, hillbilly accent. Darrin prefers Skeeter. I am having a harder time. I am still not sure of his expectations."

Jacqui laughs politely. Darrin is moving closer, listening, getting antsy. Either I am talking too long or getting the day's event wrong. "Darrin wants to talk," I tell Jacqui. As I walk away, he fills her in on the finer details. I smile and leave him to the mosquitoes.

The sleeping bag soothes my aches and pains, reminding me of my fifty-eight years and being out of shape. Perhaps the daily workout will, in the end, have a positive effect. Sleep is instantaneous and a deep REM begins immediately, causing my heart to pound.

A vivid nightmare has kicked into high gear. A train is bearing down upon the tent. Darrin has mistakenly pitched it in the middle of the railroad tracks. Its whistle shrieks as screeching wheels try to halt. The ground shakes and rumbles. The quake is gaining momentum. A thousand-plus tons are about to flatten me. I have got to get out. Flailing and clawing at the bag's zipper, I can't move it. Then I find myself fully awake and trying to get out as a whistle howls for me to get off the track.

I bolt up. "My God, it's real." The shaking ground and terrifying whistle have me moving in earnest. Quickly I roll out the tent door and toward the river. I turn back to look. My mind is going in a million directions. My heart races fast. Am I safe? Fully awake, trying to comprehend what is actually happening, I see the roaring monster passing no more that fifteen feet from the tent. As I watch cars roll by, my heart begins to slow and I recall our request for a quiet spot.

I knew Interstate Two was only a few hundred yards from the campgrounds, but the train tracks next to the tenting area are hidden in tall grass. It is the Chicago to Montana route. Too late and too dark to move, the next six hours are filled with screeching wheels and banshee whistles. I toss and turn, falling asleep only momentarily before the next train passes. There is no end to them moving through Grand Rapids, at least one per hour. The sounds and rumbling are what the 1950s movie theaters had hoped to accomplish with "Dolby Surround Sound."

Growing up a half block from a main east-west train route never bothered me, even though those old, coal-burning behemoths shook our house: I slept right through it. I had lived there since birth and didn't consciously notice it. Whenever a friend would sleep over, he would insist he hadn't slept a wink. If I said I hadn't heard anything, he would think I was pulling his leg. Now I understand.

Dear Diary,

5/30/02

Warning! Stay away from the Pokegama tent site. Although beautiful, it is fit for only one purpose: Operation Iraq. It is an ideal place for Guantanamo detainees. They would be wrecks, confessing to anything within a week. Either there is such a creature as the "ditzy blonde" or I am experiencing karma for having laughed at those jokes.

At least the birds have much to cheer about this morning. Darrin must also. He is sitting up. Before I am fully awake, he speaks, "I've been thinking…can we talk?"

Shaking my head and rubbing my eyes to ensure wakefulness, I mutter, "Sure."

"I expected some tension between us, and I knew about Schalleen's concerns, but my back is really bothering me."

I say nothing for a moment, pausing to collect my thoughts. Then, "I knew about Schalleen and expected some tension over leadership issues, but the back thing I don't understand."

"Taller people can't take the stress of leaning forward so much. The bending is killing me, and I'm in good shape. The paddling also hurts because of the crapped leg room. This canoe is narrower than what I'm used to."

I hesitate long enough so as not to blow it. "I appreciate your honesty. I had some pretty negative thoughts yesterday, figuring you were thinking I wasn't carrying my weight."

Before I can continue, he interjects, "Are you? I can't feel yer paddling making any difference."

I pause longer and take a deeper breath. "I told you how I can't use the J-stroke. I've tried variations, but only straight strokes work. It's the first time I've been a power stroker without variety. By the way, I counted our strokes yesterday. I'm doing six to your five…your change is noticeable. I didn't dare say anything 'cause I thought you'd get mad."

"I woulda."

"Look, I'm giving it a hundred percent."

"I know. I just want you to know I have three things challenging me. It's a pain."

"Darrin, if this trip hurts either of us, I'll regret it. I'd rather not finish than get hurt physically or emotionally. Honestly, I don't know what to say about your separation. I'm feeling caught no matter what I say. As far as the paddling goes, if you want to paddle stern sometimes, I am okay with that."

"No, I'm getting use to the legroom. Originally Schalleen didn't think the trip would bother her. On the honeymoon she began talking, said our pre-marital telephone conversations made her feel you were more important, that I shoulda been more supportive of her. This is new stuff. I tell her how much I love her and how keeping my promise to you is a good example of how well I'll keep the marriage promise. My comments don't make any difference. Her pain is affecting me. I love her."

"I'm sorry. If you want, I'll change the goal."

"That's the part I can't figure. Is this a joint trip or something I'm doing for you?"

"Are you asking?"

"Yes."

"I want it to be a joint trip."

"Well, when we were repacking at Itasca, you told that guy we'd do fifty miles some days. You never ask me how I felt about that."

"Your right…I am sorry. And I am okay with the thirty-five you said yesterday."

"Good."

Fifteen minutes later we hug. I have agreed to match him stroke for stroke: fast or slow. We believe only a little is resolved and the waters are still being tested. As the canoe is loaded, he says, "Perhaps the wind at our backs will help." I agree.

A couple blocks downstream is an inlet to nearby businesses. A dilapidated dock, heaved and twisted by Minnesota winters, deteriorated from exposure to snow, wind, rain, and sun, hangs onto life precariously. We step aboard gingerly. Twenty feet away is the Blandin Paper Mill's chain-link fence. Inside are logs stacked twenty to thirty feet high and being watered down by sprinklers. It is either a fire concern or the first step in pulp processing.

A block away is Highway Two. The Quick and Easy turns out to be several blocks east. The coffee is decent. "How much gas?" We smile and explain.

Once on the river, it is only a couple blocks to the Blandin paper mill and electric dam. Although no portage is shown on the map, Darrin believes an easy one should be on the right. It is not!

The left shore, right up to the water's edge and running down to the dam, is being held hostage by the Blandin/Electric company's eight-foot, chain-link fence. Blocking the right shore are iron posts, driven in and pointing upstream. On a small scale, it is what the Germans did to the beaches at Normandy. The well-manicured yard is also strewn with no-trespassing/no-portaging signs. Additionally there is a billboard claiming the portage is upstream. What a mess! The company and neighbors have a strangled hold on the Miss, sealed her off in a raffish and vulgar way.

Although the upstream bank does not seem amenable to a portage, we go anyway. After much searching, we find a neighborhood path children use to reach the river. It is straight up a steep embankment. After unloading and hauling everything up, we have no way of knowing how far to portage. Darrin volunteers to scout it out. Upon returning, he is not encouraging.

The portage is several blocks long and crosses a busy highway bridge. As we are about to begin, a pickup pulls in across the street. When the driver steps out, Darrin holds up a water jug and calls out, "Can we fill it at your place?"

The man looks somewhat bewildered. "Why didn't you guys call the power company and get the free taxi?"

"Taxi?" The word literally falls from our lips.

"Yeah, the park rangers are instructed to tell canoeists." Another fact that slipped the blonde ranger's mind!

Despite sounding critical, our new acquaintance is quite friendly, making up for the frustrations of a lack of sleep, a ditzy blonde, and a long walk for groceries. "Hey, what say I drive you to the landing?" His voice is upbeat and caring. "Besides, calling a cab will take forever." He then looks at the water jugs Darrin is carrying. "Where'd you guys get that muddy water?" We look and wonder too.

Once the gear is in the pickup, we find the canoe too long for its bed. Darrin heads off on a half-mile trek leading to Blandin's main offices. In their backyard, a friendly groundskeeper helps out with a launch site. After profusely thanking the pickup driver, the groundskeeper takes our picture at the river's edge.

Soon the riverbanks are five to ten feet high and filled with plants normally found in bogs. Either the river often floods here or the present water level is lower than low. A third option is the power company releases large amounts of water at various times, momentarily flooding the bank plains.

The outer bank of the bend ahead is a forty-foot sand cliff. Today's winds, funneling down this narrow valley, are hitting it quite hard, causing swirling clouds and mini-dust devils. They begin near the base and rise vertically, collecting sand. After hovering ten to twenty feet atop the cliff, they drop swiftly, picking up speed and more sand. Hitting the water, they scoot across and downriver, racing to see how far they can get before the rapids cool and sink them. It is a pleasant quirk in Mother Nature.

The Blandin groundskeeper talked about last summer's high waters. The erosion from it is obvious. In many places, ten to fifty yards of shoreline, fifteen to thirty feet wide, have broken off, forming new islands and separating the main channel. In one case they transplanted several three to four-foot diameter trees, a testament to Mother Nature's awesome powers.

Millions of gallons had to pummel these banks to do such destruction. Even now, huge chunks of earth fall off, melting into the fast current. On a miniature scale it is like the Alaskan glacier special where huge chunks of ice were breaking off, sending waves rippling across the bay. The dirt here is doing that. While not as spectacular, it is a great experience for a small river.

At lunchtime we decide to take a swim. The temperature is about 75. This is my first plunge. Darrin has been doing daily swims since Bemidji. It is definitely springtime weather. The trees are filling out. A set of goslings appeared earlier. No baby ducks yet. More importantly, few mosquitoes!

At about 6 PM, Darrin spots our campsite. It is atop a sheered-off, thirty-foot river bank. Last year's waters broke off more than ten feet of its shoreline, leaving the fire grate dangling precariously over the edge, awaiting its fate. The landing spot is some forty yards downstream.

After stowing the canoe and lugging up the gear, we find an outdoor toilet. Its wooden throne is literally collapsing into its own hole. These state-maintained toilets are two-and-a-half foot-high by three-foot-square boxes. A hole is cut in the top and finished off with a conventional wooden toilet seat. The box sits over a seven-foot pit. As these thrones are in the wide-open, no walls, the user is exposed to nature at her finest. If the mosquitoes or flies don't find you, sitting in a warm breeze with a 360-degree view of the flora and fauna is a rather pleasant experience. Bringing your own toilet paper is a must.

Whenever I sit down on one of these thrones, memories of my first trip to the Boundary Waters come to the fore. It was the summer after seventh grade. The first campsite was on a fairly large island. Our guide used the site because, according to his lore, bears never swim over from the mainland.

As is normal for campers after a large meal, I headed out to find a fallen log and leave behind those digested foods from which the best nutrients, vitamins, and minerals had been taken. After sitting down to cogitate nature, I heard a noise. At first I thought it was another scout looking for a spot. But as the noise drew closer, I figured someone was trying to sneak up on me. Finally I could resist the temptation no longer. I stood up and whipped around to let the sneak have it.

I would love to have gotten a picture of my expression. Prior to then I had only seen black bears in cages. This one was standing on his hind feet, pawing the air, not twenty feet away. Fortunately the downed tree separated us. I screamed and ran back to camp. Being the youngest camper, I was teased. "You're just imagining it." I swore on my mother's grave. To no avail! They were not about to let the greenhorn off the hook.

At length I could take the ribbing no longer and returned to finish what I had started. In my young mind choosing to go back must have been both a manhood thing, or I couldn't take a ribbing. Returning to the previous log and no bear in site, I prepared myself and sat down. Within moments I heard a rustling. Standing and turning, I again encountered the bear, big as ever, only five feet closer, with paws resting on the branches that separated us. He must have found a cache of grubs beneath the decaying tree. I had neither seen nor heard him. Now peering over the branches, looking directly into each other's eyes, it was time for me to leave.

I didn't finish my calling that night. Running back to camp, I didn't care what they said. As expected, the bear entered our camp after dark and tried to get into the food packs. The guide had placed all of our cookware atop them. The clanging awoke us, temporarily scaring off the bear. The leaders then took turns tending a fire and scaring off our visitor. No one ever again questioned my lack of manhood. Such are the growth experiences awaiting those who love the out-of-doors.

Life on the Mississippi has its own surprises. Last night we were in civilization and had showers. Tonight we are in the middle of nowhere. Darrin left to explore a duck blind someone put up in the middle of a nearby slough. He is also looking for a place to heed Mother Nature's call. As he couldn't find his TP, I loaned him mine. Now I need it.

Today turned out to be what I prayed for, an enjoyable thirty-two mile paddle. We wrote postcards two days earlier but still have not mailed them. How easy it is to let go of home and the job. Darrin has returned. Tomorrow...fewer prunes.

Seven days and 204 miles. I am still dressing warmly in the evenings. Bringing a winter sleeping bags was a good decision. Although this campsite is called "Swimming Bear," there is no good swimming hole, only mud. I am going to bed dirty.

SKEETER'S HOME

Mark Twain was right, river life is carefree; it shuts out civilization and adult worries. But the peculiarity, the oddity, is that it allows river travelers to be within a step of "real" life and yet be held hostage and confined by narrow banks, dikes, and floodplains; and the relentless ablution either bypasses snags, problems, and worries, or washes them away. Nothing withstands the Miss' constant refining, purifying, and purging. Those who don't recognize this will be washed asunder. It is a jarring reality.

Although still a babe, the Miss is already more dangerous and worthwhile than we had originally thought. She is giving reality to romanticism. Right now the cold, morning air is causing fog to rise from the river, mysterious in the early light. It is hiding something. The birds are out-of-sight, but their merry chorus is loud and clear. Fern fiddleheads, perfect for eating, proudly stretch their delicate necks amidst elder brothers and sisters whose fronds are a canopy of protection. Mother ducks love to nest in the soft materials left from last year's growth and the hidden privacy this year's greenery affords.

Our secondary treat this morning is a gourmet meal: oatmeal, raisins, prunes, an orange, tea, two rye crisps with peanut butter and jelly, and a multivitamin. One packet of oatmeal is enough for me. Even with heavy canoeing, only a mid-morning energy bar is needed. The simplicity is satisfying. It fits the experience.

As Darrin emerges from the tent in a long-sleeved winter shirt and jacket, I suggest, "Let's get pictures as a reminder of how cold it is."

After canoeing three hours, we take a short break on sands no human or animal ever trod. The spring flooding brought a fresh mix. This clean, pure sand beach reflects the cleansing being done by the Mighty Miss. There is also a trickle of cool water coming up through the sand and moving to the river's edge. On the southern portion of this trip we will use these springs for relief in the ninety-degree heat. Filtered through the land above, they make ideal places to bury water bottles and dig wallowing holes.

Noon finds us climbing a bank leading to Jacobson, Minnesota. Atop is a co-op building proudly proclaiming 1928 as its establishment date. Along side is a billboard asserting the Minnesota Highway Department is stealing twenty-five feet of its prime river shoreline.

We have come to investigate and eat lunch. The co-op appears to be a thriving business.

With lunch over, a walk-about begins. The first person we meet is Skeeter, a tall, lanky, retired man who is dressed for landscaping. A smile of delight crosses Darrin's face. He has met his namesake. Soon talk turns to the local co-op. "Last good manager retired a few years back. No real successor's been found...." As Skeeter's voice trails off, there is a hint of sadness.

"Did something happen?" I ask.

"Yeah, you could say that. The co-op was thriving until the manager retired. Left the store in great shape. We hired a young guy fresh out of college. He didn't last long. Skipped town with ten grand." Skeeter pauses, tightening his face into a pained expression before adding, "The guy left the safe door open...hasn't been caught."

Quickly Darrin muses, "*American's Most Wanted* should profile him. Contact them."

Skeeter doesn't hear Darrin. He is in deep thought. "The incident was the proverbial straw that broke the camel's back. The store's been closed ever since."

"Looked open to us."

"Well, it did re-open. But it's different. It's being renovated. Not to sell food or wash machines, but to give dance and karate lessons."

"Can we visit?"

"Don't bother. The owner's away. Too bad, too. There's a 'Great Room' encompassing the entire second floor. In the old days town meetings and dances were held there."

Skeeter proves to be a living historian for the life and times of Jacobson. As a young man he moved away. As so often happens in rural Minnesota, he migrated to the big cities: Minneapolis and St. Paul. 3M (Minnesota Mining and Manufacturing) lured him into a lifetime career. As with all small town heroes, Skeeter's roots were just too darn deep to keep him away.

Over the years he returned faithfully, eventually fulfilling a childhood dream: fixing up the old homestead. As the town's population dwindled, his passion carried over. Not wanting Jacobson to look like a ghost town, he began purchasing vacant homes. The salvageable ones became rentals. The really bad ones made way for a piece of Americana.

In the big city, Skeeter began attending auctions and visiting antique dealers, purchasing grand old streetlights, ornate ones with curlicues and timepieces. Some have outstretched arms with hands holding globe, much like Robert Frost's described the "prehistoric" neighbor holding stones in "Mending Walls." Others, with two, three, or four arched arms, have long metal fingers palming globes like the Harlem Globetrotters do basketballs.

"Let me show you around." Skeeter leads the way, explaining how he amassed his collection of lawn ornaments and mannequins. They cover three city blocks west of Highway 200, north to Highway 65 and east to the Mississippi River. While some are engaged in golf and miscellaneous activities, others lounge around on park benches.

"What's the story with the Marian shrine?" It is one of those typical bathtub shrines dotting the Wisconsin landscape.

Skeeter blushes. "Oh that. I wouldn't want you to get the wrong impression. I'm a good Lutheran. I got a deal on it." Other urns and statuary are suspiciously similar to those stolen from the cemetery I manage. How many of Skeeter's urns came to auction in that fashion?

"Hey," Darrin breaks in, "you should give Dave Letterman a call, invite his road crew over." Skeeter laughs and changes the subject.

His real name is Sid. His folks nicknamed him Skeeter and his brother Scooter. "Let me show you my sign collection." Rounding a storage garage, Darrin stops dead in his tracks. He has hit a bit of hog heaven. There is an old, gas station sign post sporting in big letters, "SKEETER."

I laugh. "Go stand under it. I'll get your picture."

Sid is in love with his hometown. Unfortunately some on the other side of town don't always live up to his standards. Their side is…well…run down. We noticed it when we came in. By Sid's standards, they just don't have a deep love for Jacobson. But he quickly adds, "The new co-op owner does. He is single-handedly restoring it…putting new life into old Jacobson. However, the state is frustrating him."

"Yeah, we noticed the twenty foot by twenty foot billboard. It's impossible to miss. What's the story?"

Skeeter's voice takes on a note of excitement. "The state is trying to rip him off. MnDot (Minnesota Department of Transportation) condemned twenty-five feet of prime Mississippi shore for the new bridge. Offered him a measly amount. He turned it down. The state is now trying to make amends."

After thanking Sid for the tour, we head out. Five hours of paddling then bring us to where Libby Township Campsite should be. There is no sign for the sight. It has been either taken down or lost in last year's flooding. Darrin insists, "I did the map check right. We passed Libby." As we won't backtrack, it is on to Big Sandy via a short tributary.

"It's the halfway point to Minneapolis!" Darrin declares. "We'll make it (the Twin Cities) in fifteen days." Big Sandy is a well-known recreational area with great swimming beaches and fishing.

The landing area is adjacent to empty campsites. "Before unloading, let's register. Maybe we can get one of these spots. We wouldn't have to portage." I like Darrin's thinking, but this is another Corps campground. Who knows where they put canoeists.

"Hi, guys. Looking for a site?" He is young, perhaps a rookie.

"Yeah. We're canoeing."

"The tent sites are a half-mile portage." Great! Are the rules here the same as Grand Rapids? "I see no reason to camp there. The trailer sites are open. Too cold for most campers. Tell you what, I'll give you a doublewide for the cost of a tent site." We smile appreciatively and offer profuse thanks.

While unloading a Duluth pack at site nineteen, a muscle spasm stabs the lower-back. Aches and pains appear to be taking turns nailing different parts of my body. As one disappears, another appears. I am now adjusting my paddling posture every half hour or so to help ensure some muscles are not being over used.

After dinner and showers, we take a walk around the campgrounds and find a memorial garden called Mikwendaagozwag. Four hundred Anishinaabeg died of cold and starvation here during the blizzards of 1850–51. Listed are the loved ones lost by each band of Ojibwa. This is a unique place. In the early part of the nineteenth century both Indians and whites were buried side by side in the cemetery. For three years prior to the Indians being forced onto the Fond Du Lac reservation, the settlers and Indians lived in peace. Together they ran a school where Indian and white children studied side by side.

A large sign says it is 2,348 miles from here to the Gulf. At Itasca the sign said it was 2,552 miles. If true, we have traveled 204 miles. However, the DNR map (besides showing each mile traveled) claims we started at mile 1347 and are now at mile 1109. Thus we have traveled 238 miles. Somewhere between here and Itasca are thirty-four missing miles. Secondly, if it is actually 2,552 miles, with the thirty-four miles missing miles and the 238 paddled plus the 204 fewer miles shown on the DNR map, this means we have actually covered 476 miles. Not bad for a few days work. What is harder to imagine are the eighteen steamboats plying these waters between 1870 and 1920. Enough deep thinking, it's time for bed. The mosquitoes are out in full force.

A light shower is beginning as we push off. It is Schalleen's birthday. Darrin's will be the eleventh of July. Both will miss celebrating their first birthdays as husband and wife. I won't bring that up.

The flood plains are presently twenty to thirty yards wide and solid with ferns. It looks like those specialty greenhouses where a single species is planted. The hills behind the ferns are thick with dogwoods in full bloom, a delightful smell and an unexpected visual treat. If the Mississippi Valley is to be perfumed from here to Tennessee, it will be more than a bit of paradise. The river channel is now narrow and deep, no more than 100 feet across.

Evening finds us camping in a small, well-maintained park on the edge of Palisades, Minnesota. Darrin is anxious to hike into town. He has wisely put a high priority on wishing Schalleen a happy birthday. My gift is staying with the gear and catching up on much-needed sleep.

Darrin's return awakens me. "How is everything on the home front?" I ask. He says nothing so I roll over.

While unrolling his sleeping bag he says, "Schalleen still finds it hard for me to be gone."

"I'm sorry." As I am not ready for more, I switch. "How was Palisades?"

This question stirs up his testosterone. "You wouldn't believe the bumper stickers on the trucks…tough talking. Between rifle racks and stickers, it felt like redneck country. Four guys with a full rifle rack in their pickup checked me out several times, cruising and staring. I was glad to leave."

"That's interesting. While you were gone I thought about how little civilization we've seen in the first three hundred miles."

"Yeah, it feels like the boonies." While sliding into his bag, he stops, shines his light directly into my face, "You still hoping to do fifty miles a day?"

"No, thirty-five's fine." I use my hand to shade my eyes, squinting to get a look at his facial expression.

His response surprises me. "I've been thinking. My back no longer bothers me so much. Maybe fifty is doable."

Even though his voice sounds upbeat, I am skeptical. We are still tiptoeing through verbal minefields. Only a few differences have been worked out. He has taken to calling me Muskrat, always with emphasis. I rarely respond. Right now I am not sure how to respond. "Maybe we can talk about it at breakfast?"

"Sure."

I roll over and snug the drawstring tight around my face. It is cold. The temperature is back in the low 40s. Despite paddling becoming more demanding, the river still feels like a Huck and Tom dream. It asks so little while constantly refreshing my psyche. Just a week ago I was harried with business details. Now it feels as though they never existed.

FRESH ROLLS

"Let's stop. I wanna map check." Darrin is considering a short-cut around Aitkin. Handing me the map he says, "It cuts north of Aitkin."

"It's a flood control channel. There may be little water. I'm not interested in hitting bottom halfway through. Those ditches are usually lined with boulders and cement chunks."

"We can take a look. It cuts off eight miles."

"Fine, but remember Winni."

It turns out to be a fifty-yard portage into a shallow and rocky channel. We stay with the main river and quickly realize the wisdom.

The extra miles fly by. The narrower river is higher and swifter. It is the reason Aitkin dug a flood diversion channel.

At Aitkin we begin looking for a payphone. As a pre-1950s brick courthouse with massive stone steps and arched entrance look inviting, we enter. Beyond the double doors and down a dimly lit hallway is a telephone booth straight out of the 1940s, identical to the classy one in the old Hotel Albert.

Darrin offers me the opportunity to call first. As the bi-fold door closes, a Dr. Who effect takes place. I am transported back in time. Swirling around are childhood memories, bathing me in comfort. Quickly retrieving each is a unique pleasure. A knock on the door ends my trip, "You okay?"

He looks perplexed. How long was I daydreaming? "Never better!" I respond, the memories fade. I dial the office of Darrin's older brother, Greg. His answering machine says he is in Tokyo. We leave a rousing rendition of "Happy Birthday." After reaching Jacqui, she is pleased to hear my voice again. When finished, I hand the phone to Darrin saying, "I'll get us coffee and rolls." He nods okay.

While surveying the downtown area from the courthouse steps, a bakery and a coffeehouse are spotted sitting side-by-side, a half block away. Perfect! It is a blessing to be able to partake in simple pleasures like bakery goods. The fat and calories will burn off in the next couple hours.

"I'll take three Bismarcks and three Long Johns. How's the coffee at Hawkeye's?"

"They make the best."

Hawkeye's is a contemporary coffee shop. As I head out the door with two cups, Darrin is crossing the street. "Schalleen needed to head off to work." It is back into Hawkeye's and a place to sit.

I am going to enjoy this. I take a huge bite. What the? These rolls gotta be two days old. "Take a bite. Someone has a funny idea of what fresh means." I turn to the young women behind the counter. "What do know about the bakery?"

The brunette with the pleasant smile responds, "They bake every other day." Fortunately not all is lost. Hawkeye's coffee is as great as are the counter crew, two young women. They join us—another chance to be Huck and Tom.

Back on the river, the narrow banks continue to provide a fast trip. "If this keeps up we'll do some serious miles."

Darrin only nods. His eyes are glued to the map. He is casting short, darting glances to the right. "Just ahead is an old Indian village. Wanna stop?"

"Sure, we're makin' good time."

At the designated point, three men and a boy are fishing. "Is this where the historic Indian village is?" Darrin asks.

Their replies are in marked contrast to the young women at Hawkeye's. Not only are they uneducated as to its presence, their tone-of-voice is hostile. "Never heard of it!" To press his point, the self-appointed leader snarls, "Historic Indian Village, ha!" His comrades concur.

Darrin decides to educate them on its significance. The portly leader lets him know they are not interested in knowing about "no Injuns." Some serious hostility has arisen. We decide against going ashore to explore.

Downriver, out of earshot, I ask, "Do you suppose the Red Lake logo had anything to do with the cool reception?"

Darrin smiles, "Not at all."

When the canoeing day draws near its end, daylight is fading fast. The next campsite is five miles away. As I am too tired to continue, Darrin's words are a relief, "Let's open up a site." He chooses a spot twelve feet above the river, figuring the breeze and coolness will keep the mosquitoes away. Below is a rocky shoreline. As mud has gotten into everything today, clothes, packs and canoe, this is a welcomed relief.

The hill's limited tenting space is a good reminder as to our wisdom in tent choice. Darrin broached the subject during one of our long-distance telephone chats. "A lot's happened in the fifty years since you began camping, Dad."

Much has happened since my first canvas lean-to. Today's tents are a real luxury. That first tent was a square piece of canvas with grommets in the corners and middle of each side. Called a "two-man tent," it was straight out of George Washington's army supplies. The argument was always whether it was a World War I or II foot soldier's tent. It is amazing that sometimes no forward progress is made in an area for a hundred or more years. Then, bam! The changes explode. This happened to tenting after the 1940s.

My first tent, that old army tent, had a three-foot pole for each end. A sixteen-penny nail stuck up a half inch on the top. After placing the nail through a middle grommet, and holding the pole straight up, a partner would drive stakes through the corner grommets. When this action was repeated on the other end, the "A" frame tent formed. The end flaps could be tied back to let the breeze through or pulled together to keep rain out. There was no floor. Two boyhood memories standout: the tent was heavy and emanated a moldy odor. After a rain, it could never be folded. It needed to be thoroughly sun dried. A canvas two-man tent would not be good for a Mississippi expedition.

As a teenager, when cars became available, I camped at Lake Okabogie, Iowa, or Green Lake, Minnesota. Both were the summer haunts of beautiful girls. If the truth were known, the only requirement my buddies and I had was being out of parental reach and in close proximity to said girls.

On those occasions, we borrowed a bachelor neighbor's tent. Eddy had been tenting nearly all of his life and had the best equipment around. Sometime before WWII he built a wooden box for carrying pots, pans, and cooking staples. It was designed to fit neatly into the trunk of cars being built in the 1930s. When taken out of the trunk, four wooden legs fitted into corner slots and the box stood chest high. The front opened to a ninety-degree angle. Held in place with chains, it became an ideal meal preparation surface.

Eddy's tent, a modern marvel in the post WWII era, took him to some of the best fishing and hunting spots between Minnesota and Montana. When Eddy's father died, Eddy became the breadwinner for an aging mother and bedridden sister. I never actually had the privilege of meeting his sister, but caught fleeting glimpses through parted lace curtains that quickly closed when she saw me looking. The neighborhood kids considered her a saint as she had never succumbed to the temptations of cigarettes and the like.

Eddy's one respite during those years was fishing and camping. It gave him the privilege of being a pioneer in Triple-A travel and camping. He got in on the early days when the automobile began bringing people to sites they had only imagined. My story, like everyone else's, was growing up too late to be an early adventurer.

It seemed to me those campers were truly roughing it. Of course my children know my 1960s camping equipment is beyond ancient.

Compared with what they purchase in the 1990s, it is. But in the fifties we camped in real style. Queen Stoves had already invented a cook stove powered by white gas. Everyone knows what a great improvement gas stoves are over splitting logs and cooking on an open fire.

But even better than Eddy's cooking utensils was his tent. It was a much larger canvas tent than my two-man. It could easily sleep six people and used only one center-pole. The wooden pole came in three three-foot sections. They fit neatly together with the top section sporting a twelve-penny-thick rod driven into the center and sticking up about an inch.

After staking down the tent's four corners, one person crawled through the doorway with the pole's top section. Placing its metal rod into the roof's center grommet, back and leg muscles lifted the tent's weight. After it inched up five feet off the ground, a partner would add another section. Once all three sections were together, it took the strength of two to hold it up while a third placed a square one-by-eight inch board underneath. This prevented the tent's weight from tearing a hole in the floor. Yes, Eddy's tent had a floor. Pure luxury!

Once up, it had the feel of a small circus tent. But like the two-man tent, if not properly dried before storing, its musty smell would discourage entry until the mold had thoroughly dried. Of course today it would be against the law for teenagers to be exposed to tent mold. Poor Eddy. He would be sued for having exposed the neighborhood children to toxic mold.

It surprises me that some smart lawyer hasn't filed a class-action lawsuit against the U.S. Army on behalf of WWI, WWII, and Korean vets. Surely Uncle Sam carelessly and with reckless abandon exposed our fighting men to toxic mold. There has got to be millions at stake here. Somewhere there is a psychologist who can help my brothers and sisters remember how mold caused our father to get angry and abuse us. If my dad were alive today, the psychologists could help him remember how being forced to sleep in one of those moldy tents, while seeing action in the Philippines, caused post-traumatic toxic mold shock syndrome. It would make great headlines.

Well, the good old days are gone forever and so are those moldy tents…thanks be to God! Eddy's tent had great space for four guys on the loose and looking for a great time. However, it could only be carried by car. It was definitely too heavy and bulky for a canoe.

As a Boy Scout executive in the mid-1960s things hadn't changed much, at least in scouting. I remember the scout execs at the home office in Mendham, New Jersey, promoting an old heavy canvas two-man tent. Like the camping I had done with my buddies, these tents were great if the scouts were being bused or ferried to a campsite. They were horrible for back packing. Still the older scout execs extolled their glories.

The more they talked, the more I wondered. I knew there were better tents around. Finally I asked. Immediately I got the low-down; the scouts held the patent on these tents. Still the pushing seemed more than a little strange. There had to be another reason. I queried further. "Why are the sales so important? I've seen better."

Frustrated with my interruptions, the instructor blurted out, "Cuz the profits go to the scout execs' retirement fund!" The pregnant pause among the trainees was deafening. So that is how our retirement is being funded. What a great incentive. Certainly tents added more coin to the retirement pot than cooking kits. No, those old Scouting tents were definitely not right for a canoe trip.

By the early 1970s Minnesota Outward Bound was in full swing, using quality camping equipment. Their tents were made of lightweight nylon and had separate rain flies. They had floors, dried quickly and were stuff-able. Pockets were sewn into the walls, a great place to store small items while sleeping. There was room for both personal gear and stretching out. These tents were closer to what a Mississippi expedition needed, since tents are set up and taken down, wet or dry, daily. As Darrin's long-distance biking and camping caused him to research and purchase a good two-man mountain tent, we opted to take it on the first leg.

Although small, it is perfect for cool evenings and makeshift campsites. As spring floodwaters are still receding, it is still necessary to bypass the muddy floodplains where most river campsites are located. More than once we have climbed to higher ground. Because of the tent's small sleeping area, personal gear and Duluth packs are stored outside, under the canoe. For the Minneapolis to New Orleans portion, we will use a lightweight, four-person tent. Comfort and extra room are important on extended camping trips.

Recently I purchased new four-person tents for the youth group. They are easy to put up and tight around the corners. Their greatest feature is the door and window design. Both are large openings, opposite each other, inviting in the slightest breeze. During a rain they can be left wide open as the fly extends well over the openings. This should prove invaluable in the South's 100-degree nights with ninety percent humidity.

"Do you think Father Pat contacted the Brainerd TV station?"

"Why yah asking?"

"It's okay if he hasn't," Darrin says. The stops for food, water, and telephoning are beginning to wear. Besides needing to do more miles, grubby, smelly attire makes us less anxious to do PR. Recently, Darrin has taken to sleeping in later. I get the water boiling and breakfast set. He takes down the tent and repacks the Duluth bags. It is turning out to be a good division of labor.

THE DAIRY QUEEN

There is frost on the tent. The thirty-eight degrees bites my nose and cheeks. My body begs to stay put in the warmth of this winter sleeping bag. I will trade it in for a summer weight in the Twin Cities. That bag will better fit my watertight pack.

The location of this campsite makes up for the cold. The exquisite sunrise, bright and crystal clear, is warming the tent and our hearts. The best part will be later when Zeke (Yes, I have taken to calling myself Zeke to avoid Darrin's moniker, Muskrat), when Zeke and Skeeter don't have to tramp through calf-deep mud to begin a morning paddle.

I noticed Darrin journaling yesterday morning. Earlier he was angry at me for doing so. Somehow he equated my journaling to Lewis and Clark getting all the glory for their trip. What he failed to disclose was his journaling.

Once up, it doesn't take long to get water boiling. "Breakfast's ready." The current out front is slower than yesterday. The downriver bridge is teeming with "snowbird" swallows. They have returned to their summer condos adjacent to the mosquito-infested backwaters. It is an ideal place for raising young. The wood ticks are also out in force. I took four off this morning and five before bed last night.

As Darrin emerges, he is singing, "All the ends of the earth have seen the glory of God." I didn't know he knew that hymn. It is appropriate on another glorious day. With breakfast over, Darrin is dawdling. It is 7:15. He must have an agenda. I am keeping my mouth shut.

It is now two hours since we left camp in silence. Only essentials pass between us. Ahead is Paul Bunyan's favorite resting stump. It is under a canopy at Paul Bunyan Land, Brainerd, Minnesota. "There goes our first mama duck and brood!" Another sign spring is here to stay.

Although the day started out in the middle thirties, it is now sixty-nine and clear. The canoe is nosing ashore under a bridge near Brainerd's Dairy Queen. Darrin leaves to call Schalleen while I shop. On the way back I can't resist stopping at the Dairy Queen. "I'll have a small raspberry/banana shake."

The young man looks perplexed and turns to looks up at the flavor board. After a moment he turns back. "I'm sorry. We don't have that flavor."

"The board shows banana and raspberry. Just put in a shot of each."

"Can't…only allowed one shot per shake."

"Okay, put in half shots."

"Can't…it's not offered. The owner's strict about what we serve."

"Really?"

"Yes."

"Okay. Make me a Pepsi freeze." Again I get the quizzical look. Now he turns full around to the menu board. With his back to me he says, "It's not on the flavor board!" He has gotten a bit testy.

Once he turns around to face me, I say, "I'm not asking you to give me any flavoring, just Pepsi." There is a pause. He looks over his shoulder into the backroom. Someone is there. Finally he looks back sheepishly. "I don't know how." He appears ready to step out of the box.

"Sure you do. You know how much milk you use in a shake?"

"Sure."

"Just use that much Pepsi."

"I could do that." He smiles.

"Thanks." He has found a new attitude. As he begins making his first Pepsi freeze, I wonder who is to blame for his initial inability to make decisions.

"That'll be four-twenty-six."

I do a quick check…10 ounces…4.26…that's $52.82 a gallon. "Tourist prices are in full swing!"

"Yeah." He laughs.

The high price brings images of owners sunning themselves in Florida, October through March. Ray loved his Dairy Queen business, six months off. Can't say I blamed him! As I turn to leave, Darrin is heading down the street. He is cheerful. I am happy for him. Before he can speak, I call out, "We're off the hook."

"How's that?"

"I called the TV station. They hadn't heard of us and can't send anyone until four…told them we'd be long gone."

Darrin's smile brightens, "Yes!" Although he says nothing more, he is still holding back, like at breakfast. We paddle in silence for forty-five minutes. Out of the blue comes, "I've been thinking…." I hold my breath. "Let's combine oatmeal packets into one bag." That's what is on his mind? I think not, but I'll take it.

"Fine. How about mixing lunch and dinner items?" He agrees.

Although my back continues to get stronger, the aches and pains come in earnest around 3 PM. They enjoy moving around my body, as if to throw it off. Foregoing painkillers forces adjustments. However, my main concern is how my body tires by mid-afternoon. In the past, tiredness always showed itself in poor canoeing posture. I cannot allow that on such a long trip.

The rocky riverbanks are gone. Despite our best efforts, mud is entering the canoe. Going barefoot and washing our feet before entering is now a must. I took off my long-sleeved shirt a while ago and was confronted with the fact I stink to high heaven. Paddling and sleeping in winter clothing, without bathing in between, produces a rather pungent smell. As we pull up to the campsite I inform Darrin, "My first order of business is a bath."

Darrin joins me. We pull the canoe in for a cleaning and a bottom inspection. While doing so, he says, "I'm still struggling with how hard it is for Schalleen." I just listen. Later, after dinner, he says, "I'm going to call." Not only is that twice in one day, it is a two-mile hike. I'll take that as a sign he is doing some serious fence mending.

We are camped at the group site in Crow Wing State Park. As I camped here before, I knew it would provide some small creature

CAMP RIPLEY'S SAFE   97

comforts and a telephone. The sleeping mats and bags are spread out on picnic tables in a small, screened, log pavilion. The ten-by-ten shelter is pure luxury over the previous three days. I will not wait up for Darrin.

CAMP RIPLEY'S SAFE

"What day is this?"

Darrin looks at me queer. "Wednesday…why?"

"I'd lost track. I'm trying to figure out when we'll arrive in the Twin Cities. If we paddle fifty miles today and the next two, we could arrive on Friday… spend the weekend."

"I'd like that." I knew he would. We shove off to begin a twelve-hour day.

After turning several bends, the first interesting artifact appears. It is an old, rusting, metal steam shovel. "Dead and dying" is what I would have said as a young boy. Somehow it seems appropriate. Parked on a flat, sandy stretch of beach, a quarter mile long, it is obviously from another era. Although rusting badly, the look and feel is that of the little red one in a children's book.

After passing under the bridge that takes reservists to Camp Ripley, a large object can be seen in the middle of the left channel, where the river divides around a small island. "Look over at eleven o'clock… what do you see?" Darrin's eyesight is better than mine. I am hoping he can tell me.

"Your guess is as good as mine."

"I think it's a safe." My assumption comes both from an overactive imagination and its general shape. "It looks like the door is open and lying on its back."

"What would a safe that size be doing in the middle of the river?" He pauses and stares. "It can't be." I have piqued his interest. "Let's go see!" Yes, another diversion.

It is indeed an open safe and fairly new. After peering in and finding it empty, Darrin lifts the door and lets it clang shut. Only then do we notice it has been drilled. Now the juices of speculation really begin to flow. Someone drilled it, emptied it, and dumped it in the river.

Why here? Was it a burglary by Iowa reservists up for two weeks of summer maneuvers? Was it drilled open on base with government tools? Were they trying out new army skills? Perhaps it was local boys trying to throw the sheriff off by dumping it here. Even if we could lift it in, the weight would sink us. With no more time for speculation, we move on.

"Ever been to Camp Ripley's museum?" I ask.

"No."

"Seeing how you're going into nursing, it might be worth a visit, lots of World War I and II medical vehicles, uniforms, and surgical instruments. The youth group enjoyed it."

"How does it compare to Fort Benning?"

Jacqui, Darrin, and I visited Fort Benning's museum when Darrin was stationed there. "No comparison. Fort Benning's at least four times larger."

The paddle past Camp Ripley becomes more and more relaxing. There are as yet no maneuvers on or near its twenty plus miles of shoreline. The camp is designated a state refuge and wilderness area. Paddling in the middle of the river now allows us to come upon deer without scaring them. Whoa! We both stop paddling. A group of twenty deer have stayed their morning drink to watch us. Fifty yards downstream is another group of nearly fifty. This is a deer hunter's paradise.

While vacationing near Brainerd in the 1970s, I visited the local bar where Camp Ripley's weekend warriors partied. They told tales of using deer for target practice. Claims were made the "brass" used the base as a private reserve, not the preserve the state claimed it to be. However, I am sure those were just tavern stories.

Once again there are many eagles lining the river's edge. They have made appearances for twelve straight days, always poised and waiting for some unsuspecting breakfast morsel to swim near the surface. The banks of Camp Ripley have nearly as many eagles as the shoreline between Cass and Winni.

As noon nears, Little Fall's dam and portage, with a treacherous re-rod gauntlet, challenges us. With the water level low, the hazard becomes easy picking. After checking the map, we decide to eat at a park in Little Falls.

After arriving and settling in on a shoreline bench, I turn to view the city. "Hey, does that guy speeding across the street look like he's headed our way?"

"Yeah. He sure seems intent, like we've got something he wants."

The elderly gentleman looks up to see us staring. Before we can speculate further, his long strides bring him aside the bench. With outstretched hand, we are greeted, "Hi, I'm Harlan Jacobsen. I live in that apartment." He points back across the street to where he came from. "I keep an eye out for canoeists. Come out to greet them and hear their story."

As he stays behind the park bench, we don't get up. Curious, I ask, "Are you writing a book?"

"Oh, no," he laughs. "I just do it for fun. Three days ago I met a guy canoeing alone, said his name was James." So we are catching up.

"Yeah, we heard he paddles a red, Mad River canoe." Mad River is the name of a quality canoe manufacturer that proudly proclaims its name in large letters on both the bow and stern. "He left a week before us, must be good. We've only closed the gap to three days."

Harlan nods agreement. "Told me he was sixty-three, just retired, and living out a lifetime dream, canoeing the entire Mississippi. He's been on the lower portion, St. Louis to New Orleans, twice."

"We're looking forward to meeting him," I say. So James is no stranger to the lure and power of the Mighty Miss. Perhaps he can tell us what to expect on the lower portion, prepare us for problems. After additional bantering, Harlan bids farewell. He is just beginning his daily walk.

As he leaves, three boys in the fourth or fifth grade pull up on bikes. Fishing boxes, rods, and bait dangle from handlebars. They have the same carefree demeanor I had at their age. However, they seem purposeful in setting up in front of us.

After casting out lines, they begin speculating about the quality of fishing on a small island some thirty yards out. As they seem to want to involve Darrin and me in their conversations, it transports me to boyhood fishing days. Those were glory-filled days. Like my friends and I, these boys can't take their eyes off a forbidden zone, a place impossible to reach without a boat. It is probably the one spot their parents forbid them to fish.

They are huddling up now, whispering, looking back at us. Finally the youngest is pushed out of the circle. Coerced by the older two, he takes willful steps and stops directly in front of me. "Hey, mister, would you and your son take us out to that island?"

Perhaps my age and appearance give a grandfatherly look. Patsy may be more accurate. "How would you get back? We're leaving shortly."

Back he goes to the older boys, huddling for a second conference. Upon returning he says, "We'll yell back. Someone will come and get us."

Right! Visions of frantic parents calling the police come to mind. Once rescued, the boys would fess up: "Yeah, an old, bald-headed guy and his son took us over…said they'd bring us right back…just took off." No, we don't need that kind of publicity.

"Sorry, you'll have to find another way." After several more minutes of futile pleading, Darrin and I want no more. We pack up and leave. The afternoon passes quickly.

Landing for the evening, we find a canoe and tent already occupying the only useable site. The other is a mud pit. We pitch our tent near a park bench overlooking the river. Either the other canoeist is sleeping or out exploring; his site is quiet. Although he is soloing (a fifteen-foot canoe is parked beside his tent), one thing is for sure, he is not James. This canoe is white.

After dinner, while washing dishes and still hearing no sounds from the tent, Darrin and I kibitz about him. Only after the dishes are done, and we have said plenty, does he emerge. We fall silent. Howard is his name. He is in his sixties. He has been patiently waiting to introduce himself. He must have had a few good laughs listening to our comments.

Flint, Michigan, is his home. "This is my second year on the Miss. I'm spending two weeks each summer, picking up where I left off." He is calm, relaxed, and friendly. Physically he is in great shape for someone a few years past retirement. His clothes are a darn sight cleaner than ours. His crisp demeanor and clean, light-colored, khaki clothing are reminiscent of a movie scene where the actor steps out of a safari tent, clothing pressed and creased, holding an evening cocktail. He makes me look like a hobo.

I am not sure how I would feel about doing my adventure in stages, coming back and picking up where I had left off. It does have one advantage—Howard can enjoy this magnificent river annually for some time. But make no mistake: the camping, physical challenges, and beauty are turning this trip into pure pleasure, in spite of the pain.

Because Howard's canoeing involves the Flint, Michigan, club, Darrin asks, "You ever meet Verlen Kruger?"

"Sure, Verlen's a member."

Now our interest is piqued. Darrin has told me stories about Verlen. He is not only the Mississippi world record holder but also that of several other rivers. A year ago Verlen and his partner, Bob Bradford, won the Retts Foundation canoe race from Itasca to New Orleans. They completed it in just over twenty-four days, breaking the old record set by Verlen and Valerie Fons in 1984. But the new record was not accepted. The Iowa sheriff's water patrol pulled them off the flooding river on three occasions. Guinness counted the time off the river as part of their paddling time.

Our discussion now turns to an urban legend about two young Brits who came to the Mississippi with the idea of breaking Verlen's record. When their time was announced, someone asked how they managed to go so fast. Their reply: "Surfing the wakes of downstream barges."

"How did you manage that?"

"We called them on a marine phone, asked them to slow down so we could surf their wakes." On the surface this sounds plausible. But if the truth be known, most barge operators have a loathing to share "their river" with non-commercial traffic. This comes from years of bad experiences with small craft.

Before the start of our trip a parishioner said he feared for my safety. He passed on a personal experience. It happened while he and his wife were dining riverside near St. Louis. Although hard to believe, his wife corroborated the story.

Sitting deck-side, enjoying a leisurely after-dinner drink, they saw a man and a woman fishing, drifting, and trolling the main channel. What happened next is anyone's guess. An approaching barge captain saw them and gave off shrill warnings. The small boat would not budge. Either the occupants did not hear or chose to ignore the impending doom. The captain slowed and began turning, to no avail. Run over by eighteen loaded barges, the boat emerged a mass of twisted sticks. The bodies were recovered the next day.

The distance needed to slow down or turn eighteen to twenty-four barges is not exaggerated. At the St. Paul Science Museum of Minnesota there is an interactive, computer-generated, barge operator's game. It puts visitors behind the wheel of a towboat pushing barges upstream. The intent is to show the difficulty in turning.

Earlier in the museum I had read how towboat captains often start their turn as much as a half-mile before a river's bend. As there was a long line of young people wishing to act as captains, I stood and observed. Sure enough, each participant ran his/her set of barges aground. I began coaching them to think in terms of starting their turn one-mile before the river's bend. Those who had faith in my suggestion made their turns safely.

It was this experience, coupled with Darrin's readings, that formed our decision to give plenty of room to moving barges. We have, however, decided to attempt one aspect of the Brits' urban legend. Is it possible to surf, for any length of time, the wakes of barges going downstream? We believe the legend to be a "pipe dream" of "wacky tobaccee" proportions.

As the conversation with Howard continues, Verlen begins to feel like a true American hero. He set his latest record when he was a mere seventy-nine. His partner was a youngster of fifty-eight. In talking with Howard, Darrin and I become curious as to what Verlen and Bob did to win the 2001 race. We know they are great canoeists, but to be three days ahead of the competition by the time they arrive in the Twin Cities is no small feat. Sure Verlen's been racing competitively for twenty-plus years, but so have many younger, stronger canoeists.

When people love canoeing as dearly as Verlen and Bob, they envision new designs. Besides speedy canoes, they developed sliding seats and a rudder that could be operated from either the bow or stern via a foot pedal. These innovations meant one could stretch out and rest while the other continued paddling, 24/7 canoeing.

Another legend surrounding Verlen is his canoe trip from Alaska south, down around the tip of South America, back up the eastern seaboard to New York City and points beyond. We are told canoeists now speak his name with reverence and awe. His accomplishments remind me of a nature special that featured a woman in her late seventies, solo kayaking around the world. There is a true American heroine, a mighty Miss if ever there was one.

As Howard has met James, he gives more details. What is now of interest is why no one speaks of James' personality or behaviors. Howard and the others talk about his canoe, his retirement, his dress, etc., but no one gives a clue about his personality. Why?

When Howard returns to his tent, Darrin and I return to packing food and dishes. At times today the placid lakes behind the dams made the current appear to be resting, waiting for a final plunge from Minneapolis to New Orleans. As I look at the current now, it seems to beckon me like a stranger standing some thirty yards away, motioning me to "come on down." There is special pull, giving intense pleasure. My heart goes light in having been shown so much in so few days.

A STORM HITS

It has turned into a hard day. The wind has been in our face since early morning. Previously at our backs, cooler rather than warm, it is now a Mississippi nightmare, warm summer headwinds: backbreakers. We have discussed and tried several ways to counteract it, paddling the west bank at times and then the east. As the Mississippi Valley is as yet very small, neither side provides more protection.

Although it is getting dark, we are pushing past Montissippi County Park: no telephone. We are headed to Bridgeview Park in downtown Monticello. For nearly twenty years Jacqui, I, and the children stopped there on the way to the cabins. The children loved it. A small, familiar park, it provided a place to play and eat. Contained within narrow boundaries, the children ran freely, never out of sight. Now it will be another opportunity to re-live fond memories.

In the summer of '76 Jacqui and I sat on its banks waving to two young canoeists. I shouted the usual, "Where yah headed?"

They beamed back, "New Orleans."

"Where'd you start?

"The headwaters."

I remember turning to Jacqui. "Someday…" and pausing to let it sink in before continuing, "…someday, I'll do that." In my heart I wasn't so sure; we had four children and wanted more. As that respon-sibility came first, many dreams were set aside for another day. But I was envious of those two young men. Tonight, I will sit in that spot with the satisfaction of being two weeks into my dream.

Today's dream has taken us past Sartell Linear Park, Champion Dam, Heim's Mill, St. Cloud State University, Putnam's Pasture, Boy Scout Point (there must be a million), Oak Island (two million), and Snuffie's Landing (only one). Who could ask for anything more?

Darkening clouds are thickening in the west, and dusk is coming early. There is a dark-green, luminous tint to the sky. The tree-lined banks are casting eerie shadows. Passing the Monticello nuclear power plant doesn't help. Overactive imaginations, sci-fi thoughts, combined with fatigue, are creating subdued conversations. There is speculation on how an errant discharge of nuclear waste, should we fall in and swallow any, would affect our futures. Of particular concern to Darrin are his child-begetting years. Rumblings and lightning accompany these thoughts.

The closer Monticello gets, the darker the evening sky becomes. The cooler, northwestern winds are mixing with the warm southern headwinds. Both are jockeying for control of Monticello. The turmoil is now causing clouds to boil and move downward. As we pull up be-low the park, greeted by banks fifteen to twenty feet high, we cannot fully see what is coming. However, we can feel the north wind's light, icy rain. These things push us to land quickly and change into warmer clothing and raingear.

After dragging the packs up the steep embankment, we are de-lighted to find a new picnic shelter. However, the nagging question of a tenting site keeps popping up. The DNR map maintains there is one. In the twenty years I stopped here, I never saw it. After again mentioning this to Darrin, I add, "What if the DNR map is wrong?"

Pointing to the sky Darrin says, "It's a little late for that."

The new gazebo, with bolted down tables, is perfect for keeping gear dry and secure while riding out the coming storm. The canoe is lashed to a tree halfway up the bank. The western sky makes it obvi-ous no meal is going to be fixed. Dark, putrid green clouds have de-veloped—harbingers of tornados or straight-line winds. Why bother fixing food anyway, a burger in town and a call to the wives would serve us better. They will be happy to know we are only a day away and intending to spend the weekend at home.

I am a little concerned about that. If I go to St. John's Saturday evening Mass, everyone will want to know if the trip is called off. Worse yet would be getting caught in a small group discussion about the trip. Darrin and I still have issues to work out. Lastly, what kind of pressure might Darrin receive from Schalleen?

Darrin wins the coin flip and heads downtown. As he moves out of sight, the heavy rains, accompanied by a voracious appetite of straight-line winds, lashes the site. The storm's energy is not impressed by the downtown's three-story buildings. It slams into their southern exposure, quickly climbing the brickwork and cascading down the north faces like water over a dam. Once on the ground, the waves of water sweep across the park.

Sheets of rushing water race each other to see who can be first to wash away loose articles. Each finds new objects to pick up and carry to the river's edge, plummeting them straight down the banks and into the current. Although the winds hit me, very little rain reaches this far under the shelter.

What's that? The wind just cracked something below the steep embankment. Oh God, no! I race to the canoe, praying my worst nightmare is not a reality. The cold rains pelt me like a hail of dried peas from a close quarter pea-shooter battle.

The ropes are too loose. The heavy winds have turned the canoe over, exposing its innards, turning it into a billowed sail, slowly bending it around the tree. Digging in heels braced against the tree's trunk, I turn the canoe enough to keep it from bending more. As the first blast subsides, I quickly untie it. Heavy summer storms always have momentary lulls between the first wave and the main fury. I work fast.

Glancing around I find a more protected spot nearer the river. It has three trees to hold the canoe's length firmly in place. As I tie the last knot, the winds and rain begin their second assault. Having won battle rights to the canoe, I must now do so for the packs. Moving them to the farthest, downwind side of the shelter provides maximum protection. After lashing them to a picnic table seat, I lay out a sleeping bag behind the barrier. Curling up to ward off the cold proves to be a great way to ride out the storm.

Relaxed, I begin reviewing today's experiences and all of the park improvements since my last visit in the 1980s. There was only Biff's Outhouse then. Now there is a new brick and glass building. It must double as a winter warming house for skaters and a summer game room. The sidewalk leading from the front doors is bordered by a light brown, two-foot high, brick landscaping wall along its eastern exposure. Its built-in lights provide a feeling of warmth and comfort on this evening.

One of today's portages had large boulders and sharp, three to five foot, chunks of concrete. It was good to have a partner. A twisted ankle would have brought a quick rescue. We said prayers for Howard's traversing there and through the Sauk rapids. Two sets of eyes and paddles quickly established the best route through that rocky riverbed.

In the heat of those frustrations, we didn't always appreciate each other. Looking back, Darrin's skill and presence of mind made me truly grateful. Today's low waters, with rocks nearer the surface, made canoeing dangerous in the Sauk Rapids. The waters churned and pushed the speeding canoe within easy reach of damage. Had there been a short portage, we would have taken it. As it was, the canoe passed safely, with only a few new tattoos.

What's that? An animal is approaching. Quickly sitting up and turning, I come face to face with a raccoon brushing the foot of my sleeping bag. He is headed to the river, oblivious to the storm and me. Within moments I can hear him washing and eating something, another Disney movie moment.

After the storm subsides, I hear someone approaching. It is Darrin. He is holding a peace offering: a burger. He has been gone a long time. We pitch the tent while eating and exchanging information. A streetlight makes the job easier.

Within moments I am off in the opposite direction Darrin took. A neon sign on the north side of the bridge indicated an eating establishment. Halfway across, the pizza/beer sign becomes fully visible. It is 10 PM.

The log cabin exterior is a typical Minnesota tourist trap. The interior is smoky but friendly. While pizza is fixed, a heart-to-heart with Jacqui makes me realize how good the weekend break will be.

After dinner and back at the tent, my hopes for a good night's sleep are shattered. The rains return. Darrin poses a statement that seems like a question, "Those strikes are close."

"It's the wind that worries me. Did I tell you I moved the canoe?" Thus begins an embellished recounting of how the canoe was saved from being bent around a tree, and certain disaster. After appropriate groans, we wonder whether the tent will hold up. The present wind and downpour feel like an angry mob of locals beating upon the tent, demanding we leave town. Once again the wind is hurtling streams of rain across the park. Those hitting the tent rise like huge boulders rolling up one wall and down the other. Those missing the tent swirl around the front and back, lifting up every inch of floor except where we are seated. We are now concerned with the possibility of uprooted trees. It is not uncommon along riverbanks. With this storm, we have experienced every weather condition except snow. There was a quarter inch of ice on our water container a couple mornings.

A HERD OF TURTLES

Harriet Island, an easy rendezvous point for Jacqui and Schalleen, is fifty-two miles away. The easy push-off this morning is reminiscent of another's paddling. "Maybe we should think about canoe strokes… remember Howard?" I ask.

"Yeah, he was good…kept up the first hour."

"His canoeing seemed effortless."

"Maybe we should watch each other?"

We agree. A non-threatening observation of each other's techniques, sitting positions and pull-through strokes now begins. The feedback is mostly about what appears relaxing. It is a good reminder of how strokes in twenty-foot canoes need to be straight back. There is emotional relief in accepting advice without sensing a demand or command.

Darrin ends our paddling review with, "I'm willing to continue evaluating after the Twin City's layover." On that reassuring note, I acknowledge my aches and pains and how they move around. Darrin then acknowledges I am holding up my end of the paddling. He is upbeat, in a good mood.

Nearing the Coon Rapids Dam, the sights, sounds, and smells change. Of particular interest are the plantings and tree trimming, a marked contrast to the wild. While nature's way is giving way to man's ingenuity, she still provides a pleasant setting for urban dwellers, at least some.

There are at least a half dozen street people sleeping along the banks, bent at odd angles between boulders and around smaller rocks. Most are sprawled on the jagged, erosion prevention rocks dumped by the Army Corps. The midday sun is beating down upon these poor, sleeping souls. The man nearest is wearing long pants and heavy, woolen shirts. Lying motionless, he could be dead. It is a compelling reminder that life in the suburbs is oblivious to the pains of the homeless.

In stark contrast are the sunning mud turtles. Twenty to thirty are now being jolted out of their comfort zone. The canoe's quiet, shoreline hugging has really surprised them. Scrambling down the steep embankment, they are literally launching themselves to the river's edge, bouncing off and tripping over each other, sliding and rolling down like miniature tires. Several have hit some rocks planted in the hillside, causing them to do mid-air flips. The scene is as rambunctious as any *Three Stooges* movie. This has got to be what my brother Bob called a "terd-of-hurdles."

Most land upside-down, quickly right themselves and making a mad dash to safety. One, unable to do so as we draw near, stops moving. His head and legs droop as though he has been dead for months. It is perfect. He doesn't move or twitch a muscle. We can't take our eyes off him. We have never seen a turtle feign death so perfectly. Now that we are several yards downstream, he must feel safe. He is up-righting himself.

The Minneapolis skyline now looms large. It is the backdrop for teenagers lounging, visiting, and throwing Frisbees on the boulevard bordering the shoreline. They wave, inviting us in and calling out the inevitable, "Where yah headed?"

As the canoe glides closer, a girl of fifteen or so asks if she can go along. When her question is greeted with only a smile, she pulls out a twenty-dollar bill. "I can pay my way…you got room in that middle seat."

My reply, "Our wives wouldn't be happy!" brings a smile and wish for a good trip.

It is hard to imagine teens attracted to this particular piece of Mississippi shoreline. It is downright disgusting. Manmade pollution, bottles and trash, are in every nook and cranny of the river's edge. The pigsty is a sad commentary on what commerce and individual pollution have done.

Ahead is a barge being loaded with pig-iron. The bank supporting the heavy crane is oozing a pale-white culture. Mottled with what appears to be gray and black mold, the liquid is growing like pus in an open wound.

More bottles, more trash, more industrial pollution, it is hard to see past the filth. Even more curious is the water. It carries such a foul odor; my stomach turns. My disbelief carries a yearning to flee. If the next 1,700 miles are of this caliber, New Orleans will not be achieved.

Soon the mess is behind us as we enter a small canyon. Here the swift current is sweeping away the city's pollution. Mother Nature's power to cleanse trash and ugliness is again apparent. Replacing the river's foul odor is the sweet smell of burning logs. Smoke rises, curling upward through downriver trees. As the canoe nears, a small, sandy, bay-like cove opens up. It is hosting a group of teenagers. They greet us less than enthusiastically.

Their behavior is in marked contrast to the earlier teens. These teens barely communicate or interact with each other, much less us. Rather than happy and active, they are lethargic, somber, and aged. Their only connection to each other is the large campfire, cigarettes, and mutually shared bong. We have stopped paddling. Darrin is doing a map check.

"Is this Hidden Falls Park?" he calls out. They shrug their shoulders. As it is getting dark, he asks a second question, "Do any of you have a cell phone?" They just look at him like, "Duh!"

A young girl, thirteen or fourteen, obviously the worst for usage, steps forward and asks in a high pitched, squeaky voice, "Are you guys lost?" Before we can reply, she begins giving disconnected directions. We listen politely, thank her, and move on. There is great irony in her concern for our being lost.

"Darrin, look over there. Is that the water patrol?" It is hard to tell in the deepening twilight as the boat is on the opposite side of the river. After waving and calling out, "Can you help us?" they turn. Once near, they extend a long white pole.

"We'd been hoping to make Harriet Island." In moments they understand our need and hand over a cell phone. After getting directions to the nearest marina, Darrin calls Schalleen. From their many hikes along these riverbanks, she is familiar with the area. After helping us, the police motor toward the youth and campfire at Hidden Falls Park.

The marina's docks are a distance from its entrance, giving us just enough time to portage before the wives arrive. The newlywed's reunion is akin to the WWII celebrations on Broadway when soldiers and sailors arrived home: much hugging and kissing. My smile brightens more when Jacqui arrives and new rounds of greetings occur. Quickly the vehicles are packed and vows are made to meet Sunday evening for repacking.

HOME

Breakfast is a bit different. No gentle breeze caresses me. It is deadly quiet. Where are the birds? The dining room walls insulate me from their sounds and hem me in. Emotionally my house is a prison. The world's gifts are locked away. I am no longer held tenderly against Mother Nature's nurturing breasts. I am sanitized and quarantined. The eagles and trees, the breeze and water, the mud and grass, the sand—they are all gone. If this is the intensity of my feelings after only two weeks, what will an additional six bring? The lure to live in nature is as strong as family and job. My present feeling of emptiness comes from closed patio doors and the A/C on. From nearly forty years of marriage, Jacqui knows I am struggling. I silently move out onto the deck. She allows me the alone time.

The canoe is still tied atop the van. After approaching and admiring it, I reach up. Gently unleashing her bonds, I lay her on the grass. With love and gratitude I caress her smooth body. She feels alive. My strong desire is to reach out, hug and kiss her, let her know how deep my gratitude is. She brought me home safely.

Retrieving the hose, I begin her bath, washing away mud and checking for unusual wear. I am still unsure as to how much punishment a Kevlar can take. Close inspection shows nothing but a few scratches. The many beaver dams, rocks, and downed trees did little damage. Finished, I wander the yard, searching. The apricots are still too green for picking. They will ripen while I am gone. My desire is to stay within the confines of the yard. I know why. I am trying hard to hold onto the canoe experience, perceiving this day as a wilderness layover, a regrouping before a major assault.

After evening church, I enter my office to sort mail. Okay, here is something I failed to plan for. I write more detailed instructions. The office and grounds are in great hands. A couple months before leaving I hired a new maintenance supervisor and bookkeeper. They are outstanding additions to an already great office staff. Ed, George, Mary Ann, Christy, you make dreams come true. What is happening to me? I am backsliding. I'm working at the office!

Sunday, another perfect day for canoeing, calm and cool, brings zero miles. The weatherman says Monday's departure will be stormy. I set up the new tent. It is missing a pole.

EVADING DEATH

"Walk me to the van. This is the last pack."

After tossing it in, arms enfold me, "Happy anniversary!" Oh, no! I promised I wouldn't forget our thirty-seventh. Hugs, kisses, and words flow from many great memories, yet my mind is elsewhere. Darrin and Schalleen will be here any moment.

"Did you notice if I left anything?"

"No, but don't count on me, double check."

"Come with. If I have forgot something, your thoughts may jog my memory." With arms around each other, the short walk to the door is slow, soon to be parted for thirty days. "Will you and Schalleen fly down to meet us?" Before Jacqui can answer, there is a honk.

"Schalleen and I can discuss flying down. I'll let you know our plans."

My mind is back to the packs and water jugs: I piled them all in the living room. "I feel like I've forgotten something."

"Didn't you check everything last night and place it together?"

"Yeah, but still it seems like something is missing. Well, if it's important, I can always buy it. We'll be hitting Red Wing shortly."

Another honk! Darrin and Schalleen are turned around, ready to head out. With windows rolled down they yell, "Good morning!" Their tone means, "Get going!" Still, the nagging feeling of having forgotten something will not leave.

Darrin leads as we turn east onto Highway Five. We will get back on the river a quarter mile upstream from where we got off. "Now I remember. One of the water jugs rolled behind the corner rocker when I tossed it on the pile."

"We can go back. You know how Darrin wanted to make sure you had enough water."

Yes, Darrin insisted on two five-gallon jugs. "I know, but I can buy one downtown."

"That's not a good idea. Please go back."

"He's already a block ahead. I can't flag him down. I'll get a new one. They don't cost that much."

"That's not the point. You know how he feels. It would be a mistake not going back...Please."

That's twice for me. First the anniversary, now this! What else have I forgotten? Jacqui is right. I should go back. I just hate to let a small mistake set me back.

Remaining quiet, I weigh the pros and cons. This could be a more grievous offense than forgetting my anniversary. Two jugs are important to Darrin. He researched water needs and knows five gallons will not last long in the southern heat. We argued. I didn't want to carry the extra forty pounds, but he convinced me. Now my heart says turn around, but the guy in me just hates self-imposed delays. "I'll tell him immediately when we get there."

After arriving I grab the water jug and approach Darrin. He beats me to the draw, "Where's the other one?"

"It got…" He had argued so strongly and articulately for a second jug, he has jumped to the conclusion I deliberately left it behind. He has cut off my explanation. Not going back is now causing a major delay. The heated discussion saddens me as he believes his leadership decision is being obviated by the "old man" using trickery. His words and frustration remind me of the times I thought someone was playing a game with me. To him, I have.

"Gimme that!" he shouts, ripping the jug out of my hands and destroying it.

At that moment a vanload of youth pull up. It is a surprise send off. Excited and happy, they are jumping out and unfurling a banner. Cameras are ready to roll. I look to Lisa, the driver, and shake my head. She calls the kids back and pulls up to the other end of the lot. It is obvious we aren't ready for a send off. Darrin's "#%* sure we aren't leaving until two water jugs are in our possession.

Schalleen now intervenes and the two walk away. After a few minutes of discussion, they return, willing to go and purchase new ones. My credibility is shot. As they drive away, the youth get out sheepishly, once again unfurling their banner. Pictures are taken. They need to get back. All I can do is apologize. They let my weakness slide.

"Who's that?" one of the youth points to a canoeist landing just behind me. I turn to see Howard from Flint, Michigan. His two-week canoeing ends here. I introduce him and more pictures are taken. Life is curious. Had we not argued, I wouldn't have a picture of Howard. Unfortunately my partner is not in any of the sendoff pictures.

The Van Pelt/Vanderlinde banner is impressive. Some have canoed with me. All spent a great deal of time putting together the two-and-a-half-foot high, seven-foot banner. It features a huge "OOHAA," surrounded by prayers, good wishes, and reminders of NCYC (National Catholic Youth Conferences), Summer Bible Camps, and other events we have done together. My shame is increased.

OOHAA is a favorite water call. It carries well. Brigade leaders during my time at Outward Bound used it on the large lakes as a warm hello to others across the lake.

The group's send off is a blessing in an otherwise challenging beginning to phase two. It is a clear reminder that even though Darrin and I are making the trip, others are involved. God sent a clarion message via grace-filled people. The youth are helping to put me back on track.

When Darrin returns, we leave in silence. For a while stabs are made at discussing what happened. Each fails. It is obvious the mud will need to settle before a healing begins. Not an auspicious beginning. Hopefully it won't last long. I have a feeling we will need to be shoulder to shoulder as the river widens and greater challenges arrive. The water is deep now, the current swift. Mistakes can be deadly.

At Lock and Dam Two we are greeted by someone who is either having a worse day or is a total jerk. He is topside, leaning over the railing, walking along the lock deck, shouting abuses as we paddle through. One of his milder statements is, "I hate canoeists…they shouldn't be allowed on the river." We look at each other incredulously and pull our hats down more, shielding our eyes.

Because all previous lock experiences were pleasant, this guy is scary. And, neither of us is about to respond to his stupidity. We listen and continue paddling, too stunned to respond. As we are the only traffic going through, he continues to spew out his rantings even after we stop to wait. Finally he leaves.

Fifteen minutes go by. The gates are closed but the water is not going down. "We shoulda been outa here long ago. What do we do?" Darrin asks.

"You're taller. Stand up and see what's going on."

Leaning against the lock retaining wall, Darrin slowly rises, as if sneaking up on someone. After peering over, he slides back. "He's doing odd jobs. Sweeping and straightening up." We go quiet again. The dragging of time compounds our nervousness. Are we being set up?

"I've got to confront him. This is ridiculous!"

As I begin to rise, someone barks, "I thought you had a boat in the lock! Why the hell haven't you emptied it?" Immediately hurried steps cross the pavement. A slamming hit to a lever or button can be heard. The lock begins to drain. As the gates open, he reappears, yelling more insults. He ends the one-way conversation with, "I sure as hell am glad it's Monday."

Monday? I can hardly suppress my laughter. People normally say, "TGIF." This lockmaster (if he is worthy of the title) is now saying, "I have next week off. I'm looking for ways to kill the rest of this week."

His choice of words is chilling. If this is how he feels on Monday, what will Friday be like?

"I hate this &*%#^%# ing job," are his final words. They are the first honest thing he has said.

Immediately after leaving the lock, we pull over and transcribe what we heard. We feel incredible disbelief that a lockmaster would be so bold, so blatant about his dislike for canoeists and his job. He must be carrying a lot of pain. After pushing off, Darrin wonders aloud, "What do you suppose that guy was smoking? It must be some pretty bad weed."

"What I'd really like to know is why he kept us in the lock so long. What could he possibly gain?"

"We called him on the marine radio. Could that have bothered him?" Darrin suggests.

"Let's monitor the next lock through. Maybe we'll get a clue."

Darrin stops paddling and turns. "Do you think the Indian logo and St. Mary's Mission had anything to do with it?"

"Your guess is as good as mine. We just need to monitor lock conversations. If something is going on, we need to know. If there are others like him, we're in trouble. Did you run into anything like that in your readings?"

"No."

Although nothing prepared us for the lockmaster's greeting, it has united Darrin and me. We are speaking civilly. Lemonade from lemons!

Soon the scenery is spectacular. The right-hand riverbank is carved out of rock. It reminds me of the narrow gorge where we last met a towboat. The operator slowed down while passing. The rock walls on either side of the river were some fifty feet high. Not only did he slow down, he moved as far as he could to his side of the river. We did the same. That has been our sole contact with barges this trip. Last year we met a couple barges on a day trip from Chaska to Harriet Island. Both operators slowed down to share the narrow river.

"Barges coming."

I look up. Ten are rounding the bend, two wide and five deep. Twenty yards to our right is a fifteen foot high shoreline carved out of limestone. As it is impossible to land on this side, we move closer to the wall for a wider loop. The river is fairly wide here. Passing will be easy. If the barges were on our side, their wake would bounce off the wall and send us battling to stay afloat. Although the lock experience has left me a bit leery, I discard negative thoughts to concentrate on the moment.

The towboat operator has nearly completed his turn. The shipping lane buoys on his side are nearly on the opposite shore. There are no buoys on our side, meaning it is navigable right up to the rock wall.

"Darrin, am I imagining it? Are those barges headed our way?"

"He is turning."

"Yeah, but why? He'd be crazy to turn and head straight for the wall." I look back upriver. The towboat operator has clear sailing. No one else is around. If he continues, we will be forced to cross the river just to avoid being hit.

Darrin's words now mirror my thinking. "If he keeps coming, we'll need to cross. It won't be safe."

"He seems to want this side. Let's cross while we still have a chance," I say. The minute we make our turn and head across the river, the towboat captain begins turning his barges back upriver, toward our new course. It is now impossible to safely cross in front of him.

"I'm turning us back."

Immediately after this second course change, the captain makes another course change, again heading directly upon us. "We can't be imagining this!"

"Dammit!" Darrin's voice is beyond angry.

"I am going to stand and wave. Steady the canoe!"

It changes nothing. We are in trouble! We both frantically wave our paddles, the universally accepted method for telling others to take notice. I again stand, motioning him to move away. It does no good. He keeps his barges on a collision course. As we can see the captain, he can clearly see us. We are literally trapped between fifteen barges and a rock wall.

"We've got to paddle hard before it's too late." In my heart I believe we have already waited too long for our maneuver. We must paddle as close to the barges and as far from the wall as possible. I cannot believe the captain is willing to risk hitting us directly; it would cause him to hit the rock wall. He obviously knows his craft well to risk any maneuver in these close quarters. If his timing is good, ours will need to be perfect. We are rapidly picking up speed for something no book learning prepared us.

Darrin's fear is beyond my level. "What the hell are you planning?"

"Trust me. Don't panic. I'll explain later. We need speed."

"If there is a later!" His anger allows him to dig deeper and paddle harder, expending newfound adrenalin. I do the same. I am sure the towboat operator will not expect us to pick up much speed. But it is the only way to avoid his wakes and get enough momentum to quickly ride out the coming rapids, the turbulence, the wash created by his propellers.

"We need to hit the wakes at full speed." As I am saying this, our canoe is already skimming just inches ahead of the barge wakes and well ahead of their reverb off the rock wall. We are some fifteen feet out from the wall and ten feet from the barges.

Darrin's fear continues to grow. "Why the hell'd yah get me into this?"

"Shut up and paddle!" I scream. It is a command. Darrin gives in for the moment. There is no time to talk. The barges loom larger than life. They appear empty, riding high in the water. We are passing in their late afternoon shadow. Our fate seems worse in the dim light. We cannot afford to get broadsided by the upcoming towboat wake and rebounds off the rock wall.

Again Darrin yells, "What the hell yah gonna do?"

"As we pass the towboat, back-paddle when I yell. Pray to God your paddle doesn't break."

"That's cutting it too close!"

"Now!"

The canoe responds quickly. The breaks are slammed on through back paddling. A little ruddering does the rest. As the towboat's stern passes, our bow misses it by inches. I cannot comprehend the fear Darrin must now feel for the ninety-degree turn heads us directly into the wake and churning waters. My neck muscles and blood veins are pumped to bursting. I must get the towboat's name. This maniac needs to be grounded. I glance up at the wheelhouse. The captain is watching, laughing and pointing, clutching a canned beverage. This is funny?

"Darrin…quick! Read the name. Don't forget it!"

As the engine's wakes collide around us, lifting the bow and crashing it down, waters rush up and over the sides, filling the canoe at will. However, the worst is yet to come—the reverb off the shoreline wall. In a moment successive waves from the towboat's engine and the reverb will lock beneath us. Only God knows what will happen then.

Perhaps it is sheer terror combined with survival instincts, but we are panicking very little. There is no time to think as the two sets of waves, the reverb from the shoreline and the additional towboat wakes, are tossing us. Darrin is now doing draw strokes on both sides of the canoe, as if paddling to miss boulders. He is going with the natural flow. It is precise, beautiful, and instinctive.

By switching paddling sides rapidly, we are avoiding the larger haystacks. Although water's coming in from both the bow and stern, we aren't capsizing. Several inches float our packs and slosh with the action. Darrin's got choice words for me. "Damn you, you nearly got me killed. I'm so angry I can't stop shaking!"

"Don't talk. Just steady the canoe. We need to get the water out before it soaks the packs."

As the rocking slows, bailing cans (doubling as pee cans) go into action. With ninety-eight percent of the water gone, sponges come out. Completed and exhausted, we try to piece together what just happened. Paranoia drives my thinking. Did the sadistic lockmaster make contact with this barge operator? Is that why he detained us so long? Did they figure an old man, even with a strong partner, would be unable to outmaneuver the man-made rapids? Why would any barge operator want to sink a canoe? He knew his action would pin us against the wall.

The wall, although it represented disaster, was far better than the alternative, being run over. My heart will not slow even though everything, or at least what could be hoped for, went well. Our Guardian Angels, the prayers of loved ones, God, someone is watching over us.

Now more than ever barge and lockmaster transmissions will need to be monitored. If there are additional nightmares, we need to be prepared. With the canoe dry, I rummage through my pack. Diary in hand, I ask, "What name did you see?"

"Eckstein!"

"That's what I saw. We'll need to avoid him when he comes back downriver. That was no fricken' accident."

We fall silent to fathom and write about such a close encounter. Soon Darrin has the map out. He wants off the river. "There's an island site at mile 807. 'Gore's Wildlife Area' is a couple miles beyond." We choose the island site.

When the island comes into view, we go down the right-hand side. Midway down is a roughly built, three-level dock jutting out about four feet from the island's twenty-five foot embankment. As we draw closer, we see stairs connecting the landings. Atop the hill is a two-story, log structure draped with a shredded, blue, plastic tarp. The tarp covers some roof and the north side of the building. It must be a windbreak for the cooking/eating area. There is a picnic table beneath it. It garners our interest, but exploring is out of the question. It is getting dark.

"It looks like some teenager's Shangri La," I say. "It reminds me of those structures back of Minnetonka West Junior High." Behind West was a pond of fifteen to twenty acres. Beyond was a magnificent stand of pines. Originally intended as Christmas trees, they were allowed to grow too tall. The dense grove shielded everything in its inner sanctum. This is where students built crude shelters and put up tents for pot smoking. Their parents believed them to be staying at a friend's house. According to one student, it was the favorite summer 'runaway place.' "Hey, Shangri La even has a potbelly fireplace."

"It's called Tanglewood. Look at the sign." Darrin seems a little sarcastic.

Sure enough: Tanglewood, Open 24/7

"So what's Tanglewood?" I ask.

He comes back with, "What's Shangri La?" He then adds, "It was probably built by Wisconsin teenagers from Prescott." I take these two comments as a sign our relationship is continuing to heal.

"Yeah. They probably borrowed the parent's boat, loaded it with neighborhood lumber and came here, miles from any adults." It appears to be a modern day "Jackson's Island," built for twenty-first century Huck and Toms. The only difference is the pipe tobacco. Our modern youth wouldn't be caught dead smoking Prince Albert.

As the water is moving swiftly, Tanglewood is gone in an instant. The island will be too if we don't stop. The downstream point is just ahead. With no campsite appearing, Darrin demands we pull over.

We beach the canoe in the nick-of-time. The bow comes to rest firmly on the very southern tip of an extremely narrow, sandy, reedy point. The canoe is hugging the sands just enough to be grounded. Darrin steps out and pulls the canoe further ashore. Once I am out, we pull the canoe fully out of the water. We do not want the current dragging it back into the river. Getting stranded here would not be good.

We walk through the tall reeds in the direction of Tanglewood. Soon it opens up into a flat, sandy opening. Although it appears to be the campsite, there is no fire grate or table.

"This has got to be the campsite!" Darrin is emphatic.

"Perhaps the people of Shangri La raided this site, hauled it up to their shelter."

"Tanglewood!"

"Okay! Do you want to continue up to Tanglewood? I didn't see or hear anyone…seemed deserted?"

"Yeah. Gore's site is too far. The sun's already setting."

Tanglewood is another fifty yards up the island, twenty of which are up hill. Upon entering the Tanglewood campsite, we note the land surrounding the two-story log structure is cleared of small saplings and underbrush. Further out it is surrounded by Red Pines. They are tall and spindly, like telephone poles. "Well, what do you think?" I ask.

Darrin smiles. "It's got the Corps' picnic table and fire grate." As these items are labeled Corps property, there is no question as to ownership. "There's a dock for unloading," he continues.

The blue, plastic tarp is stretched between four poles and pitched over the picnic table and cooking area. "It looks like rain. This could be good protection." Darrin agrees and we return to the canoe.

The fifty-yard, upstream paddle to the river deck proves challenging. This is probably due to the combination of swift current and fatigue. Within moments of hauling the canoe and gear up the two sets of stairs, the skies open up and the rains begin.

While Darrin sets up the tent and stows personal packs, I prepare dinner in the northwest corner of the log shelter. The Corps table is stationed here. We decided against using the second-story sleeping area as its roof is not fully covered by the tarp. The wisdom of that decision is now apparent. The sleeping shelter, located above this dining/cooking area, is leaking in every conceivable place. Water is pouring down on all sides of the table and grill. The surrounding black earth, trampled bare of vegetation, is quickly becoming a mud pit.

After calling Darrin for dinner, he appears with a sign in hand. "Look," he says, "someone threw it on a garbage pile." It is the Corps' campsite sign. The raid on the Corps site was complete.

The truth is the Tanglewood people found a more suitable site. The breeze on this knoll keeps the mosquitoes down at the sandy point. In those tall grasses, they can hang out and breed undisturbed. As the Corps does not look fondly on this type of man made intrusion, I expect this "unauthorized" summer getaway will soon to be torn down. With its demise will go some of the romance in the souls of men and women who dream of Tanglewoods, Shangri Las, or Jackson Islands.

As I serve up Hamburger Helper fortified with chunks of smoked summer sausage, the heavens open up a second time. Relatively speaking, we are enjoying our meal in luxury, no mosquitoes or mud. As we eat in total darkness, we agree there will be no cleanup. We stow the packs under the picnic table and crawl into the tent.

Falling asleep is difficult. The wind and rains pick up a third time. There is no real security under the tall, willowy trees that break the wind. Both Darrin and I have lived through heavy storms that toppled pines this size. However, I know if I don't sleep, I will be dragging in the morning. Considering Lock Two and the Eckstein, today's thirty-two miles was good progress.

THE MISS TAKES A BATH

Even though it is foggy, Tanglewood's potential is obvious. The camping site is spoiled only by Swinus Americanus. Huge piles of waste: assorted beer cans, bottles, aluminum foil, and cooking leftovers litter the back forty. In all other ways Tanglewood is a boyhood fantasy, a scaled down Robinson Crusoe island. The two-story, roughly hewn log structure, placed among towering pines, and the climbing ladder leading to a lookout platform are a boy's dream. The three decks and two rope swings over the river add a final romantic touch. The clay, pot-bellied stove is a curious ambiance to an otherwise wilderness setting.

We are eating breakfast on the middle deck of the three-tiered dock system. A rope swing here and one at the higher level are knotted on the end with a sloppy version of the "Gordian or Monkey Paw Knot." The morning is quiet. Not even the animals are moving. Perhaps it is the coolness and slight, northern breeze that keeps them tucked cozily in bed. On a less structured trip that is where I would be.

Morning tea is complemented by mist rising in curls from the fast-moving current. The island channels the Miss into two narrow paths, sending her waters flying to the gulf. A hundred yards downriver is a stirring on a dredging barge. In the fog a shadowy figure is standing on the riverside edge, relieving himself. The workers must be bunking on the dredge; no motorboats have approached in the hour since we got up. We will greet them when we pass by.

Right now the bug has bitten Darrin. After setting breakfast aside, he strips down and climbs to the upper deck. "I'm going for a double jump!" is the enthusiastic explanation. His swing out from the third level will take him far out over the river.

The middle level would land him closer to shore, but he wants to try the "big boys' rope." I am tempted, but the cold holds me back. Darrin, however, is intent on not missing any opportunity. As he swings out over the river, his Tarzan call echoes along its banks. Perhaps the cry works up the necessary testosterone to ward off the shock of the cold, swift current.

Hitting the river nearly dead center, the current grabs and pulls him downstream so rapidly he nearly misses the island's point. The steam rising from the river gives me over to meditating. Multiple curls rise and melt into a fog hovering ten feet off the water's surface. The pattern is fascinating and captivating; it comes from a fast current and northerly breeze.

Darrin's second swing is from the middle deck. To ensure a quicker return this time, he swings up river, allowing the current to bring him to the lower deck. After a third jump, he stands beside me shaking like some waterlogged mutt. Smirking, he asks, "Aren't you going?"

"No, I'm passing. Too cool."

"Getting old, eh!"

I smile. The challenge is not enough to move me. Soon we are on the river and my thoughts are of Lake Pepin, another infamous lake indelibly etched in my memory. Years ago a brother-in-law's vicarious introduction made it so. His stories were of huge waves and barges. Will reality verify his fish stories?

With the wind at our backs and fog beginning to lift, Golden Wings slides silently past the dredging operation. No sounds emanate. The positioning of this barge indicates a fair amount of silt is rushing around both sides of the island, colliding and filling in the shipping channel. The removed silt is being dumped inland, adjacent to the parked barge.

Quickly the barge is forgotten as the fog's hidden secrets draw attention from speculating on workers to catching glimpses of animals. There are both small and large shadowy figures moving about, ghosts running from past hunting parties. These may be deer, fox, and badgers. Groups of wild dogs are also known to roam the Mississippi Valley. Gazing intently, passing in silence, we hope against hope to see secret behaviors.

As the current is swift, the miles pass quickly. Soon Lock and Dam Three is in sight. Darrin wants to portage. I want to lock through. Although a set of barges is just starting in from the downriver side, Darrin reluctantly agrees to wait.

As the half hours tick away and our canoe sits dead in pooled waters behind Dam Three, stress mounts. What was billed by the lock master as a short wait is now nearly two hours. The fog burned off over an hour ago and the morning sun is now blistering. Darrin's careful research on dam portages, coupled with disappointment on the long wait and yesterday's water jug blunder, is causing a melt-down. As his tensions rise, my request to lock through is seen more and more as laziness. To counteract the mutinous grumblings, I give a solemn vow to follow his advice on future dam portages.

Our delay has come mainly because a towboat captain can't keep his barges in a straight line. The marine radio reveals his foul mood. After getting the first half through, his crew, apparently green horns, couldn't secure them properly. As Lock Three is smaller than most, larger sets of barges must go through in two sets. Darrin and I are salvaging some time by eating an early lunch, a decision bound to affect us later. It is now clear any Lock wait beyond a half-hour must be a portage.

After finally moving out of the lock, I rationalize some quirk of fate is doing us in. "Perhaps the river gods don't think we have enough stress!" Within fifteen minutes I am convinced. "Check those barges." Darrin looks up to see a set of six barges crossing the river and heading directly toward us.

"You weren't watching where yer going."

Whoa…he can't really believe that. Fortunately there is no sheer rock shoreline to hem us in this time, just mud flats. This means there will be no major reverb. As this captain and his barges bear down upon us, the wide open space makes it easier to maneuver and adjust. If necessary we can easily land. This captain won't catch us in his crosshairs.

Now fully aware the captain means to run us off the river, Darrin digs deeper to give us more speed and maneuvering ability. As we move toward shore, we know it will soon be too shallow for the barges. After yesterday's nightmare, we are calm and prepared to take any and all appropriate actions to counter a towboat operator's stupidity. This captain's movement out of the main channel and into our space is as obvious as the last. But we won't be hunted down this time.

How would we fare in an aluminum canoe, riding out man made wakes? Our every movement toward shore causes the towboat captain to make even greater turns. The stalking feels like a whale hunt, an attempt to head us off, harpoon us at the last possible moment. But this whaleboat is a monster. We are merely a minnow. Why are we even experiencing this? The captain will have to make a last-minute turn to avoid grounding. Our last-minute turn will be to ride out his wake. Perhaps whales feel sadness when seeing the glint of a sharpened harpoon waiting to pounce. It is my present feeling.

Even though Darrin recognizes it is not me who created this situation, his fear is again turning to anger. It is more like a son expecting a father's protection and being disappointed when the evil doesn't magically disappear. Although our speed and the river's width allow us to stay farther away, there is still a need to do a quick ninety-degree turn into the turbulence caused by the towboat's props.

"Now!" I yell. Once again our graphite sticks are tested in back paddling against a swift current and forward momentum. Headed into the engine's wake, the first wave curls over the bow, entering just above Darrin's seat, soaking his shoes and daypack. Fortunately it is a small amount of water. We look back to catch the name: Mike Eckstein.

"That can't be a coincidence!" I add.

"Look at the captain. He's laughing and pointing," Darrin says. Although a high sign is the preferred reply, we give him thumbs down. "Dang…he really went out of the shipping lane. Why would he want us off the river?" Silence follows before Darrin adds, "I'm sorry I blamed you. I really thought you were being lazy."

Okay, that's a backhanded compliment. As the super sponges come out for a second time, all because of one shipping firm, I add, "My concern is when he comes back." Darrin and I both know how silent barges run when moving downstream. Mississippi books indicate towboats sound warnings if another craft is unaware of their presence. Will the Ecksteins? The upside is we are strongly united against a common enemy.

As river life returns to normal, the peacefulness makes it hard to remember the incident. We are now trying to make the moments linger as the sun continues to rise and plow through the morning clouds. It is an odd sensation to observe the sun's heat create a pathway between a huge bank of clouds, forcing them to move rapidly north and south.

Not only is the rising sun parting and dissolving clouds, it is a notification of greater heat. Even though the present blue skies, coolness, and wind at our backs invigorate Lake Pepin's twenty-plus mile paddle, it is offset by my right shoulder and chest experiencing a minor charley horse. To take my mind off the pain, I am counting the strokes between here and the next bend. It will give me some idea of the effort needed for Pepin.

At 3,200 strokes I get the picture. There is no sense counting the uncountable. Besides, counting a forty to fifty-mile day will make it unbearable. Before the trip began, I expected the current to help more. That notion is gone. The only way forty or fifty miles will happen is by hard paddling. The strong currents are few and far between.

Right now Lake Pepin is a like a wide, flat prairie, light brown in color from the Minnesota River's clay-silt entering at the confluence below Fort Snelling. Pepin's shores, right to the water's edge, are marshland plantings nourished by the silt and fertilizers from Minnesota farms and lawns. The trees and solid land are more than a mile away. Already reflecting the sun's rays, she is as harsh as any desert. My skin is beginning to bake. I need to stop and put on sunscreen and lip balm.

It is now two hours since entering Pepin. "What say we take a break and swim? The water's clearing up." I like Darrin's thinking.

I, too, noticed the lake's new clarity. In general the lake seems more like a large, shallow slough. "Perhaps it's acting like a filter, taking out all the garbage."

"It's definitely getting cleaner…see any good swimming spots?"

"Let's paddle closer to the western shore." Although still over a mile away, I am not interested in looking on Pepin's left shore. It would mean over a half mile paddle just to get there and the shipping channel is definitely on the right side of the river.

With the wind at our backs, we are making up lost time from Lock Three. Now after mid-day, the first sandy point is in sight. After plunging in, the heat of the day is quickly cooled. The river temperature proves ideal for swimming. Once dried, I feel dirtier. The silt, and whatever chemicals it holds, has left a film on my body.

The wind continues to pick up and push Golden Wings across the mighty Pepin. After what seems a short time, three hours, we are nearing its end. As the day's heat has us sweating, we are ready for another break.

"Wabasha is coming up. There's a shower at the city park. Wanna stop?" Darrin asks.

"Was I talking to myself?" I mumble.

"What?"

"Never mind, I like your idea."

Even though Pepin was an easy paddle, no head wind but plenty of tailwind, I am hurting. Quickly I maneuver us toward the clean, inviting park. After unloading, showers take precedence. We can call home later.

"Oh my God that's cold. There's no hot water." Darrin hesitates at my announcement. At first the shower feels good, cooling the heated body. Quickly though, chill sets in. Stepping out to lather down is a must.

After showers, we lay the tent out to dry and call home. An hour later the relaxing warmth of the park has a hold on us. We are feeling lazy. Paddling and the sun took out more than we realized, and pleasant spousal conversations created more laziness. We are dawdling.

"We gotta go." Darrin is right.

After pushing off, discussions on a campsite begin immediately. "Drury Island is a possibility."

"Not after today's experience," I quip. "It isn't worth the attitude." We go silent and I contemplate eagles. They are still with us, been flying overhead every day.

"Do you realize the eagles have been leading us downriver? It's a sure sign the river's healthy."

"You read my thoughts." I laugh. We both laugh when I tell him the coincidence.

We go silent again, basking in the comfort of eagles and the chance to cogitate how things are going. The meals continue to go smoothly. I am eating less while Darrin eats more. I am happy there are no leftovers or anything extra going to my waist.

After setting up camp and eating supper on an island near mile 756, there is quiet time for journaling. We did forty-nine miles under mostly blue skies, and the waters are once again sky blue. The Miss' mud is left behind in Pepin's shallows.

MISSISSIPPI'S MT. RANGES

There is a fishing barge anchored in the swift current below Lock and Dam Four, the Alma Dam as the locals call it. The fishermen tell us lunkers abound in these waters. They must, the fishing barge and shoreline below the dam are lined with fisherman. There is a Towboat and its barges locking through. We are portaging around the dam on the western shore.

"Hi, guys."

Staring down from a river path footbridge is a youngish looking, middle-aged woman. Her lyrical sounding voice reminds me of a singer. She is straddling a bike and dressed in full-length pants, long-sleeved shirt and broad brimmed hat. As it is hot, her sweat piques my curiosity.

Without further introductions, she continues, "I've done a number of Duluth to Minneapolis MS (Multiple Scleroses) bike rides... ended up in the hospital last year...didn't drink enough water. How about you?" Her comments and question, accompanied by heavy perspiring, seem more than a bit odd. She jumps to UV rays.

"You're dressed inappropriately. The hats and shades are okay but give up the t-shirts and swim trunks, cover-up!" She is nonplused by fifty sun-block. "I'm a nurse," she states with much authority, intimating we must heed her advice.

After thanking her, we quickly move out. Downriver we discuss her interest in our health and that which others have shown. Her authoritarian tone, however, reminds me of Tom Black Bull's private nurse, Mary Redford, in Hal Borland's, *When the Legends Die.* Mary Redford wanted a controlling relationship. Why would this woman? It must be from a deep-seated need to care for people.

Soon Lock and Dam Five are in sight. Lock Five "A" will come shortly after. The barge that went through Lock Four is now coming up behind us. As neither of us want to wait for him nor portage, we are paddling hard, racing ahead. As we near the lock, the gate opens. This is a lockmaster I can appreciate. However, our sail through is not quick enough for Darrin. He says, "I don't want to lock through Five "A.""

"I didn't mind it. It's a break."

"I don't care if you're tired." It must be the heat. Darrin is in no mood to be slowed.

Soon Five "A" is in front of us and I ask, "Whadda yah think?"

"We aren't close enough!" is his terse reply.

True, but don't fault me for trying. There is no lock traffic. "Okay, where to?"

He points and I turn the canoe. It proves to be an easy portage. A few fishermen are on the downside. Our arrival attracts interest from a man my age. We stand and talk. After the usual questions, I ask him, "Do you canoe?"

"Some. My best experience was Minnesota Outward Bound. Heard of it?" We now begin exchanging "war stories" and his blood really begins to pump. "God, I wish I could join you." His envy reminds me of an earlier day. I want to say more but Darrin's anxious stare tells me to end it.

Our personal water intake today is nearly double yesterday's. Dipping my hat, filling it with water before replacing it, happens about every half hour. The quick cool down and rapid evaporation is refreshing.

Soon we are passing some pretty awesome cliffs south of Winona, Minnesota, I ask, "Have you read Fr. Hennepin's journal?"

"Yeah, why?"

"This must be where he thought the Miss passed through a mountain range. The cliffs and towering trees remind me of California foothills." The beauty of the mature trees hemming in a narrow river valley is majestic. Silence takes over. We quit paddling. My mind wanders to all the places a canoeist could stop: Fingers Lakes, Zumbro River, Buffalo City, Cochrane, Fountain City Bay, Merrick State Park, Teepeeota Point, Minneiska, Hershey Island—so much to see and so little time, perhaps another trip?

The cool, north breeze has slowed. It is now softer, gentler, and more sporadic, like a child gently pushing a toy boat. It is a nearly perfect day, unfortunately Darrin set his watch-alarm for 4:30 AM. The heat and early start did cause us to take a longer lunch break. Now we are quitting earlier, heading to Perrot State Park in Wisconsin. Darrin wants to camp next to Mt. Trempealeau.

Perrot is everything Darrin imagined. He is pleased. "Here, take my picture with Trempealeau in the background." We set up the tent on a level area at the bottom of a gently rolling, wooded hillside. The slopping lawn is well manicured; its picnic tables are placed far apart. The trailer campsites are up the hill and to our left, out of sight. There is a shower there. We will get some creature comforts tonight.

The local mosquito patrol welcomed us last night, this morning a symphony of birds feeding upon them. In front of the tent is nearly a square mile of marsh. The lush greenery carpeting this backwater begins less than thirty feet from the tent door. It extends to the foot of Mt. Trempealeau. Three level plateaus stepping down the eastern slope mark the beginning of a panoramic setting.

The trees lining our site swing around behind the tent, enclosing it in a small, stage-like area, focusing attention on the lush, green, marshland plants. The wind rustles the broad-leafed lily pads just enough to suggest the appearance of concertgoers scurrying back to their seats after the dimming of foyer lights.

Now seated, the audience fans out to Mt. Trempealeau's tree-lined base. Above and behind Trempealeau's darkened theater is the deep blue, night sky, moments before sunrise. The eastern sky offers up a sliver of baby blue, pre-dawn rays. Four sets of white, flat-bottom clouds hang like theater flats. Each is evenly spaced, one above the other, stretching from east to west. Rays from the rising sun project onto the highest layer, giving them a tinge of pink. The bright green, the deep blue, the clean white, and the faint pink are Mt. Trempealeau backdrop. Overloaded senses call for prayer. Breakfast can wait.

Before slipping quietly out of camp, nature's litter confronts us. The sandy beach where we landed is strewn with thirty to forty turtle eggshells. Rocky Raccoon uncovered two caches last night. He feasted.

His first attempt to satisfy hunger pangs was our food. Packs piled high with pots and pans scared him off and alerted us. He soon returned for a second try but was confronted with our howling. After a third attempt, he stayed away. We could hear him near the beached canoe but were too tired to investigate. During breakfast we speculated. Now we know.

There is minimal river traffic. It is a peaceful, leisurely paddle through La Crosse, Wisconsin. "Now, there's an interesting place. What say we stop?" Darrin's voice carries a curious excitement.

Looking up, I understand. The large come-on sign reads, "BYC, Bikini Yacht Club." "It's a little cool for bikinis," I comment.

"Come on. It's lunchtime. It might be our last opportunity to celebrate a taste of the river."

Right, a taste of the river! I love rationalizing. Darrin is probably right, though. There have been few restaurants with outdoor, riverside eating decks. The maps indicate there will be progressively fewer towns near the river. Besides, the stop will give us an opportunity to call home and tempt imaginations.

"Yeah," I say to Jacqui, "it's called BYC."

"What does BYC stand for?"

"Why yah asking?"

"Just curious."

"Bikini Yacht Club."

As always Jacqui is quick with a comeback. "Tell me, Deacon, how exactly are the waitresses dressed on what you describe as a 'cool' morning?"

Taking a tip from "The Body," Governor Ventura, I skirt the issue. "Honey, the temperature's in the thirties. It's been raining since mid-morning. Do you really think the attire matches the name?" After more weather details, I am given a tentative okay.

Back on deck, we are the only customers. Two waitresses bring water and menus. Soon two others join them. Now this is service. The meal is fixed quickly and all four sit down, anxious to hear about two men wandering the river. In truth they are mostly interested in the younger guy. At any rate, we are the only specimens around.

"What does it take to make such a trip?" one asks. The question is a searching, a mulling over. Perhaps she is wondering, "Is this something I might do."

The dreaming of young people is always a fire in the belly, something to do. Older people's questions always seem softer, further away, more relaxed and peaceful. Their adventures have already shaped and changed their lives.

The excitement from both the young and old often forces me to wonder, "Am I more like the old, enjoying successes, dwelling on dreams fulfilled? Do I still have fire enough to enjoy the risks and dreams of youth? I appreciate, with deep respect, dreams fulfilled. The aura of both dreams fulfilled and those yet to see fruition permeate me as I watch the glow on faces and the tautness in body expressions. People are vicariously enjoying this trip. I cannot decide whose passion is greater, the old or young, nor do I wish to.

The love others have felt and their desires for what is to come lure me into the secret recesses of their hearts. The sharing is always humbling. I still fondly recall a very short conversation with a woman the week before leaving. After hearing of the trip, she stopped in passing at the church door and gave me a hug, allowing me to feel a longing in her soul. Softly, and with passion in her voice, she said, "Make the most of it." The dream in her eyes, the deep love for the out-of-doors, instantly became a part of this trip. That brief encounter allows me to more fruitfully enjoy and understand the gift God is providing on this Mississippi experience.

My dreaming stops. One of the young waitresses is staring. "Was I drooling?"

"No." Her smile turns to a blush.

"Darrin, let's toast the future." We do. The young women raise water glasses.

Once on the river we find a powerful warm front is again challenging the north wind. Soon the clashing creates a downriver thunderstorm over a large lake behind Lock and Dam Eight. We are somewhere between Upper Deadman's Slough and Coon Slough Daymark.

The colliding winds are like the meetings of the old Viking Purple People Eaters and their chief rival, the Green Bay Packers. The lightning strikes rumble and shake the water much like their pugilistic head butting did the grounds of old Met stadium. Sufficiently impressed, we head toward shore, but not quickly enough; Mother Nature has other plans.

A huge gust grabs the canoe, momentarily holding it in place and then, like the flick of a wrist, spinning it ninety degrees. She seems to be saying, "Oh, no you don't." We are now facing upriver, being driven back to where we came from. Immediately life jackets go on. Then, harnessing some of Mother Nature's power, we do a 180. Tacking begins, but it is not enough. The inching toward shore is too slow. The north winds push us closer and closer to the lightning. Finally, five feet out and hugging the shore, the risk too great, we get off.

Overhead circling winds bring back an early morning river experience: hawks flying in formation. Four were equidistance apart, balanced in a circular formation. Were they hunting? Was it a game or spring mating ritual? They forced us to stop and enjoy several minutes of their company and acrobatics. Moving in perfect unison, they flew high and low circles before swinging wildly to the right and then left, finally disappearing over the tree tops. They were a clear reminder that there is no sufficient way to explain Nature's gifts.

After the storm subsides, we soon find ourselves approaching the King and Queen bluffs. They tower a hundred or more feet above us. It is the beginning of the Great River Bluffs State Park in Iowa. The Mississippi Valley grows more beautiful with each mile into Iowa.

With only one state behind us, it is an odd sensation to realize our Mississippi expedition is nearly one-third completed. But the lower portion of the Miss, Iowa to Louisiana, will be nearly a straight shot compared to Minnesota's zigzags.

Noticeable also is the distinct beauty each river town has or lacks. Red Wing is not marred by the industrial pollution of Minneapolis and St. Paul. She gets an "A," they get a "D minus." Winona is somewhere in the middle. Her biggest drawback is a drab, aging warehouse district. LaCrosse, twenty miles downstream, is more picturesque and park-like with a neat, clean riverfront.

The afternoon quiet and daydreaming draw attention away from aching muscles. Darrin has both the upper and lower body strength needed for this trip. I am grateful my biking built up leg muscles. In all my years of canoeing, I never realized how important legs are. On this trip, with lots of time to notice every aspect of canoeing, my daily dress (shorts) allows me time to notice such things as leg muscle movements. The leg skin ripples up and down as the muscles move with each stroke. It is amazing. One would expect upper chest, back, and arm muscles to see that much action, but it is the legs that give major power to the strokes. Still, my chest and back are reaping pain for failing to build strength there.

Ahead is the Blackhawk Corps Campground, a hot shower and bed.

IOWA TO CAIRO VIGNETTES

MAP TWO, 675 MILES

Dancing with Carp — Blackhawk Park
Harpers Ferry

WISCONSIN

Guttenburg — Huck & Tom,

Dubuque

Sleeping with Barges

IOWA

Clinton

Davenport
Muscatine — Mike & Dee
Iowa River — James

Burlington

Fort Madison — A Red Cooler

ILLINOIS

Canton
Illinois River

Hannibal

MISSOURI

A Hotel Rest
St. Louis

Missouri River

Crystal City

Ohio River

Cape Girardeau
A Wing Dam

Cairo

DANCING CARP

The marine weather channel's rude awakening is: "It's thirty-six degrees with stiff breezes out of the northwest."

"Turn it down," I plead, rolling over and covering my ears.

"Just wanted you to know."

After unzipping the door flap, I see my freshly laundered t-shirt hugging frosted grasses. The night winds blew it off my drying tree. It looks stiff and frozen. My body heat will have to finish the drying.

Now standing naked except for tennies, I shudder while pulling it on. "Oh, God that's cold!" My shorts remained suspended during the night. "Ahh…that's better.

Despite some strain in decision-making, we still feel excitement and look forward to daily mini-adventures. While peeling his orange, Darrin seems to be mulling something over. "I can't believe we haven't seen James."

His comment doesn't stir me about James, although I am still impressed with his Mississippi retirement solo and how quickly he is moving. Yesterday a lockmaster said James was still about two days ahead of us. He also talked about another, older gentleman. As the lockmaster didn't know his name, Darrin and I immediately dubbed him, Bottle Man. He left the Twin Cities a week ago on a raft of plastic bottles and is rowing to New Orleans. His desire is both for a place in the Guinness Book of World Records and a confrontation with America's lack of recycling.

Bottleman's anger over a lack of recycling in America sounds strange to us; we have been recycling since the early 1970s. Nearly every plastic used in America today is recyclable. Perhaps he is just late in being introduced to it. But how can that be, he is older than me? Perhaps his corner of the world is more polluted by Swinus Americanus. As he can't be going very fast, we should soon find out.

"Hey, Dad, there goes another barrel." Quickly I look up to see it sail past. Since entering Iowa there are enough discarded fifty-gallon drums, metal and plastic, floating or stranded, to fill a small barge. Where they are coming from is anyone's guess. Maybe docks torn away by last year's flooding?

"Hey, listen to this." Darrin reads another description of a place we will pass. This trip is beginning to feel like a whirlwind. It would take months to do it right. Today we'll pass Bad Axe, Diamond Jo, Broken Arrow, Hammond Chute, Pigeon Island, Indian Camp, Betsy's Bend, Atchafalaya Bluff, and the list goes on.

After getting on the river, we soon find ourselves approaching Lansing, Iowa, on a side channel. The main channel is shorter, but we are looking for a distraction. Without our river maps, we would never have known about this side channel. My original response to Darrin's map request was, "Maps, who needs them? We'll be going downstream the whole time."

True, but river camping for forty-five days calls for finding fresh fruit, vegetables, and drinking water. On some stretches of the Mississippi, towns are few and far between. On others, towns are a quarter to one mile back from the river's edge, making lugging food and water a major chore. Yes, maps are important. As Darrin is our navigator, he plans for re-supplying. My leadership is in guiding the canoe on the water. This sharing of power is proving to be a good mix.

To convince me to take the two large maps, Darrin explained it this way. "You know how highway maps show a town adjacent to the freeway and you get there only to find it a mile or two away? We can't afford to carry food and water that far." He went on to say the width of the floodplains on the Lower Mississippi can be a quarter to a half-mile or more wide. "We'll need to look for towns truly on the river. See these light brown areas? Those are dry floodplains during low water times."

Our two Army Corps maps show dike roads and bridges leading into towns as well the backwater areas. As the scale of these maps is two inches to the mile, and each mile is marked, the map is an easy read on the canoe's bottom. The scale led us to believe we will be able to see some downtown areas from atop dikes but not be able to visit because the connecting bridge is too far away. Imagine carrying forty-plus pounds of water in a cube container, with a suitcase-style handle, a mile or more. Five-gallon camel backpacks for carrying water would be far easier but none were available.

The only drawback to the Corp maps is the size. The larger is fifteen by twenty-two inches and takes up valuable canoe space. These maps are really designed for the wheelhouses of towboats and ships, not canoe bottoms. However, we always know where river traffic will be coming out of locks and around bends, the shipping channels are clearly marked. Knowing the shipping lanes will be especially useful on the lower Miss where the river is wide and abundant with islands and side channels.

The Corps maps also explain navigation regulations, types, and uses of buoys, and the radio frequency used by towboats, locks, and the weather channel. Harbors, private and public marinas, bait shops, bridges, coast guard stations, campgrounds, and levee dams are all noted.

Levee dams are important for us as some Mississippi locks and dams don't extend the entire width of the river. In those instances, levee dams cover the remaining distance. These smaller dams hold enough water to keep the locks operational year around. Their cement deck is flat and fifteen to twenty-feet wide. During high water times canoeists simply paddle over them. Due to the unusually light winter snows and spring rains, the water level is presently four inches below the levee dams. Unloading and portaging across them takes about fifteen minutes.

We already know there are places where boaters can look down-river and see two or three channels. In those places we will know exactly where upstream barges are coming from. Knowing the routes of downstream barges allows us to stay out of their way. This is important as the distinctive roar of towboat engines can only be heard from those coming upstream. Often towboats and barges coming downstream are upon boaters long before they hear them. Seasoned captains know this and signal small craft with a horn blast or two.

The Corps maps come in two sets. The first covers the upper Mississippi, from Coon Rapids, Minnesota, to Cairo, Illinois. This section ends where the Mississippi and Ohio Rivers join. As mileage is always counted upstream, mile one is Cairo and mile 866 is the Coon Rapids Dam. The second set of Corps maps is for Cairo to New Orleans. It is called the "Lower Mississippi" map. Actually, for canoeists, the Upper Mississippi Corps map is more closely akin to a middle map, for prior to Minneapolis there are 560 miles of river.

While Darrin researched and purchased Corps maps, I ordered fourteen pocket-sized Mississippi maps from the Minnesota DNR. These free maps cover the first 673 miles. They, too, give mileage, campgrounds, resorts, rapids, islands, and water stops, plus historical and natural resource information.

Sometimes just the names of places are enough to evoke images of past glory and historical adventure: Smiling Joe's, Gambler's Point, Fort Snelling, Pig's Eye, Maiden Rock. By the time we hit Bad Axe Point, the last piece of Mississippi River land in Minnesota, we had paddled over one quarter of the river. Most people have no idea so much of the Mississippi lies within Minnesota's borders. They picture the Mississippi as that portion navigable by large craft, the Minneapolis to New Orleans section, where the river can be one or more miles wide.

Because of the Corps' maps, we are now on a side channel that has unique faces carved in Mother Nature's limestone cliffs. One appears to be an old man peering from behind several trees. His huge, protruding nose parts them. "Hey Darrin, two giants standing at attention, guarding an entrance."

Not to be outdone he responds, "There's a pan of Paul Bunyan's freshly baked bread."

Hugging the shore, as we are now doing, means never being sure of what is beyond the bend or point ahead. Darrin sees them first. Perched in the trees, on the downriver side of the next point, is another family of hawks. They take off directly overhead. The two mature ones, surely the parents, swoop down and make threatening gestures, putting us on notice: "Don't mess with our young." Perhaps it is indicative of this lifestyle. We are no longer apart from nature's business; we are a part of it.

Today's coolness is causing numerous potty breaks either with the pee can or in wooded areas. The latter stops are always happen on the upstream side of a point. The positioning shields us from what lies ahead and gives a sightline to what is coming from behind.

Darrin has requested a stop. He drank too much morning tea. It is time for a little funnin'. Presently he is standing with one foot in the canoe, the other on land. Somewhat nonchalantly I call out, as though someone is approaching, "It's okay ma'am. He's my son." After pausing a moment, I resume, "Yes ma'am. He does this at home all the time." Now a second pause for dramatic effect and, "Yes, I know it's hard to raise kids right."

Not to be outdone, Darrin shoots back, "Yeah, tell her who taught me this." We continue the bantering men are wont to do on camping trips. Soon Darrin finishes. After shoving off and taking no more than two strokes, we hear, "It's rough out there today. You boys best be careful." It is the deep voice of an older woman. It shatters our joking. The quiet that follows is uneasy.

Peering into the underbrush on the hillside, I see nothing. Darrin is blushing. Hesitantly I call out, "Where are you?"

"I am up here…in my summer porch." Darrin and I look at each other. We can see no one or any building. We are speechless. She calls out again, breaking the tension, "Where you boys from?"

Sure enough, there on the other side of the point, just up the hill and fifteen yards from where Darrin was standing, is an octagonal, screened porch, about ten feet in diameter. It blends in perfectly with the vegetation.

"Minnesota," we call back, continuing to paddle and put distance between us. We don't want to give out any more information.

Keenly aware of how well sound travels on the water, we are well downstream before beginning a discussion on this latest turn. As she had to have heard us, she must be having a good chuckle. Mississippi shoreline cover may feel like the Boundary Waters, but it isn't.

"She must be one of those polite Iowa women we read about," Darrin says.

We both doff our caps in her direction and say, "Thanks."

By noon it is quite hot. After using a shady spot for lunch, we head out with a breeze at our backs. Once in the open sun I suggest, "Let's hug the shore." Darrin nods and switches sides. Quickly the canoe pulls into the shade of overhanging trees. As if by magic, dancing carp appear.

In the shallows, carp will jump once in a while but not dance. The timing is perfect. The shady area is inhabited by hundreds, if not thousands, of carp, either on a feeding frenzy or trying to get out of the heat. Trapped between the shore and canoe, their herd instinct takes over. There is a mad scramble. As the bow reaches the first of them, they rise out of the water head first. By mid-canoe, ninety-nine percent of their body is upright and out of the water, riding the surface like dolphins at Sea World. As the stern passes, they slide back down. Packed tightly together, like dancing sardines, they are quite entertaining. We both saw *Dances with Wolves*. Now we are experiencing slam dancing with carp.

The slam dancing goes on for over a half block. Asian Silver Carp were imported to Mississippi fish farms in the 1960s. Over the years some escaped through flooding and poor management. The Mississippi became an ideal breeding ground and is now infested. These are Asian Silver Carp.

The experience rivals the best slapstick we have ever seen. Most are bouncing off each other, as happens in slam dancing. A few ride atop the gasping lips of others, crowd surfing, as in a mosh pit. So far none has landed in the canoe. If we paid a price for canoeing the Mississippi, the reward just quadrupled. It is an event I shall never forget. We are laughing so hard it hurts.

All of those pulsating carp lips remind me of a great assistant principal I once worked with. The students who needed regular disciplining found it easy to blame him, via pictorial name calling. One particular student coined, "Carp Lips." Soon it caught on. Whenever the guilty left his office, stage whispers of "Carp Lips" could be heard. The more he held them accountable, the more they pursed their lips and gasped, looking like guppies at feeding time. The irony was obvious—these were final gasps before heading to detention.

"A fishing boat's headed over." Darrin's heads-up is because of two near mishaps. Mississippi boaters understand how quickly the current grabs a floating object. When they visit, they zip right up to another boat before shutting down their engine. While their wakes have little effect on flat-bottomed johnboats or large pleasure craft, they cause enormous problems for us.

It catches boaters by surprise to see anxious faces and canoeists waving them to slow down. When they don't, our canoe takes on a small amount of water. After profuse apologies, they offer a beer for Darrin and soda for me. It is happening again. After some friendly conversation, we move on, deciding to bypass Lock and Dam Nine by taking Harper's Slough to Harper's Ferry. We like the name.

At Harper's Ferry we are greeted by the "Delphey Brothers Marina, Gas, Bait, Repair and Ice." It is a proposition too good to pass up. The Delphey Brothers Marina is a good-old-boys place. The owners are friendly and portray a living history of a slower, more leisurely lifestyle. We enjoy our time with them.

On the river again, Darrin reviews the map and asks, "Wanna stop at Hanging Rock? It's right next to Effigy Mounds National Monument." He figures there must be a connection.

"Any other choices?"

"Guttenburg."

"Sounds better."

Darrin agrees and we hurry on past Marquette and McGregor, over the wing dams adjoining the Upper Mississippi River National Wildlife and Fish Refuge, sailing past Cat Fish Slough, French Island, and Lock and Dam Ten. Once secured at Guttenburg, we climb the protective levee knowing fate has something in store. It does. Halfway up we spot a canoe parked downriver. Its owners must be in town. We will look for them.

Guttenberg turns out to be the quintessential, Middle American town that Norman Rockwell loved so much. It is Everyman's dream. The streets are clean, the houses neat, and the fences freshly painted. The people are friendly and the food is great. Everyone seems to have a good job. Proverbial Iowa at its best; the corn is tall and the children smiling. To top it off, a river runs through it. Okay, alongside it. But good people clearly live here.

After calling our wives, Darrin seems upbeat. Schalleen must be feeling less pain. With groceries in hand, we return to the canoe. While repacking, I see them. "Darrin, look up," I whisper.

Strolling toward us on the river-walk, cigarettes blazing and smoke swirling in huge, billowing clouds are the spitting images of Mark Twain's characters Huck and Tom. I cannot believe our good fortune. I knew they'd be on the river. I knew we'd find them sooner or later. "If I ever get the chance to cast Sawyer, those two guys will be my models." Darrin smiles in agreement. They have got to be modern-day youth looking for adventure.

Darrin stands up, hand outstretched, "Hi, guys. That your canoe?"

"Yup." The response isn't exactly a challenge, but it isn't overly friendly. Perhaps suspicious!

Darrin continues, undaunted by their curt reply, "Where yah from?"

"Indiana," the younger, dark-haired one replies. They relax a bit. They are wearing clean jeans and polo shirts, not exactly river attire. As

I open my mouth to engage them, they purposefully turn their bodies away from me, toward Darrin. My age difference seems to be a turn-off.

Huck, who has light brown hair, asks, "You guys been on the river long?" He is slightly thinner than his buddy, but not by much. Both are slight of frame, identical in height, maybe five-foot-eight.

Wanting to be a part of the conversation, I step behind and around Darrin. Now facing the boys, I answer, "Yeah, we left Itasca the Saturday before Memorial Day. Laid over in Minneapolis two days. How about you? When did you start?"

The dark-haired one glances at me but refocuses on Darrin. "We started a couple weeks back at Coon Rapids." As of yet no introductions have been offered. Darrin and I look at each other but keep our facial expressions in check. It is a long time on the river for so little progress.

Without hesitation Huck volunteers more information, as if he had answered our questions many times before: "We just graduated from high school…taking the summer off…headin' tah college in the fall…flew to Minneapolis…took a taxi to Elk River and the nearest Wal-Mart…purchased a canoe, two paddles, a cooler and some groceries."

Incredible! These guys really fly by the seat of their pants, and Huck has developed his own patter. The tone is clear, "Don't break in until I'm done." He goes on to say that with food and craft in hand, they called a second taxi to take them to the Coon Rapids Dam. They started there to avoid portages; locks all the way for these boys. They simply got on the river and are floating or paddling at-will. Their paddles are those cheap plastic blade and aluminum shaft models. They usually don't last too long. Their bright red, ice-chest catches my attention. Turning back I introduce Darrin and myself.

Quickly our modern day Huck and Tom tell us they are Chase and Marc. They are in no hurry to get anywhere on this day or any day. Five, ten, or twenty miles a day is fine. They are not interested in any physical exertion. Stopping often, they take in the local sights and cuisine. The latter is because they don't want to burden themselves with too much cooking. Their youth makes me realize my age. They are so young looking, so innocent. Unfortunately they are also very naïve about the river and canoeing.

This is Marc's first canoeing experience. Chase spent two summers at a camp in northern Minnesota. He has made two short trips into the Boundary Waters. They are even less knowledgeable, but not by much, than my lifelong buddy Danny and I were when we spent a week on Lac La Croix. Neither of these guys is your typical Boy Scout or outdoorsman. However, for adventure, their hearts are in the right place, but will that be enough? I decide to offer advice, "Have you guys…."

Chase sees it coming and abruptly turns to Darrin. "We met a guy named James. Mighta been a bit older than yer dad. He wanted to give us advice about the river. We cut him off." Chase stops there. Marc is eyeing me.

They are not naïve about everything. I will push no further. It is too bad, I think, I bet James has a wealth of information. I still can't believe we haven't caught up with that old river rat. Maybe he will share some of his knowledge with us. I don't mind learning a few things through the college of hard knocks, but this trip has already thrown enough curves.

Chase and Marc continue to light up one cigarette after another. Indifferent to the smoke clouds hanging over us, they are almost arrogant. Their actions say they won't be listening to anything we have to say. In fact, they are anxious for us to let them by. Wishing them luck, Darrin and I step aside so they can continue to their craft.

After finishing packing and taking off, when out of earshot, we express concerns for their physical health. Besides chain-smoking, they appear to lack enough canoeing experience to have a long life on the Mississippi. Our conclusion: pray for them.

James and Bottle Man are still ahead of us. We are anticipating those meetings. From what we have heard, I am surprised we haven't already caught Bottle Man. Maybe we are slower than I imagined. Maybe he is traveling day and night. Certainly James is doing well for paddling alone.

"Darrin, can you read the sign on that barge across the river?"

"Miss Restoration, the sign says they are on a mission to clean up the Mississippi." On deck are barrels and an odd assortment of chairs, re-rod and other garbage found on the riverbanks. As they are too far away for a visit, we continue on.

With fatigue again catching us, we discuss renting a paddlefish. While the Minnesota DNR rents beavers, muskrats, and walleyes, the Iowa DNR allows the rental of paddlefish. It is Iowa's version of "catch and release." Fishermen snag them in the rushing waters under the dams and place them in live-wells built into the sides of Iowa locks. Every Fridays at 4 PM a private auction is held for bait shop owners.

In Guttenburg we talked with a local bait shop owner who hires Amish farmers, from Harmony, Minnesota, to cut and sew leather harnesses during the long winter months. These harnesses are a miniature version of the larger horse and buggy ones. A fish harness sells for $10 while the paddlefish rents for $3 a day. As the bait shop owner was sold out, Darrin is now more anxious than ever to see a paddlefish.

He is asking every fisherman we meet. They just shrug and raise their eyebrows like he is pulling their leg. Now he is finding out why. We have pulled alongside and old-timer in a Johnboat. He was so perfectly still before arrival, he could have been mistaken for a river memorial statue. The old man is patiently responding to Darrin's question about paddlefish. "The odds of you seeing a caught paddlefish are something less than zero."

It seems this great eating, boneless fish, is rarely caught in the usual way. It is even rarer to see one caught in the summer months. Ninety-nine-point-nine percent of the time these fish are snagged, not caught. Most often they are snagged in the rushing current of dams and waterfalls during the late winter/early spring thaw.

It has been about an hour since leaving the fisherman. After turning to check for upstream traffic, I moan, "Oh, no! Iron Mike is back." Darrin stops paddling to look. Ever since our last run-in we have been watching over our shoulder. We know what goes up must come down. We have vowed to avoid the Ecksteins like a plague. The name has become synonymous with danger. It is easy enough to spot them. Each company has its own colors. The Eckstiens are blue and white. We are now giving Mike a wide berth in extremely shallow waters. He will ground long before getting near us.

We wonder if others have trouble with the Ecksteins. We have composed ballads and tearjerker, country westerns, depicting the havoc they wreak upon canoes, small boats, and little children. We could be wrong. Maybe the Eckstiens are really a great company to work for and all of the other river captains admire their daring. Yes, and the Corps is selling Lock and Dam Ten to the lowest bidder.

As dusk nears, we are anxious to find a campsite. Ahead is a sandy beach. As we land, Darrin calls out, "Fifty-eight! Our best day yet. Must be the current!" I agree.

BOTTLE MAN

The sun's rays are just beginning to light the horizon as we push off. A mile downstream, Huck and Tom's beached canoe and red ice chest come into view. We begin calling, "Marc! Chase!" It is quite a din. Tiring of it, Chase drags himself to the tent door. He waves halfheartedly and hastily beats a retreat to the waiting arms of Morpheus. We yell again, encouraging them to get an early start. Our chiding is an upstream paddle. Their minds are made up. They are going to go with the flow.

After a short while we come upon the first of several wing dams. One after another, we shoot them. Yesterday we compared notes with Marc and Chase. They, too, are using wing dams as short cuts. Yesterday the rapids didn't have much power because of the river's width. Today, however, the river is narrowed and pushing more water over these dams. In the last two hours we have nearly capsized twice. If the rough water is becoming a challenge for us, and our canoe hugs the water, what will it be like for Marc and Chase in a top-heavy, aluminum canoe? Darrin suggests we pray for them.

"Let's also pray they quit smoking," I add. "Do you remember how hard it was for me to quit?" He shakes his head, "no." True enough, I quit smoking before he was born. "Each of those guys has to be going through a couple packs a day. Did I ever tell you about Marge?" Again Darrin shakes his head, "no." He is neither engaging nor disengaging my conversation, so I continue. "She was our school secretary and a dear friend. It was a great loss when she died of emphysema in her early fifties. It was my wake up call." My words are like smoke dissolving in the wind. Darrin is off daydreaming. I won't disturb him anymore.

We haven't seen Iron Mike's barge today, but here comes Penny. Although she is from the same fleet, this will be our first encounter with her. As the river is wider and shallower here, it is easy to move away as she turns in upon us. We aren't worried. We can easily paddle where Penny fears to tread. Shortly after she passes as near as possible, sending only minor waves, another lock appears on the horizon. It is decision time. Do we portage? Before Darrin can decide, I blurt out, "What's that?"

As we stare at the boat next to the lock, I hear myself proclaiming, "Bottle man?" Although more than a mile and a half away, the craft's odd look can be no other. We scrap portage plans for the long awaited encounter.

Alex is a kind, grandfatherly man in his seventies. He is quiet but filled with a zest for life. His daughter immigrated to the United States first. He followed from Belarus a few years later. He attempted this trip a year ago but the Coast Guard stopped him the first day out. He didn't have the proper registration and approval for a "non-approved" boat design. Ah yes, I love the way laws are written. Approval for the non-approved must first be approved.

Alex says, "The Volga have no restrictions." To get a license, his craft needed to be seaworthy. He slaps the right breast pocket of his coat. Therein lay the approval papers, stashed within easy reach. He has already been stopped several times. "During winter months, I wrote Admiral. I get reply. Now nothing stop me."

"Nothing!" I wonder.

Alex's dark, solid colored t-shirt and light, woolen jacket, opened three buttons, are tucked neatly into workpants. His attention to clothing details leaves me feeling he is ready to work at a moment's notice. Reinforcing this feeling are his eyes, constantly darting over to the gate. He's like an animal ready to pounce.

His rowing-craft consists of one-hundred and twenty-eight two-liter, plastic soda bottles. They are bound together by ten-gauge, wire fencing; the same style fence used to separate my childhood back-yard from the neighbor's. The wire-loop openings are about four-inch squares, just wide enough to put a foot in. My dad hated that. Our climbing constantly broke down the fence. But for binding bottles it is perfect. The wire causes neither too much drag nor adds too much weight.

At the center of his craft, securely connected but one layer lower than the top deck of bottles, sits an aluminum webbed chaise lawn chair. It must double for sleeping and working. Immediately behind his "captain's chair," within easy reach, is a cooler. Stacked around the cooler are provisions: bottled water, clothes, a sleeping bag, etc. Immediately to the right and left of Alex's chair are two oars, wired in place.

When the craft was first described to us by a lockmaster, I thought surely he was mistaken. He said, "When he stops rowing, the boat immediately comes to a full standstill." Knowing how watercraft drift a bit after being shut down, I found his description hard to visualize. Now, as the lock open, I will see for myself.

Immediately Alex begins rowing. From previous experiences we know lockmasters will stop us if we begin moving before the gate is fully open. That is not happening to Alex as he rows hard and fast. In truth he seems to need a jump start to make it through in a timely fashion. He just stopped to move something on his deck and the craft did stop dead.

As the lock doors close, we are barely in. Normally we would be on the other end and resting, holding onto a rope thrown down by the lockmaster and attached to the top railing. On this trip though, the lockmaster is not requiring any of us to stay put. It is obvious Alex will need all the time he can get just to make it through before the gates opens on the other end.

It would take only one or two strokes to sail past him, but etiquette and interest keep us from doing so. He arrived at the lock first. He gets first choice of where to stop. However, that is not going to happen. He is rowing non-stop. As he works hard, we drift and make small talk, listening as if hearing someone's profound secrets.

When the exit gates open, Alex is still rowing feverishly with yards to go. He does not want to keep the downstream boats waiting. He rows like a madman paddling upstream against rapids, yet the waters are placid. I can't imagine working that hard for any length of time. He must do a lot of drifting. How dangerous is that with barge traffic? Then Darrin asks it, "Do you drift a lot?" Alex says nothing. He is a good man with a dream to get in the Guinness Book of Records for floating down the Mississippi on a bottle raft. He also hopes to help put an end to pollution.

Before entering the lock, Alex told us that as a boy in Belarus he had dreamt of floating down the Volga. The Russians, according to

Alex, "destroyed dream by way Volga managed." He does not want that to happen to the Mississippi. He now lives with his daughter in Edina, Minnesota, fifteen miles west of the world's fourth largest river.

Safely out of the lock, we pull up to the right shore. Alex wants to exchange addresses and telephone numbers. "Let's meet in fall and talk about trips." He is very proud of what he has already accomplished. He should be.

He is particularly proud of his stomach muscles. He emphasizes this by lifting his shirt, patting them while saying, "When I begin, I am fat and bulging. Now it is muscle." It's true. His revelation is of a slim, muscle-bound stomach. "True six-pack," he proudly proclaims. The implication: People in the infomercials have artificial six-packs. Slim and fit looking, nicely tanned, excess fat melted away, a cheerful demeanor, all make him a great model for a senior's magazine. He is giving me hope. But as my workout is not so strenuous, I doubt I will ever develop his six-pack.

Darrin asks, "You eaten lunch?" When he shakes his head "no," Darrin turns around and rummages through the food pack, grabbing three portions of everything, passing around fruit, granola bars and a sandwich. Each time Alex accepts an item, he packs it away in his food bag. At first it seemed he was waiting for the sandwich. Not so! It, too, is packed away, routinely, almost un-noticeable, except he is not eating with us. We say nothing. This may be a second reason he is so slim. He must be doing his trip on a smaller budget than we.

"I average twenty-five mile a day. I go late." He is hinting at night travel. There is no other way to make twenty-five miles in his craft. After eating lunch, we turn to go our separate ways. Alex wants to head into town for supplies. His tone and hoarding behavior lead us to speculate he is going to seek handouts. He remains the main topic of our conversation for the next couple hours.

By mid-afternoon, despite the wind at our backs and having traveled only thirty-five miles, we call it a day. The Dubuque Public Campgrounds, just ahead, offers us a shower and shave before Saturday evening services.

While unpacking, a man in his fifties stops at the edge of the site. He is dressed in dark shorts, white t-shirt and a straw hat. "Hi…that your canoe?"

"Yup." Seeing an opportunity, I don't hesitate. "Say, you wouldn't know of any Catholic churches in the area?"

His name is Steve. "Sure, there's a five-thirty Mass at St. Mary's. I'm going to town later. I could drop you off…can't pick you up." After additional conversation, he promises to be back at the appointed time.

With the tent up, clothes washed, and a shower taken, I am, for the second time since leaving Minneapolis, wearing totally clean clothing. It feels good. I brought two sets. The first is for church, the second for New Orleans. As our ride passes over the bridge and out of the campground, I point to a sign at the Greyhound Race Track, "All You Can Eat Buffet."

Darrin agrees, "Sounds like dinner."

In my best Minnesotan I respond, "You betcha!"

The walk back from church proves pleasant and leisurely. It is too hot to hurry. Walking through an older section of town, we are encountering many empty industrial buildings similar to those I remember from my youth. In their heyday, before forklifts and air-conditioners, the large overhead doors would be wide open. Men would be hurrying in and out using two-wheel handcarts to load and unload manufactured goods.

As we near the racetrack, wild rabbits freely roam outside the fence. They seem intent on finding a way onto the lush, green, track grass. "Do you suppose they ever get on the track during a race?" While Darrin cogitates an answer, I continue, "When I was going to school in Sioux City, Iowa, a classmate said it happened there. I always wondered if it wasn't an urban legend. My friend said all hell broke loose whenever a wild rabbit got on the track. Some dogs chased it while others stayed with the track rabbit."

"Sounds like a legend. They've fenced them out pretty good." Darrin is right. There are plenty on the outside, none on the inside.

The buffet is great. With a keen appetite from paddling, the greasy foods slide down easily. As the calories will burn off by lunch tomorrow, it matters little. After dinner we return to the campground via the scenic route, between the campground and racetrack grounds. Once back we head up to visit the camp manager, Pat. She has a picnic table, a place to comfortably write postcards. Thankfully my postcards are not yet from the edge.

Pat is both the friendly, motherly type and a bit of a flirt. After offering her picnic table, she disappears only to reappear with Pepsi and popcorn. She begins by sharing experiences from previous canoeists. I should be writing this down. Her anecdotes would make a great book. Perhaps she keeps a diary. Whether she does or doesn't, we will now be a part of her lore. With the canoeist topic exhausted, she shares another tidbit. "You guys know this camp was under six feet of water in May?" We shake our heads "no." "We're still cleaning up."

"I noticed a pile of mud chunks near the Vietnam Memorial." The memorial both impressed me and caused me to fight back tears of joy and sadness. For the first time I was truly humbled as I touched the names of those who gave their lives. It was a heaviness I hadn't felt when visiting the D.C. Memorial. Perhaps I was still too immature. Today all I could think about was my protesting while classmates were being shot at.

During my childhood, WWII vets lived in the two bums' camps near my home. They never talked much about their war experiences, only that life hadn't worked out the way they had hoped. Now I have a classmate in that situation. Perhaps it was Darrin's stint in the army and being shot at in Kosovo that finally allowed me to clearly feel the cost of freedom. My initial sadness was tempered by an overwhelming joy: Darrin was home, alive and beside me on a lifetime experience.

"Gary, you still with us?" I look up. Pat's quiet smile is inviting. I can't respond. Tears are again welling up. I smile and nod. She knows something is happening and turns to Darrin, beginning a new conversation.

After postcards, pop, and popcorn, we thank Pat and head back to the tent. We still have a campfire invitation waiting. As we near our site, a man and his two children are standing near the canoe. Upon arrival, the father says, "The children and I are wondering how many times a day you capsize, and how you keep your food dry?"

His question is not a joke and I respond caringly, "In the twenty some days we've been out, we've never capsized."

The father's look is one of incredulity. He speaks again, "I'd always understood tipping was a routine part of canoeing." It would be tempting to believe he is pulling my leg for the children's sake, but he is not. He is dead serious. What ensues is a half hour discussion on canoeing. They leave with a whole new perspective.

After changing into freshly laundered and dried canoe clothes, we head for the family reunion across the road. Earlier a dad and his son invited us to join them for an evening of friendly conversation and drinks. The latter we will turn down, still amazed at how much physical stamina alcohol and caffeine take out of us. Secondly, we want to sleep as soon as we go to bed.

The next two hours are spent in friendly, campfire discussions. Finally someone turns the conversation to the history of Dubuque. "Who founded it?" I ask.

"Dubuque!" they answer in unison.

"Who was he?"

All they seemed to remember is Indians ran him off a cliff and local citizens built a memorial to him. "A memorial…why?" My question seems to startle them. When no one answers, I do. "If he was running from the Indians, maybe he'd done something to anger them. Perhaps the Indians did everyone a favor. Maybe a monument should be erected to them." The silence is deafening. Darrin looks as shocked as the rest. With damage control impossible, I decide to forthwith retreat.

Comfortably settled in my sleeping bag, the park now seems noisy. Previously I had thought it fairly quiet. The noise is not coming from the neighbor's party. It is from two different sources. From the race track's kennel near the opposite end of the campground emanates a constant yelping, whining and anxious barking. Having gotten used to the solitude and quietness of river camping, the dogs seem deafening.

However, the dogs aren't alone. Someone has let the kids out. There is a live rock concert a few blocks away. As the hours pass, new songs re-awaken me. At 2 AM I comfort myself with thoughts of returning to the river's quiet. It normally teems only with the sounds of friendly wildlife.

A BAD DREAM

Despite a lack of sleep and the early hour, we decide it's time to leave. This is not due to the chilly morning or the yelping greyhounds wanting to be fed. It is the ranting of their caretaker. The dogs are doing their best to bark over her. She is berating them in a higher-pitched bark: "stupid, bad dogs." Between these words come threats, "You'll get no food if you keep this up. They should shoot the whole lot of you." Her nonstop barrage is far more irritating than the dogs' barking. We leave without breakfast, resigned that neither the dog's pleas nor the gods are going to change her approach.

The early start is relaxing. There is a slight breeze out of the north. No strong, warm, southern headwinds have yet appeared. Right now the current is above average. These are all welcomed factors. My strokes are getting longer and more rhythmic; this bothers me. They feel like the stroke of a tired person. Will we ever catch James and his Mad River canoe? Perhaps he is truly a canoeist of mythical proportions. Have we unwittingly passed him and missed an opportunity to meet a great river rat?

At Savannah, Illinois, the river traffic becomes heavy, like a Monday morning beltway rush. "Let's paddle over to Sabula (Iowa). Perhaps it'll be quieter," Darrin suggests.

Once there I exclaim, "Let's stop for lunch. I'm buying" Home Port is the place. It is a mom-and-pop riverfront, three/two beer joint/ pizza place with johnboat rentals. More importantly, the operation offers a place to tie up and observe our canoe and belongings from deck tables. Once inside, the stale smoke and beer smells remind me of Fink and Marie's, my Uncle Frankie's old beer joint in New Prague, Minnesota.

After ordering pizza, we begin visiting patrons. They are the same good people I remember from Fink and Marie's. Yes, Home Port offers that same momentary friendship and camaraderie. Most memorable at Fink's was a sign over his bar mirror, "Free Beer Tomorrow." When I was finally old enough to read, I asked Frankie, "What about soda… will you be giving away free sodas?" As I sat on the bar stool waiting for his reply, the other patrons went silent. Frankie offered one of his warm, friendly smiles and said, "Come back tomorrow, I'll tell yah." This was followed by more silence. I could feel the other men, including my dad, watching, waiting for me to speak. Nervous in the silence I asked Frankie, "How yah able tah give away free beer? Isn't it expensive?" The sounds of laughter began to cut through my naiveté.

Frankie leaned closer and gave me a quick wink and a whisper. "Come back tomorrow…I'll tell yah." I knew Frankie was trying to give me a hint. I looked up at the sign again, thought of the snickers, and realized his friendly joke.

Years later, as a teacher, I made a similar sign. I hung it over the front chalkboard: "Free A's Tomorrow." One fall I found it torn down, ripped to shreds, crumpled into a ball and stomped upon. It was two months into fall semester. Classroom space was at a premium. I was sharing my room with a floater, a teacher who had no permanent classroom. With the banner utterly destroyed and in plain sight, I asked my students if they knew what happened. No one had a clue. Some were disappointed. It had become a conversation piece, a constant reminder not to take life too seriously.

The next day I stood outside the room during the floater's dismissal time. I asked some former students if they knew what had happened. Big grins stretched across their faces. Indeed they did. It seems students had been bugging the new teacher for their "free A's." In vain he assured them the sign was not his. Knowing it bothered him, they continued. Finally he wanted no more of it. He yanked the sign down, tore it up in front of them, wound it up into a ball, and just to make his point perfectly clear, he stomped on it. Naturally everyone thought this great entertainment.

"Hey, Dad. You with me?"

"What?"

Darrin has met the adult children of Home Place's owner. They have brought their children for a Father's Day pontoon ride. Presently the grandchildren are moving in and out of granddad's bar as freely as I did Fink's. Back then I would ask my folks for a nickel to play the pinball machine. These kids are asking for quarters to play the video games. Mostly, however, they are staying on an upper deck overlooking the outside dining area, a place to which Darrin and I are now retreating.

Taking up positions at a picnic table near the water's edge, away from the upper deck, we breathe cool, fresh air. Life seems perfect. The entrance to the deck above is a pair of sliding glass doors from Grandpa's living quarters. Nearly all of the children are decked out in life jackets, constantly leaning too far over the railings while pushing each other. They are antsy for the day's activities to begin.

While waiting for pizza, we are entertained by the children taking turns calling out in loud voices, "Grandpa, when are we going?"

Or, "How long till you're ready, Grandpa?" There is a regular rhythm to it. When one tires, another begins. It has been going on since we returned to the deck. It now appears Grandpa and one of the mothers can no longer take it. Basically they have told the children to, "shut-up and wait or else."

Apparently Grandpa Pat's relief person called in and is arriving late. Grandpa, for his part, had promised the grandchildren a Father's Day pontoon ride on the Mighty Miss. Their promised boat ride is now running more than an hour late. Even though things are out of Grandpa's hands, the children know a promise is a promise. Fortunately the beer is keeping the adult children mellow.

It is now a good thirty-five minutes since the children were told to "shut-up." As Darrin and I stand to leave, the children have been asked to come down from the upper deck and receive a present, "for being so patient." I am unsure as to how yellow cheese and chocolate ice cream go together, but on this Sunday afternoon they do.

As each is handed cone and cheese, he or she immediately begins marching single file behind the first child. They mimic this older child's rhythmic stomping on the hollow deck, as though it were a large drum. The drumming is whipping up emotions. Holding cone and cheese in outstretched hands, like demonstration placards, they turn the peaceful outdoor seating area into chaos.

Stomping and winding among the tables is great payback for the challenge they faced not long ago. Even though all of the cones have been distributed, and they have been repeatedly asked to board grandpa's pontoon, the request is being ignored. What started as a rag-tag operation has grown into a full-fledged cry for retribution. Their movements are no longer random.

Captain Pat now takes a firm stand behind the wheel, asking his adult children to do the same with their children. When the grandchildren don't respond, Pat again conferences with the other adults. The children, sensing the end is near, stomp louder. Soon the hollow drumming, the cacophony, breaks down under the threat of police action. It is family life at its normal best. As we pull out, the adults are gradually getting each child under control. Life is good!

In spite of new twinges in my upper back, it is a marvelous Father's Day. Darrin is cutting me extra slack, allowing me to linger and enjoy every moment of Home Port and other places along the way.

As evening nears, we are again drawn into heavy river traffic. We definitely stayed too long at Home Port. Weekend boaters are clogging the river, racing each other to the landing. As there are no lanes, the fastest will get there first.

The speeding boaters are oblivious to the tranquil river islands which are in much the same state as when Huck and Tom plied these waters. These low-lying islands, where spring flooding is inevitable, make building impossible. The islands are great bird sanctuaries. Perched in the trees, at the water's edge, these birds and their ancestors will forever be giving river concerts.

Each evening there must be a call to all the most talented singers in this locale, asking them to take part in a grand, evening concert. Their singing is a delight. It accompanies the beginnings of a glorious, mosquito-free sunset—probably due both to voracious bird appetites and the cool evening breeze. In spite of the boats, our paddling is on a mostly smooth, glasslike surface. The pace seems paradoxical. We move swiftly on a still surface while boats race by to an upstream landing.

"These small river towns remind me of my boyhood." When Darrin nods, I continue, "It's almost too good to be true. The deck at Home Port brought back memories of the Casino on Fountain Lake. That was enjoyable. Maybe I'm just getting old, but the shape, size, and condition of those buildings and the dock are from another era."

Darrin's reply gets my attention. "I am glad you're enjoying it. It's what we came for."

Yes, Darrin, I think to myself, today's more like the vacation and camaraderie-building I'd hoped we could do. After forty-six miles, too tired for anything else, we retreat to a campsite and bed.

I don't know how long I have been asleep, but in my dream, men are running around, yelling at each other. I find myself screaming at them, demanding to know, over the roar of a towboat engine, "What the hell's going on?" I bolt up; awakened. Instantly voices surround me. "Darrin!"

"Go back to sleep."

"Something's wrong…listen! We're being raided!" The fear in my voice matches my mind racing processing a hundred different scenarios. What's going on? How do I prepare for what is about to happen? Desperately searching for my eyeglasses, I find Darrin's flashlight and shoot a beam out the screen door. I can't move, momentarily paralyzed by fright. Less than ten feet away is a grounded barge. This just can't be. I'm dreaming.

"Darrin, wake up!" I scream.

"What's wrong?"

"There's a huge barge looming over us, it's...it's huge," I stammer!

"No way! Go back to sleep. You're dreaming."

Although he would like to roll over, I won't let him. "It's not a dream!" As the reality hits me, I shout, "Darrin, I swear! We've nearly been run over." He fumbles for his glasses. After joining me looking out the tent door, we both stare in disbelief. The huge, metal hulk, towers over us. Neither of us speaks. Fear and the realization of death are too great. It is not one of my wild dreams. We are wide awake.

The lead barge is grounded some fifteen to twenty feet up our sandy beach. How could it be grounded so far up? Perhaps the captain is asking himself that question. The deck hands are cursing him. "What the — was he thinking? He must be the dumbest — around!" The cursing continues. The engines roar in reverse to pull the barge off the beach. It is to no avail.

The ship's megaphone comes to life, "Disconnect it!" The crew begins uncoupling the grounded barge. The other barges must be backed off and parked while the towboat pulls at the grounded barge.

After the others are safely parked, the engines again roar in reverse, struggling to get the grounded barge off the sand. The men continue swearing and shouting orders. It takes them over an hour to finish and get on their way.

The scary part is this beaching happened while we were sleeping. We heard nothing as it slid silently up the shore, like a tsunami rolling across some peaceful, south sea island. Had we tented in our normal spot, ten to fifteen feet back from shore, we would now be flattened. Had we secured our canoe in front of the tent, the normal practice, it too would be gone forever.

"This has got to be a fluke. No one would be stupid enough to scare us in this fashion, would they?" Darrin doesn't answer my question.

After they leave, we are too shaken to sleep. Until now I never really comprehended how huge those barges are, so much is below the water's surface. I don't want to be paranoid about barges being our nemesis, but these incidents are getting to me. No one ever came to apologize. The captain knew we were there. Several times the powerful spotlight lit up our tent and the men commented on how close we were.

MIKE AND DEE

Needless to say, our near demise is breakfast conversation. We want to leave quickly. On the river and still shaken, we push hard to put it behind us. We head for the Quad Cities: Davenport, Rock Island, Moline, East Moline, Silvas, and Bettendorf. I guess they really can't be called the Quad Cities anymore.

We waited too long. The floodgates are barely holding back morning tea. Perhaps animated conversations caused us to forget nature's call, but calling she is. With civilization on both sides of the river, and lots of traffic, we have no alternative but to head in. We are uncomfortable using pee-cans while so fully exposed. Darrin has spotted a boat landing with what appears to be a public restroom.

After tying up, we head to the first building, The Buffalo Bill Museum. The public restrooms are still a half block away. This museum is about 1/30 the size of the Buffalo Bill Museum in Cody, Wyoming. Being in greater need, I am in the museum first and moving quickly around paying guests. I am about to meet the museum's hostess. Unshaven, dirty and, in general, looking more like a bum than a river rat, my first words of introduction are, "Hi, do you have a restroom?"

Her back is turned, so she begins giving directions while turning to face me. "It's over around…" She now sees who is addressing her and stops in mid-sentence. Quickly moving a couple steps back, she confers with a gentleman taking tickets. I would like to shout, "Lady, I can't wait much longer!" but I know it will be a mistake.

Turning back, a bit flushed and reticent, she says, "I'm sorry. The public restrooms are at the end of the parking lot." It is as though I affronted her. She liked the sound of my voice but not the cut of my jibe. I feel sorry for her. She doesn't have the integrity to stay with her initial gut-level instinct. Her posture also changes. Apparently I am not acting quickly enough. She becomes emboldened and points to the door. She wants me to leave the foyer immediately. Her paying guests stare as her voice turns from sweetness and welcoming to cold and calculating, "Leave!"

I want to stay and fight, show my business card, and tell her about the trip, but the experience will do my ego good. She provides a gentle but firm reminder of how judgmental I have been. I am experiencing what must be very common for street people: fear and embarrassment on the part of the establishment.

On the way out I pass an elderly guide telling of a rivalry between Le Claire and Port Byron. They are on opposite sides of the river. "They shut down the river traffic once a year and stretch a rope across. The two towns have a tug-of-war," I hear him say. I don't bother to stop and ask who has won the most. I need a restroom.

On the entrance ramp I meet Darrin coming up. Quickly, without stopping, I explain the situation. Within moments we are nearing the boat landing restrooms. The outside walls are painted in modern graffiti. A large padlock adorns the door. A small sign greets visitors, "Closed due to vandalism."

Quickly exiting right, I am running up the adjoining street, racing toward a restaurant another half block away. Upon entering I do not ask for directions but head directly to the back. Everyone stares at the speeding bum who interrupted their leisurely breakfast.

Back on the river, the real heat intensifies. The cool weather has ended. Summer has arrived in earnest. The sky's brilliant blue allows the sun rays to beat down, arousing warm winds out of the southwest. As of yet they are still soft, like an aroused lover's heavy breathing, they gently caress our face and necks. The flushed feeling of this southern comfort is inebriating. The foreplay wants to numb us on what is coming: ninety-nine percent humidity and one-hundred degree heat.

The river and its scenery are changing, mostly due to the parallel, three-pronged delivery system of barges, trains, and semis. The commercial picture makes it clear what is keeping our great country going.

Last night we stayed on an island in the middle of the river. Today many islands are a part of the scenery, big ones and little ones. It feels very wild again. We are paddling in the middle of the river, about a half-mile from either shore, just north of Clinton, Iowa.

"I wanna call Schalleen." Darrin is unsure when we will again have easy access to phones.

As we move toward shore, I wonder how many townspeople voted for Bill Clinton simply because of his last name.

Clinton turns out to be a nice, clean-cut, all-American town. We spend an hour. By the time we return to the river, the wind has changed. It is now buffeting rather than caressing. We hug the western shoreline. Although it blocks most of the wind, the paddling is still hard work. Darrin nods agreement when I say I hope it is not the beginning of the southern headwinds.

The day turns into a noon-to-dusk push. Potty breaks and calls home set us back. Adding to that stress is a lack of good camping areas. We are now arguing over the dumbest things. Just ahead is Lock and Dam Fifteen. A quarter mile before it, on our left, is the first sandy area we have seen in the last couple hours. Some campers are setting up tents. As we approach to join them, a large white fishing boat races across the river and cuts us off. With beer in hand, the driver gives a friendly wave, "Hi, guys. Where yah headed?"

"It's gettin' late. We need to camp…gonna join those people."

Immediately his tone changes. "No you're not! That site's taken. It ain't big enough for more. Besides, I want to be alone with my family." Darrin and I both study the site. It is over forty by thirty yards, plenty big for all of us, but now is not the time for a rational discussion.

"You boys'll find some good, sandy sites jist about two miles downriver," he slurs.

Ten miles south of Lock and Dam Fifteen, reality sets in. The tale of sandy sites is pure fiction. The fisherman is probably still having a good laugh at our expense. Discussing it only exacerbates our attitude. We now blame each other for not having camped while it was still light.

Darkness came with a bang. The thick woods along the western bank intensified the blackness. We are trying to peer into near total darkness. Added to the misery are mosquitoes. It is so stressful we are trying not to speak. It only brings blaming. Between verbal jabs Darrin asks, "Are we looking into people's backyards?"

Some fifty yards ahead, about thirty feet off the ground, two tiny lights break through the pitched darkness. As we close in, the faint silhouette of a woman leaning over a deck railing can be seen. Her stance seems relaxed and comfortable, as though she has been there often. As she seems to be peering in our direction, I call out, "Do you know where the campsites are on this side of the river?" My question holds urgency. I am beyond begging. There is only a moment for her to reply. The current is swift. We will be gone in a second, even though we have quit paddling.

"Yes!" is her eager reply. Darrin is dumbfounded. He thought I was wasting my breath.

"Where?"

"Right here!"

"Are you serious?" I give this question more than just a hint of jubilation and jam the rudder for a ninety-degree turn.

"Yes!" comes her friendly reply.

Already past her home, the swift current's broadside gently turns us another ninety degrees, pushing us sideways and onto the neighbor's shoreline. With the canoe safely grounded, we walk back to her deck railing.

"Hi, I'm Gary. This is Darrin. We are attempting to canoe the Mississippi."

"I'm Dee. Mike will be out shortly." Instantly he is beside her, looking relaxed, as though these invites are a normal part of his wife's life. As they look down at us, our smiles must seem as broad as a Cheshire cat's.

Mike and Dee own a typical, Iowa, flood plain home. The living space is one story up. Underneath is a carport with a small storage room. The doors and windows of the storage room are designed to allow spring floodwaters clear passage through, ensuring the home's structural integrity. The yard is strewn with large trees, grown randomly to help stop or slow down flood debris that might hit the basement walls or deck pilings.

"Sorry the yard's such a mess." In the dark we hadn't noticed. "We're still cleaning up. Two weeks ago the river was ten feet higher," Dee says. Unbelievable! Quickly our hosts stop the chitchat, leave their comfortable perch, and come down. Their greetings continue to be gracious and from the heart.

After handshakes, Darrin asks, "Where do you want us to set up?"

"Pick the best spot," Mike replies. "When you're done, come in and join us for drinks."

"I'll fix you a meal," Dee offers.

Darrin looks at me for direction. "Thanks, but we've already imposed enough. We'd be happy to join you later."

Their hospitality has caught us unprepared. We are still dealing with hurts. Imposing personal pain would not do. Our doing the routine, pitching a tent and boiling water, will help us prepare to forgive each other. That preparation began with being rescued so quickly and completely. It has brought a sincere feeling of humility. The stress of the darkness and the lack of a campsite, deepened by the anguish of slings and arrows tossed since Lock and Dam Fifteen, are now miraculously washed away. Mike and Dee, literally and figuratively, have plucked us out of deep waters. "Thanks!" just doesn't seem enough. We need to be at peace with each other.

Before turning toward the house, Mike asks, "What would you like to drink?" After taking orders, they disappear. Before we can get the water boiling, they are back. The after-dinner-drinks are now before-dinner-drinks. Dinner is rushed in anticipation of their third invitation: hot showers.

After taking a moment to thank God and seek forgiveness from each other, dinner is rushed. With quickly prepared food under our belts and peace restored, we are ready for hot showers and good conversation. Before reaching the house I grab Darrin's arm, "We just blew it."

He looks at me like I'm crazy. "I don't understand."

"Remember the crunchy bits?"

"Yeah, so what?"

"It was half-cooked!"

"So?"

"The number one rule for dehydrated food is 'cook it thoroughly.'"

"Get to the point!"

"Undercooked, dehydrated food causes volumes of the nastiest gases imaginable. You don't want to be downwind or in the same tent. Beans are minor compared to the sounds and smells from partially cooked, dehydrated foods."

Darrin says nothing. He knows our Bear Soup, which is a great soup, wasn't thoroughly cooked. As reality can't be changed, we change the subject, marveling once again at how readily Mike and Dee took us in. While climbing the stairs leading to their river sanctuary, we agree it is quite a contrast to Buffalo Bill's.

After a shower, shave, and change of clothes, we are human enough to inhabit their living room. The soft leather couch is comfortably overstuffed. The smooth, slippery surface begins massaging my body. Aching muscles begin to fade. It will not be long before sleep takes over. I struggle to stay awake and rejoice in the moment as drinks, hors d'oeuvres and marvelous conversation begins.

Periodically Dee goes to her porch light switch, flashing it on and off as a "hello" beacon to the evening barge traffic. Although names are never exchanged, Dee and many barge operators are on a first name basis. She fires off friendly "hellos" and "good-byes;" they respond with a powerful beam that floods the home. The lightshow goes on for about thirty seconds. It is all part of her evening routine.

Mike begins the first series of questions with, "How long do you plan to be on the river?"

When our answers seem to satisfy his questions, Dee asks, "And tensions, how do you deal with them?" Leave it to the woman to be direct and concerned for our emotional health.

Tension? Who said anything about tension? Darrin and I look at each, hoping the question will go away. We turn back. She is waiting. There is no ducking it. She must have heard harsh words floating down the river. Sound dances all too well across water and up to elevated places.

Darrin responds, "Some of it we don't deal with. We just recognize it and move on. We both know there is more than one solution, and we also know when we've crossed the line." He pauses, looking for some agreement from me. Feeling it, he continues. "Heated exchanges come with the territory." Dee seems pleased with his responses.

Not able to leave a good response alone, I jump in, "I explain it this way. I'm an old man trying to hang onto youth and leadership. Darrin is young and strong, coming into his own and willing to challenge me. I just pray I don't meet the same fate as Idi Amin's father." Darrin laughs. We relax more.

Mike is a lawyer, judge, and racecar driver. His colleagues encourage him to either preside or take the prosecutor's position for murder trials. I am not sure how any these points correlate or why they came in the same breath. Perhaps it is part of the excitement Mike feels for life.

All too soon I can no longer keep my eyes open. I stand to thank our hosts for a wonderful evening. After crawling into my bag, I roll over and stare out at the stars. "Other than salvation, we may never receive a finer gift…human love. It's awesome."

"You got it right!"

Tonight was a perfect mimicking of God's love, an ethereal moment with awesome power. My sins were forgiven by an energy force that lifted up my body. I roll back, prepared to sleep, but turn to Darrin instead. "Again, I'm truly sorry."

"Me too."

How much more effective are patience and praise, unconditional love! The world seems right at this moment. We are resting comfortably in God's arms, ready for a deep sleep.

MAD RIVER JAMES

Something has awakened me. Someone is outside the tent. I lie still. Nothing! It is literally the crack of dawn, well before 5 AM. Yesterday, before wishing us goodnight, Mike said he would bring us coffee to see us off. Perhaps he is actually up at this ungodly hour. Unzipping the door and poking out my head, I find Mike, coffee in both hands. How long has he been there? He and Dee are the epitome of good neighbors, living life as George Elliot suggested, "What do we live for if not to make life less difficult for others."

After breakfast, washed down with more of Mike's great coffee, we say a fond farewell to Horse Island. It is so named because the Indians wintered their horses here. Today's residents call it Enchanted Island. Indeed, it is enchanting. The fast, subsiding floodwaters quickly scoots us past the bottom tip where the truth sinks in, this friendly neighborhood is an island. Originally the entire development seemed more like just another nice, friendly, suburban, riverbank community.

Crookston, Minnesota, has at least three neighborhoods formed from the Red Lake River's snaking through town, looping off sections of land. These entities are named after early settlers. Ours was the Jerome's Addition. Another mark of a true river town is naming her sloughs. The one behind our house was "Aunt Polly's." On the Mississippi, all the sloughs and backwaters have names.

Flooding is another condition river communities seem to endure. Those are scary times for people living next to levees. At the water's peak, the rumbling and rushing can be felt and heard in nearby homes. The trembling levee walls means nerves of steel are needed to walk them during flood watches. The sound and fury of a twenty-five-to thirty-foot wall of water crashing and pounding against each bend in the river is like stampeding buffalo thundering across the plains. The rushing water, just inches from the top of the levee, is also spellbinding. It looks and feels like an industrial conveyer belt that can be stepped onto and ridden like fliers do airport people movers.

Flooding rivers have this strong desire to burst their levee walls. They rumble and shake the dikes, pummeling the high, narrow, artificial banks. A thirty-foot wall of water, squeezed between banks fifty yards apart, literally tears downstream in hot pursuit of an opening. The river demands release and freedom from its barriers. It wants to dissipate its rage by crushing everything in its path. The fury is absolute. A leveling must happen before calm can return.

The excitement of so much raw power can lead to blunders. Once in the early 1990s a Washington, D.C., weatherman built up the flooding on the Mississippi by showing graphic video of destruction on all three of Minnesota's major rivers: the Red, the Minnesota, and the Mississippi. He was having a field day. He turned up to high the recorded volume of roaring waters.

He must have been a neophyte, fresh out of broadcasting school. He was so eager in extol the amount of water and damage being done, he embarked on a detailed explanation of how the flooding Red was flowing into the Minnesota. He explained how the two churned up great damage while relentlessly moving on, adding to the Mississippi's destructive powers. "People along the Mississippi are getting the brunt of the ravaging Red and Minnesota rivers," he said. I am sure he got the brunt of ravaging office jokes for weeks. The Red flows north into Hudson's Bay, not south into the Minnesota and Mississippi river valleys.

But imagine how thick a book it might take to tell the history of flood damages on any major river in the United States. It would take even more volumes to tell of the summer adventures of young people living along those banks. Then add in the history of the sloughs, islands, and floodplains named by settlers and riverboat captains. Finally, think of all the scalawags who made a quick buck on the river.

"Look at those trees!" Darrin's laughing brings me back. The trees just beyond the flood plains are filled with two-liter bottles, old tires, children's toys, and other odds and ends. "Let's pull up and see what's on the other side." I like his idea.

Atop the riverbank and looking into the woods, we are amazed. Truck fenders, cans, docks, barrels, car doors, strollers, and so much more, once carried in the Miss's arms, are scattered about and spilt from venting rage. Mother Nature aided the Miss by sending those raging waters to sweep clean the sandbars and islands. She helped clean up the Miss's mess. She helped sweep away, out of sight, over the banks and down under, the Miss' garbage. Mother Nature and her daughter are great co-conspiracy here. They make each traveler feel as though he or she is the first to set foot on the clean, warm sand beaches and islands.

Beginning with southern Minnesota, we have seen many man-made sand piles, places where the Corps has dumped millions of tons of dredging that the Miss used to clog channels. These piles, often thirty feet to forty feet high and two blocks long, dwarf many land quarry piles.

Although the river's sand gets into everything we own, we don't mind. Its cleanliness is much more refreshing than mud. We prize the soft, sandy stretches where tents set up easily and gentle, cooling breezes blow.

Unfortunately it is the dreaded southern headwinds that now challenge our downstream progress. Although not heavy, they slow us. As we are only now being introduced to them, they are not as yet frustrating. Even though the turbulence below the wing dams continues to increase, the day feels like a lucky one.

Pulling up to Lock and Dam Sixteen, Darrin grabs hold of the lower rung of the outer lock ladder. He is prepared to shove us off when the lock signal turns from red to yellow to green. These lights are identical to vertical traffic lights. Then, out of nowhere, a red, Mad River canoe pulls in front, cutting us off, trapping us between it and the cement retaining wall. It is a bit unnerving. I had no idea a canoe was approaching. Why hadn't we heard anything? Before I can think about it, I blurt out, "James!" I sound like some schoolboy meeting a celebrity.

He immediately barks back, "Who told you my name?"

As I have been looking forward to meeting him, the edge in his voice tears my expectations to shreds. My gut wants to respond in kind, but my mind remembers anticipating this moment. I take a deep breath and reply, "Actually several people. We heard you'd just retired."

Before I can say more, he cuts in with a new demand. "Who were they?" He is disturbed not only that several people have given out facts about him, but that we have collected these facts. His reaction brings to the fore how humans often share one or two random facts, opening up a friendly conversation, never thinking someone might collect the tidbits. It is easy to see how investigators piece together a profile.

"Was the first guy fat, short, and balding?" James' demeanor and continuing third degree tell us we hold far too much information.

"Not exactly. A little heavy, but not bald. I am bald." I lift my hat to show a freshly shaved head. The attempt at humor does little to diffuse his tenseness. The questions continue to fly.

"What about the second guy? How did he know my name? What else did others tell you? How come you guys are so interested in me? Who told you I'm retired?"

As we sit outside the lock entrance, waiting for the gates to open, I feel trapped. His list of questions and tone, coupled with an unwillingness to give any opportunity to answer questions, only adds frustration. Darrin and I look at each other in bewilderment. Perhaps shock and awe might be more accurate. We had been looking forward to meeting the mighty man of sixty-two, someone conquering the Miss alone. What have we gotten ourselves into?

James notices the quizzical looks and backs off a bit. But he doesn't let go of his tough, macho image, an image enhanced by army fatigues and a long wooden paddle slung across his lap, resting like a weapon ready to be fired at a moment's notice.

His paddle is a throwback to the 1930s–1950s style of steering and paddling. It is from an era when a paddle's length was judged by the paddler's height and canoeing position. The correct length for a paddle back then was the distance between one's armpit and the ground while standing erect. That canoeing lore also encouraged stern paddlers to add another twelve inches for deep ruddering. James is using the old standards.

We call his type of paddle "old thunder-heads." They usually make a lot of noise when used. James' paddle didn't. His present posture reminds me of a scene in Rambo where Stallone is sitting, resting on a log, a 44mm canon on his lap, ready to mop up troops coming from any direction. James gives the appearance of someone you don't want to mess with. As I am not ready to duke it out on the Mighty Miss, especially with a crusty old river rat I was longing to meet, I ignore his pose.

He has not shaven in days, perhaps since his trip began. Besides his camouflaged fatigues, he has another army amenity: MREs, Meals Ready to Eat. Just add water to the outer pouch's chemicals and you have an instant hot meal. Besides being easy to fix and no dishes to wash, they taste great, according to my son. When I asked Darrin how often he had eaten MREs, he said, "When the platoon was doing two-day marches or playing seven-day war games." That would explain why they tasted so good.

"My MREs are a retirement gift from a son-in-law…purchased them at a flea market. There's a military base near where he lives." Immediately red flags go up. How did these particular meals get from the supply depot to the local flea market still in their unopened handling boxes? Were they outdated? How likely is that for MRE's? Whatever the case, James is proud of his cache. I can't blame him.

Several things are evident about James. He is an excellent canoeist who loves the old ways. Secondly, because he exudes self-confidence on the water and seems to have such a depth of camping and canoeing knowledge, he would be an ideal partner for any outdoor trip. But he is a loncr. He guards his privacy. At one moment he is eager to have newfound friends, the next he is suspicious without adequate reason.

Since I can't possibly understand another man's journey, I accept James for what he portrays. After initial introductions and exchanges of information, it appears James will share no more. We, too, are leery.

One moment he cuts off a conversation, the next he starts a new one. Perhaps his mannerism is intentional, to keep us off-guard, to draw forth all that we know about him.

As Darrin has had enough interrogating, he changes the subject. "Did you meet up with a couple of young guys?" Darrin knows the answer. Huck and Tom told us about James.

"Yeah, I paddled with them for awhile. They had little understanding of the river and its dangers. I offered to share, but they weren't interested." James has just transformed from Mr. Hyde to Dr. Jekyll. His voice, posture, and mannerisms are changed. He is soft and gentle. Darrin and I look at each other in disbelief. Perhaps this is the real James: animated, caring, and friendly. "I wanted to tell them what they'd encounter on wing dams." James continues, "But they said they'd been using them for short cuts and just cut me off."

His voice trails off in sadness. It seems they treated him as if he were some "old man" who didn't know crud from shinola. They weren't any more interested in listening to him than the parents they left behind. James' voice belies a genuine concern for their safety. Once they had made their feelings clear, he moved on, leaving them to fend for themselves.

"Would you be willing to share some of your expertise with us?"

This is a mistake. Taken aback by my request, he quickly changes again, eyeing me suspiciously, like I had just set him up. I open my mouth to assure him it is legitimate, but it is too late. He is interpreting something in my mannerism or tone of voice. Perhaps it is my age. Maybe he figures anyone my age shouldn't be on the river without the necessary experience.

Without a moment's hesitation, without acknowledging my last question, he says, "I see you guys have black paddles. How do you like them?" He is a cool customer. It is as if our whole conversation has been normal and polite.

I accept the change. "These paddles are the reason an old man can paddle the Mississippi."

If my previous questions and comments were not the last straw, my answer is. He apparently thinks I am referring to his age, not mine. He is now anxious to move on. We are both in luck. The gate is opening. Immediately he pushes off from our canoe and paddles ahead. Lock etiquette is the least of his concerns. Darrin, however, is not ready to give up. With a few extra strokes inside the lock, Darrin brings us along side James and asks, "How'd we get ahead of you?"

If James wasn't angry before, he is now. This time it has nothing to do with us. He is trying to remain calm, but is seething. "Did you notice that little island about a mile before this lock?" his voice has a sharp edge.

"Yeah," we both say.

"That's where I camped. You guys passed just about the time I was shoving off…too far out to call or quickly catch up. Figured I'd catch you at the lock."

These answers seem normal enough. What's bothering him? I decide to compare camping notes, hoping to get more insight. "Did you run into the fisherman camping with his family above the last lock? He misled us on campsites." Darrin and I now relate how Mike and Dee salvaged our evening.

This knowledge heightens James' agitation. He blurts out, "I met the same —er." So James was dis-invited too. For us the man said he wanted to be alone with his family, promising sandy campsites below the dam. For James, the fisherman was a bit more blunt: "You won't be staying here. Get a site below the lock." So we both went through the lock at dusk believing suitable campsites were just downstream.

"That guy was full of — and a — damn liar." James' anger is raw. The lies and lack of campsites are too much. His next words rest uneasy. "I am so —damn mad I've half a mind to canoe back up there and shoot the son-of-bitch." Although we take his remark as rhetorical, his point is clear: Don't mess with me! He is a wily old river rat who doesn't want his honor messed with. He will defend real or imagined slights.

Some of James' mannerisms remind me of train hobos who passed through Albert Lea in the 1950s. Rail-riders was my mother's polite term for those needing food or a day's labor. With both north/south and east/west rails, Albert Lea, a hub of sorts, was blessed with four bum's camps, two within four blocks of my home. James' behavior is bringing to the fore two memories. The first is pleasant, putting a positive spin on the moment. The second is a bit scarier.

The first happened on an idyllic summer day when I was out exploring and visiting the camp near Queen Stove's Manufacturing. Queens had a rail siding where scrap metal was placed in open rail cars. The best pieces ended up in the camp, making it a premiere bum's camp. On this particular day there was only one man and his dog. It was rare to see a dog; it meant another mouth to feed.

Said his dog's name was Charlie. Never told me his. We sat there for some time and talked about life and the beauty of the day. The bum's appearance was different, not the usual camp attire. His clothes were cleaner and he had more self-confidence. I gave it little thought until years later when a high school English teacher assigned a newly published American novel, *Travels with Charlie*. Halfway through the book I began to feel as though I'd met Steinbeck, even though I knew my chance meeting was a couple years earlier than Steinbeck's travels. I chalked it up to great writing.

My second memorable encounter happened while returning from the beach. Kenny, a best friend during the elementary years, shared my passion for water, walkabouts, and whatever action might turn a young boy's fancy. On this day, after spending several hours swimming and flirting with the beach girls, the path home took us along the railroad tracks. Near the depot was a wooden, outdoor, ice storage box. It was never locked and presented an ideal place to cool off and quench a thirst.

Kenny climbed inside to chip off pieces and hand them out. From nowhere came, "Get the hell outa there. That's my ice." About thirty yards away, walking toward us, was a resident from the nearby bum's camp. We knew better than to allow a bum to scare us away. Out of the box came Kenny. We dropped the ice and picked up large rocks to make a stand in the middle of the hot, dusty gravel road that ran beside it. Our young minds believed we could retain rights to the ice.

When our threat became obvious, the man simply stopped, set down his small valise, opened it, and reached in. Out came a German Luger. We knew what it was from watching WWII pictures. He pointed it directly at us. "If you boys want a fight, I'm your man." Without a word we dropped our rocks and ran hell-bent for home. James reminds me of that man.

The water has dropped. The downstream gate is opening. As James heads out, he pauses, again changing the subject. "There's a great little bakery in Muscatine…terrific sticky buns and coffee." Sticky buns, those huge cinnamon rolls, coated with nuts and oozing with luscious caramel, best served hot with slabs of melting butter. Each bite of

MAD RIVER JAMES   171

pleasure fills a hollow spot in the stomach. Eating them on canoe trips is an added pleasure. There is no concern for calories and cholesterol. Paddling burns away every trace of those nasty elements.

After directions from James, we agree to meet and talk. It is a curious parting, more like the generic greeting, "How are you?" and the response, "Fine." We hear it and react positively whether we believe it or not. We take James' remark as a final farewell. We have no more intention of meeting him than he does us.

As we move toward the right bank, James heads down the middle, using the current for a fast paddle. Out of earshot Darrin says what I have been thinking, "Can you believe that guy?"

As he made no effort to share a good landing spot, we land close to where the downtown is located. As we tie up, we see him turning in about a mile and a half downstream. He looks back. We wave but get no response: a clear and certain sign we are going our separate ways. That is fine with us. Our run-in left us feeling less than eager to share more of our lives.

When I was a boy, the word Muscatine conjured up excitement for the down and out, those needing a drink. For Darrin and me the name has a different lure. It offers three things: a home-cooked meal, straw hats, and sticky buns.

Despite a Wal-Mart, Muscatine's downtown is still intact. The sticky buns are a pure delight as is meeting the baker. After leaving Darrin says, "That guy is young-looking for the weight he's carrying. It's a bummer. He's so friendly."

I know where Darrin is headed and add, "He's been enjoying too many delicacies."

"How long do you think he can last?" I just shrug. The sadness in Darrin's voice is really an emphasis on the baker's marvelous personality and culinary gift. He is the kind of person the world needs more of. "Perhaps someone in Muscatine will encourage him to join dieter's anonymous."

"Hopefully he won't run into the same counselor I did."

"This one of your stories?" Darrin asks.

"Yeah…thanks for asking. It happened in the early 1970s. I was sent to a drug treatment center for facilitator training. At one point we were asked to share our deepest, most intimate secrets. Apparently I wasn't doing an adequate job. The assistant began questioning me more intensely. When my answers didn't meet his approval, he became agitated. I thought he was trying to teach me a trick of the trade. Whether it was or wasn't, I'll never know. As he became more agitated, his face became flushed and his neck veins began popping out. When he could take my answers no longer, he leapt out of his chair, bounded across the center of the circle and stood towering, glowering down. It was a very dramatic gesture. He must have expected me to cower.

"When his confrontation didn't cause me to slink down and slide off the chair, melting into the carpet, he became even angrier. His arm veins bulged as tightly clenched fists shook at his sides. He then turned to the rest of the group, threw his fists up for a dramatic gesture and shouted, 'Gary will die of a heart attack before he's forty! He keeps everything bottled up! He's got so much rage he can't let it out!'

"The group fell silent. The pregnant pause was an attempt to suppress laughter. The lead counselor got up and walked out, ending the session."

"Nice story. I liked the baker's waitresses."

"What's with the smirk?" I ask. Darrin is right though. Besides being good looking and flirting with him, they showed a genuine interest in the trip, particularly the "why." It is always the "why" that shows a dream is straining for release, looking for one good reason, one good excuse, to take the plunge, make it happen. The bakery help also recommended a good restaurant.

After lunch we head out to find Darrin a straw hat. After visiting several stores and not finding what Darrin wants, a merchant tells us about a Dollar Store near the northern edge of downtown.

"These hats have chinstraps." Darrin is referring to today's wind's velocity, which now rises in direct proportion to the temperature. Every ten degrees adds two to four miles-per-hour. Although our floppy rimmed fishing hats roll up for easy packing, the wind has shown their uselessness, something James already knew.

When talking to James I was wearing a baseball cap and Darrin his floppy rimmed fishing hat. At one point in the conversation James used Darrin's hat as an excuse to move discussions off himself. He pointed to Darrin's brim being tossed about in the wind, "You need a hat like mine."

As James wasn't wearing a hat, Darrin asked with a bit of derision, "What might that be?"

"It's my 'Giv'em Shit' hat." We said nothing, eager to hear more. James rummaged through his Duluth pack before pulling out a leather hat similar to those worn by Excelsior, Minnesota, drug dealers in the early 1970s. Those young dealers fancied themselves pretty cool as they strutted down Water Street wearing leather hats and paisley bellbottoms. Like pimps in the popular movies of the day, these drug dealers knew their hats drew attention. They were like neon "open for business" signs, the equivalent of an ice-cream truck's bells and whistles.

On more than one occasion, while at the Excelsior Commons, a waterfront park on Lake Minnetonka, I spotted teenage dealers in their leather hats moving cockily along the lakeshore walk. Out of nowhere people came, handing off cash for packets. Such were my thoughts as I stared at James proudly wearing his hat. We did not comment.

After leaving James, Darrin vowed he would not leave Muscatine until he found a better hat. Thankfully he now owns a stiff, broad-brimmed straw hat with a draw string.

Once on the river, large pleasure crafts, oblivious to our size, begin halting within inches, sloshing water over the gunwales. We are accomplishing PR, but to our detriment. Darrin deems this my problem and is acting like the spouse who says, "Why don't you discipline your child?" What he actually says is, "What are you going to do about that dang lettering?"

By early evening we have had our fill of close calls with boaters and the delaying tactics of headwinds. The heat today generated plenty, causing us to hug the western shore where a ten-foot lane of calm water saw the wind blowing over our heads. Now, cooking dinner, I'd say the wind is a blessing. It both cools and keeps the mosquitoes away. Rather pleasant.

As the sun begins to set, I quickly gather up my gear and enter the tent. I will remain here until morning when the mosquitoes go to bed. Darrin, however, is choosing to stay out "in the breeze." That won't last long. Ah, here he comes.

Hastily crawling in, he proclaims, "no-see-ums."

"Did you see 'em?" I query, trying to be funny.

"No!" he answers seriously.

"Did you get bitten?"

"No!"

"Then how do you know they're out?" I am pursuing this line of questioning because he believes the area is swarming with them, and he is zipping up all the windows. "Darrin, you can't do that. I don't want to be shut up without a draft."

His desperate reply, "Without the screens blocked, we'll be invaded."

"Do me a favor. Look up." The top of our tent, all four sides, is nothing but screen. The rain fly is six inches above that. "Those screens can never be zipped. Even if you block our air flow, we'll still be invaded." My garage mechanic's logic pays off. He agrees a draft is important if they will get in anyway. Ah, gentle peace. Thank you God!

Today the eagles were replaced by turkey vultures. Large groups, six to ten at a time, took flight at several bends. If I were superstitious, they would be a sign the trip is not in harmony. I do, however, wonder where all the carrion is coming from.

Looking for an answer, Darrin is taking out his recreational guidebook. "Do not eat more than one fish per month from these waters." He adds, "If there is something harmful to humans, perhaps it's harmful to the fish…maybe it's killing them." This causes me to wonder about our swimming. Although the waters appear clean, what is really being dumped by the cities, businesses, and farms?

No, I am going to focus on the positive! The air continues to be intoxicating as more blooming basswoods appear. Many trees and flood plain blooms are at their peak, delighting us beyond imagination with overpowering fragrances. It is truly outstanding to paddle and be constantly greeted with new, sweet smells from different tree groups and plants—intense, awesome fragrances. Even as I lie here in the tent, it is as though God planted me in a perfumed garden. A gift I never counted on.

Once again pleasant memories from our visit with Mike and Dee come to the fore: the great coffee, drinks, and conversations. Dee even washed our clothes and towels as though we were family members. My t-shirt came clean. From long trips in the wilderness I have learned to forget about changing clothes. One shirt, one pair of shorts, and two pairs of socks are enough whether the trip is five or fifty-five days long.

Many were the times I put on fresh clothes in the wilderness only to have them become dirty and smelly within a half-hour. Why bother changing? It means carrying excess baggage, and who needs that? We already get plenty from stress. I wash my clothes as often as I bathe. Yes, Dee and Mike were angels. They gave us just enough reprieve from negative attitudes to be lifted back to near normal. What a blessing!

Today we reaffirmed portaging around locks. We also found the Ecksteins are still at it. One of their towboats needlessly forced us into rapids when we exited a lock. Since Golden Wings relishes turbulent waters, the challenge became a short thrill with no effect on our progress. The towboat, however, was forced to back off the lock and realign before entering. What a wasted effort!

Traveling close to shore today meant listening to the loud drone of cicadas. Now the evening has multiple choruses, at different pitches. The discordant patter grates on my ears, creating the sensation of an imminent insect attack. The numbers and tonal pitch grows louder as they close in upon the tent. The intense heat must be driving them out of the mud flats and closer to the river.

RUMBLING TRAINS

When morning comes it is clear we camped on a small patch of sand just inches above receding floodwaters. We are surrounded by a muddy slough created at the Iowa River confluence. Once on the river we begin visiting duck blind stands on stilts. Their plywood floors are covered with six inches of caked mud. As we paddle away, it feels good to leave the mud and cicadas behind.

My spirit is freer this morning. It is once again released from a self-imposed confinement, time. Humanity messed up when it carved Mother Nature into cycles of days, months, and years. Not today! The wilderness has again cleared my mind and brought me to living only in the moment. The river doesn't care what is around the bend, only for survival. No production lines, waiting lines, or lengthy meetings. Life on the river is immediate!

The sky is overcast with a slight breeze, a needed respite from the sun. Even with fifty-sun-block, hat, and sunglasses, twelve to fourteen hours of direct sunlight is draining. Still, I will not canoe in a long-sleeved shirt and pants; it's a Huck Finn's straw hat, shorts, t-shirt, and no shoes for me. So what if my skin gets old, wrinkly, and cancerous? "Blue Cross will cut it out for free," this according to a health instructor who worshiped the sun.

The overcast burned off all too quickly. The headwinds have resumed a battle with our canoe. A couple is fishing downriver. Darrin suggests a break, "What say we visit?"

As I need a break, there is no argument from me, "Sounds good."

Before we can say hello, Ed greets us, "You guys from Red Lake?" His wife Tanya is in the bow. They love to fish. Both have a beer in one hand and a rod in the other. They are, according to Ed's reckoning, "relaxing on the river with a cooler of beer." Didn't I say life on the river was great?

"You guys want a beer?" Tanya asks, holding one within reach.

"Sorry, I don't drink it. Darrin does." Eyeing me a bit suspiciously, she hands him the "cold-one." I am envious. He has an instant connection. We float and visit, holding each other's crafts as though walking hand-in-hand. Gifted with caring people once again fills me with the strong desire to jump up, pump my fist, and yell, "Yes! Yes! Yes!"

In bygone days, Ed commercially fished these waters with an uncle. They sought carp, sheepshead, and spoonbills (paddlefish) for smoking, a true delicacy. If you can't be big, be good. "Eventually the number of fish decreased as our costs increased." Ed's memories of smoked fish stir not only my digestive juices, but also my desire for more conversation. Darrin, however, is giving me the let's-move-on look. We thank Ed and Tanya.

Lock and Dam Eighteen has no portage possibilities but the dam's control gates are wide open. With no warning buoys to stop us, we are moving in for a closer look. The sun's glare on the rapids below the dam make it difficult to see how much water is actually spilling over. We have slowed our approach to make an informed decision. Before we can get near enough to determine how safe it is, the lockmaster replies to Darrin's query, "The lock will open shortly." We turn back, paddling to the entrance. I am disappointed. I was hoping for a chance to shoot a dam.

Shortly turns into forty-five minutes. After passing through, we look back to check out the rapids. To our chagrin there is only about six inches flowing over the dam, barely a ripple. We missed a golden opportunity—bragging rights for having shot a Mighty Miss dam. It is unfortunate we couldn't see the small drop from upriver. All other dams have been too treacherous. We console ourselves with "better safe than sorry."

The map makes it abundantly clear that Fort Madison, Iowa, allows no camping anywhere on its riverfront park. Too tired to continue, we visit the adjacent marina. "Sure. Set up on the asphalt near the park. If you want, we have showers. I can loan you the key."

Showered and ready to eat with civilized people, we head for the marina's North Shore Bar and Grill. It offers "Fine Dining." While eating, Darrin brings up Bottle Man and Huck and Tom. "How do you suppose they're faring?" He is referring to the headwinds the last one hundred or so miles. "It must be tough."

"I'd hate to be in Alex's craft," I add.

"He's got to be at a standstill. The winds could even be pushing him back." Judging from our progress, Darrin may be right. This is the third day of headwinds and mounting tensions.

When these discussions renew our stress, I switch topics. "Do you think The Body will really do it?" Yesterday, Jesse (The Body, now The Gov) announced he is planning to Jet-Ski from Minneapolis to New Orleans. We started a blitz campaign asking lockmasters and river residents to watch for him. "Give him a message. Tell him a real Minnesotan would canoe it." If enough people hit him, he may look us up, creating an opportunity to publicize the mission's endowment campaign. After speculation on Governor Jesse Venture is exhausted, we go quiet, avoiding any personal frustrations.

Tonight's campsite parallels three great transportation modes: rails, highway, and river. To our left is the Miss. The rails are maybe seventy-five yards to our right and the highway another fifty. This could be another Grand Rapids' night. Already the train's vibrations have stirred childhood memories of the house shaking. The kids living down the street had it worse, living within thirty feet of the tracks. We never discussed it. What's to discuss? That's how we lived.

Since dinner it seems there has been a train every five to ten minutes. Each is fifty to a hundred cars. The highway traffic is also heavy. Fort Madison must be a storied place; fire and/or ambulance sirens are going off about every twenty minutes, all harbingers of restless sleep.

Our neighbor, River View Park, sits three feet to the south of the tent. It is actually a well-manicured, two-block strip of waterfront.

Two security guards from a private firm have just driven up and are getting out, heading our way. Why would such a small park have night security?

Both are dressed in freshly laundered white policeman shirts and black pleated pants. They are about the same height and weight and walk with the same swagger. After brief introductions, my curiosity gets the best of me. "Why don't they allow camping in the park?"

"Tenting is hard on the sod." At that moment a long line of cars begins entering the park. I stare past him wondering what is going on. He turns to look. "We gotta go…got 150 cars coming."

"Why so many?"

"Tomorrow's the great East Iowa car sale."

"It looks like you're gonna park 'em on the grass."

"Yeah, they just fix the sod when it's over." His strutting away reminds me of a banty rooster trying to control a chicken yard. I wish I could see his face. As if reading my mind, the older man stops, turns around, and calls back, "We'll be here all night 'cause of the cars." What's with the smirk? After taking two more steps, he hesitates and abruptly turns around. Returning to face me directly, he is ready to say why they originally come to visit us.

"Listen, the sale starts at nine. You guys be gone by eight." It isn't a statement so much as a command. It reminds me of the sheriff's warning to vagrants passing through Albert Lea when I was a boy, "Stay the night but leave immediately after breakfast." I always wondered if anyone dared ask when breakfast was served.

As I know our present appearance is not that of world travelers who impress car clientele, I don't bother to challenge his request. Anyway, if we are not gone by eight, our day is in trouble. Besides, tonight's accommodations are definitely not choice camping. I turn to go call Jacqui.

The public phone is within thirty-feet of the tracks. As my call begins ringing through, a train of nearly one hundred cars begins rumbling past. Before I can hang up, I hear the familiar click of someone picking up the receiver. With brains rattling, I hang up. If Jacqui heard the rumble and got the dead click, she may be wondering. I'll wait before dialing again. As I begin a second dial, I hear another train approaching. Within moments after hanging up a second time, I am crawling into bed. Darrin stays behind to call between trains. He is taking no chances with Schalleen.

THE BIG SOLO

The birds must have slept peacefully. They are cheery. It is a half hour before dawn. The sun, under a pink horizon, is pushing the darkness westward. If the auto guards are awake, they are making no sounds. Sometime after I fell asleep, they placed a thirty-by-fifty-foot car dealers' circus tent on the sod. Quickly dressing and eating, we break camp. No more than a hundred yards downstream I call out, "Look to your left…eleven o'clock."

"Nah, it can't be...do you think?" Floating on the river is a red cooler, the spitting image of Huck and Tom's. Coincidence? How many new, red ice chests float down the Mississippi? Did Huck and Tom take one too many wing dams? Speculation leads us to believe so. We pray they are all right and discuss their possible fate.

Are they regretting turning down James' advice? They said they would continue using wing dams "'cause they're not too dangerous." Well, neither were the first ones we took. Of late, however, they have been getting more challenging. As the conversation becomes disconcerting, I say, "Can we change the subject?" I go quiet, wondering what we must do to stay safe.

Some twenty minutes of contemplating my fate is too much. "Hey, does it seem strange we didn't talk mileage last night?"

Without a word Darrin gets out the map. "Maybe thirty-five…we haven't been doing too well lately."

"Perhaps it's the heat and slow current."

Darrin busies himself with the map and changes the subject. "Have you noticed how the small towns offer free camping?"

"Too bad we never arrive at the right time…maybe it's Murphy's Law."

Staring intently downriver, Darrin says, "Lock Nineteen is coming up." His voice implies more. While waiting for him to continue, I recall how the Corps personnel have made a point of keeping us from landing on Lock property. They never say why. They are just emphatic that the lock and its fenced-in land area are closed to the public.

As we approach Lock Nineteen and Keokuk, Iowa, that same impression comes through as Darrin talks to the lockmaster. At first the lockmaster's voice is stern, telling us there is no way to portage around or across Corps land. Then he softens a bit, almost apologetic, "You've over an hour's wait." Immediately we begin discussing a need for fruit, meat, cheese, and vegetables.

Darrin goes back on the radio, "Is there a grocery store nearby?"

"No, the closest one's a few miles away. Hold on for a minute."

We can hear him talking to someone in the background. When he comes back on, he is definitely more compassionate. "You guys need something?"

"Fruit and meat…thought this might be a good time to stock up."

Now we are put on hold. After a couple minutes, he comes back on, more friendly and relaxed. "One of the guys is going off shift… said he's willing to give you a ride. You'll have to find your own ride back."

Darrin volunteers to go. "I'll run back," he tells me. "I'll be here before the lock-through." He is being optimistic. My gut tells me those are famous last words. He goes back on the radio. "I'll be up in a couple minutes."

I reach for my billfold. "Take this…get a cab."

With a smile and a yes, he grabs it. The radio crackles to life again. "You can come up. Your partner will have to stay put." Darrin is met at the top rung of the ladder by what appears to be a uniformed lockmaster, although I see no badge.

To while away the time and stretch my legs, I get out and stand on the Corps' floating dock. Within moments I am restless and anxious to get out of the sun. With no wind or shade, the confined area is a heat stroke waiting to happen. I begin to climb the ladder. Before reaching the top, the same lockmaster is out of the control booth and towering over me, feet firmly planted on the top step. His positioning is as authoritative as is his tone. A series of questions begin. I am being checked out.

I must have passed the test for he finally asks, "Are you interested in knowing how the locks work?" I answer affirmatively and he steps back, allowing me to climb aboard. Standing face to face and shaking hands, my guide reveals the hidden agenda.

"Since nine-eleven the Corps has made all Mississippi locks off limits to outsiders. Hearing about you from other lockmasters, we determined that if you began climbing, I'd question you." As we walk to the control booth, he is animated about his job. The gadgets controlling the gates and water flow are fascinating. At the tour ends, he asks, "Interested in re-filling your water jugs?"

The Corps' security concern seems justifiable. Imagine the havoc to river traffic if a couple locks were destroyed. From the commerce figures I mentioned earlier, it is easy to see how blowing up a lock would have disastrous effects upon the cities and farms of the Mississippi Valley. Our U.S. economy has already taken too many hits.

As my downtime ends, anxiety sets in. Another set of barges is waiting to go through. If Darrin is not back in time, and I don't take the opportunity, it will be over another hour and a half before we can try again. Three hours to four hours is far too long to spend at any lock. I climb back down the ladder and stand near the canoe, anxiously looking toward the bridge. With no Darrin in sight, I ease into the canoe. My worst nightmare is about to happen. If I do not paddle through, Darrin will be angry over waiting another hour and a half. If I solo, what might happen?

I would never hesitate to solo a seventeen-foot canoe. The J-stroke makes that shorter canoe easy to handle, even in rapids. I have been doing that forty years. It is quite another thing to handle a twenty-footer that doesn't easily respond to the J-stroke. Only once, briefly, have I tried to solo this twenty-foot canoe. Then it was not filled with packs. I begin re-arranging gear so I can paddle from the middle seat. For balance purposes, this seat is just a few feet in front of the stern seat.

My greatest concern is staying out of the rapids on the downside of the dam. The unimaginable is meeting an Eckstein intent upon showing me he has the right of way, regardless of my personal safety. As with any sinner in trouble, I pray earnestly, "Dear God, help me to remain calm regardless of the difficulties!"

While I fasten packs to the thwarts, in case I capsize, the lockmaster is standing topside telling me about the downstream rapids, assuring me it is no great challenge. I wonder whether Darrin is running hard to join me. Some Mississippi expeditions have land teams that supply them along the way. Had we arranged a supply team for fresh fruit, vegetables, and water, it would have spared us some major disagreements and this new challenge. But no, we agreed the trip would be done solely by us.

As the canoe is about to push off, I recall a short story made into a movie. One scene is set high atop a railroad river bridge. A southern Confederate soldier is about to be hanged. He looks up, praying to God, and notices the rope is frayed. When the trapdoor releases, the weight of his body and the sudden jerk snap the rope. He plunges deep into the swirling rapids below. After freeing his hands, he swims up to gulp fresh air. Bullets are whizzing all around him. He plunges back down, swimming to safety.

Moments later he climbs ashore and runs down a forest path. Arriving at a plantation road, he turns down it. His wife is out walking. In a burst of energy he begins running toward her and she to him. Soon they will embrace. The camera slows the running, allowing each minute ounce of straining to be clearly seen as they reach out to embrace. Hope and despair are painfully written on their faces. At the moment of embrace, the director snatches them apart to begin anew their sprint. After a couple of slow motion runs, the camera flashes back to the bridge. The soldier's body is twisting in the wind, a final twitching before going limp. The escape was nothing more than the dream of a dying man.

Does such a fate await me? Will my last image be Darrin running and jumping into the canoe, saving me just as I am about to capsize in the swirling dam waters?

As I push off, the lockmaster yells down, "Shortly after the lock you'll find a backwater landing spot to your right, if you make it." Hey, wait a minute, a second ago you were encouraging me, now you're saying, if I make it? He nearly shoots what little confidence I have built up. I glance back up and over my shoulder, hoping to receive some different reassurance. He has gone to shut the gate and start the process. My mind begins running possible scenarios. It won't be too bad if I stay to the right and allow the current to pull or push me.

I move slowly through the lock, using the opportunity to burn off pent up energy. Every muscle is taut. Even after twenty-some days, soloing is like partnering with a stranger. The slow paddle, however, allows me to move closer to the gates without a warning to back off.

Oh, no! I maneuvered too close. The first rush of water, as the lock opens, draws and pulls the canoe to the right, too fast. I will hit the cement retaining wall. How can this be happening? It must be my imagination. There was no more than six inches of water rushing out the opening. Fortunately, by moving slowly, I am now able to maneuver away from the wall. But momentum to offset the current's pull is also gone. My mind must be playing tricks on me.

I am grateful the exit gate is not like the entrance gate. The entrance gate is a one-piece bridge that lowers into the depths, rather than opening on hinges like all other lock gates. The upper gate doubles as a bridge to the electric powerhouse near the center of the river. If that gate had been on this the end of the lock, with the water running out over the top of it, I would feel an even greater pull.

A unique aspect of the entrance gate is its wire-mesh roadway; it acts like a huge fish net. When the gate rises out of the water, several fish get trapped, making for easy pickings. On this day the lockmaster took pity. He threw the stranded fish back into the water. Paddlefish don't always meet such a pleasant fate, especially if they have been injured. The lockmaster said they are taken home and cut into steaks.

My mind is wandering. I can't allow that! The dam rapids are tugging and pulling me left. I must offset it. Thankfully the initial pull was to the right. Between the right and the left tugging, it is easier to stay between the retaining wall and rapids. The canoe is now within three feet of the retaining wall. My goal is to catch the eddy at the end and get pulled around behind, into calmer waters.

Good fortune appears to be on my side. Wait, the backwater eddy is hitting the bow and bouncing me out and into the rapids. The undertow has grabbed the canoe and is rushing it in hot pursuit of the gulf. Quickly switching paddling sides, I turn the canoe toward the nearest point of land.

Lady Luck seems to be with me, the colliding dam waters and back eddy are now taking me to a middle ground. Remember, don't fight Mother Nature. She is in control. Go with her flow, look for an opening. Her powers are always too much to totally harness. Find a way to use her power until she runs her course.

The rapids are pushing the canoe farther downstream, toward a new point of land. In an effort to grab this new opportunity, I paddle backward on my right. The stern swings left and hits the rushing dam-water. The 180-degree swing that follows pushes the canoe backward and toward shore. As it approaches land, I do the maneuver again and swing into calmer waters, now facing downstream. As I land, I try to calm my pounding, telltale heart. How much pressure can a fifty-eight year old heart take? I don't want to find out.

A moment ago a young man fishing off the lock's retaining wall took my exit in stride, as if nothing momentous were happening. To him, it wasn't! My actions seemed normal, in control. If only he had known. If any of us really knew the moments of anxiety, pain, and challenge that others face, could our empathetic hearts take that kind of pummeling? Breaking into my concentration, the young man calmly called out, "Some guy yelled he's coming down with groceries."

From the underbrush, Darrin appears, "I'd just started over the bridge when the waters began lowering." I can hear delight in his responses as I babble like an idiot, trying to explain the exit. Once again I take my standard oath, "Never again!"

The delight on Darrin's face continues to dance impishly. "Getting a taxi didn't work, but the fruit should hold us a couple days." He is gripping two bulging plastic bags.

The day turns into another hot one. Soon we are paddling in real heat, the high 90s. Although only a couple hours away from the locking experience, it is time to rest and regain strength. The heat is taking a toll. The positive is no river traffic and we are making good progress using the main channel.

While glorying in my prone position under a shady tree, I wonder, "Will I ever again have the inner desire to go back to work?" I can see why James and others save this trip for retirement.

The rest of the day's paddling brings us to the Veteran's Camp at Canton, Missouri. The locals are out strolling, barge-watching. Canton is a small town of 250 souls. A man named Doug and his son just stopped by. "So what brought you guys out?" I ask.

"Just a way to spend some quiet time together." His son nods agreement. After finding out more about the trip, Doug offers a nice surprise, "How about if I bring Dan Steinbeck by tomorrow? He's our newspaper reporter. He could take your pictures and do a story on the Red Lake Mission."

"That would be awesome, but we'll be gone by 5:30."

"Shouldn't be a problem." The conversation now takes a marked turn. "Our foundry's gone bankrupt. They're giving out pink slips tomorrow." It is another blow to small town America and life on the Mississippi.

His son adds, "The only real claim to fame we now have is our levees didn't break in '93." They bid farewell with a promise to return.

The setting sun brings another beautiful evening. While Darrin is anxious to head into town, I want to pause and take in the moment. Some high, white-streaked clouds are cutting through a pink sky. It is totally awesome. Darrin wins. We leave.

People in town are cooling off by driving the main drag in air-conditioned cars. It feels like the late 1950s before people began purchasing window air conditioners.

Canton is a friendly town, if friendliness is in direct proportion to quietness. My "telephone talks" with Father Pat never change. He is never home. With his busy schedule and my limited calling times, it isn't surprising. I just leave messages, trusting they are being placed on the Internet. Several people have said they will be following us via the canoe's website.

Darrin's telephone conversations with Schalleen are also the same. She still wants him off the river and home. I am sorry for his added stress. Mixed with our river stress, it is not helpful. Jacqui said she met with Schalleen for lunch. The visit did little to relieve Schalleen's pain. All I can do is listen to Darrin and support his relationship with Schalleen. Jacqui's Chan-O-Laires, church liturgist responsibilities and gardening continue to keep her from spending too much time dwelling on my absence.

MARK TWAIN

It is 5:30 AM. Doug is as good as his word. He has brought Dan. Their timing is great. We just finished breakfast and packing. Dan asks a few questions and takes our picture. The sunrise, with its low 70s temperature, is still carrying a soft, velvety touch as we leave. The forecast is for greater heat and humidity than yesterday. The constant humidity is causing our sleeping bags to retain moisture. Hanging them out to dry has the opposite effect; the bags only attract more moisture.

Normally bundled clothes are a pillow when camping. Body heat keeps them warm and dry for an early morning dressing. Not so on this trip. The hot, moist Southern summer is keeping them damp. I'm too used to the North's low humidity and cooler weather. Adding to the wetness problem is the tent. It has become a dew collector. Compounding the problem are our early starts. They force us to pack it wet.

Although it is dangerous to canoe in the early morning fog, an even greater threat is the afternoon heat. On the positive side, the early morning paddles often give a suspended sensation, as if floating in a cloud.

Even though close to towns, we face a true wilderness threat: wounds. On my first trip to the Boundary Waters, a small leg gash turned into a serious infection. Due to ignorance, I didn't treat it properly, and it didn't scab over like home wounds. Within five days the entire leg was infected. Even with good emergency room treatment, the scars still haunt me, serving as constant reminders that infections in the wild are to be taken seriously.

The farther south we go, the more contaminated are the water and mud flats. Among the trash being pushed downstream are small glass shards and rusting metal objects. Both settle into the flats and sand beaches. Often a thin layer of silt or sand hides them. As summer marches on and river waters recede, shorelines become booby traps for barefooted beachcombers. I am susceptible. I loathe wearing footgear in the thick gooey mud and warm sands.

Yesterday when I stepped out of the canoe to heed nature's call, I stepped into ankle-deep mud. A shard pierced and sliced deeply into the sole of my foot. In an instant a two-inch gash opened. In deeper water, I washed away the mud, allowing the blood to flow. I used drinking water and soap for cleansing. Triple antibiotic ointment took the place of stitches. We were too far from civilization at the time.

God bless our chemists. It is clear why early frontiersmen and women feared cuts. Without antibiotics, infections often run rampant. At breakfast the wound had no redness, swelling, or soreness. Perhaps all of the fruit and vegetables are aiding the healing. "Do you suppose I'll ever be able to wear shoes again?"

Darrin stops paddling and turns, "Where'd that come from?"

I pause to think as he goes back to paddling. Finally I say, "I am trying to imagine myself back at the office, shirt open, shoes and socks off, squishing my toes in the soft carpet. There is a knock at my office door. In comes a new parishioner. As I reach out a welcoming hand, her stare goes from the open shirt to the bare feet. That's the stuff of nightmares."

When Darrin makes no comment, I continue. "I remember how fond I was of running barefoot as a youngster. Your Grandmother Hoffman scolded me for embarrassing her when I walked uptown without shoes. It wasn't until later she revealed she had been forced to go barefoot. Her parents required her to walk barefoot to school...didn't want her to wear out her shoes. Her classmates teased her." When Darrin says nothing, I drop the subject and go back to daydreaming.

Two days ago I stepped on a thorn. It jammed itself over a half inch into my heel. Pulling it out was easy. That too is healing nicely. Somehow, even if an infection ensues, it will be a small price to pay for this boyhood freedom. Those who love to analyze people will someday say I am going through a midlife crisis. Really? How many fifty-eight-year-old men can brag they went barefoot, all day, for forty-some days?

Ah, yes, the good life. Mark Twain was keenly aware of how adulthood subtly steals away the blessings of youth. Feeling an absolute necessity to thank him for enriching my life, I shout to the wind, "God bless you Huck and Tom and Becky! Don't let go of your dreams!" Darrin has stopped paddling to observe me. He thinks I've flipped. I can hardly contain what must surely be an ear to ear grin.

The trip would be better if Jacqui and Schalleen were along. I must admit though, when I'm lying in the shade on a warm sandy beach, with a cool, gentle breeze caressing my body and I am writing in my diary, I feel like I am in the midst of a South Pacific romance novel. I have no doubt that God and Mother Nature are doing their best to make this an ideal summer. Even our arguments, about who knows best in any given situation, pale in the presence of these moments.

Robinson Crusoe could not have enjoyed his island paradise more. Being a filthy river rat, sand clinging to the skin, clothes, bedrolls, and tent, is no problem. A little sand in the food isn't going to kill me. Sure it's gritty, but what vacation is perfect?

It is midmorning. Our break is a floating one. Three high school kids on Jet Skis are whizzing by, hurrying to catch up to a set of twenty-one barges, seven deep and three abreast. Now they are moving back and forth in front of the lead barges, playing a game of who can get the closest without being run over. How will they handle it if one stalls in front of the barges? It will be his demise. Maybe that is why the Ecksteins don't like small craft. But that can't hold true for canoes. Canoes can't make those rapid maneuvers.

Arriving in Hannibal, Missouri, we set aside two hours. What self-respecting river rat wouldn't roam the streets looking for Huck, Tom, and Becky. After thirty minutes we find only postcards. The locals are not interested in pointing out their homes. Perhaps they have been questioned too many times. We spot an eatery that specializes in brats.

Despite our grubby appearances, the brat master makes us feel right at home. He is familiar with unkempt looks. After walking through the door he looks up and without a moment's hesitation asks, "How's the river trip going?" After brats, it's Becky's Ice Cream Parlor to inquire about her whereabouts.

The waitress is polite, "Becky's out for the day."

We continue roaming Hannibal. "Hey, there's Twain's office." We approach and knock. No response. Perhaps he has gone fishing. Certainly it is too hot for working. Pedestrians approach.

"Do you know where we might find Mark Twain or Tom Sawyer?"

Without stopping, the older gentleman replies, "Yes, Twain's on the river with Huck and Tom." After taking a couple steps, he stops, turns full around, and comes back to face me. Smiling he says, "Once you're on the river again, you might look inwardly if you're really interested in visiting them." I take this as a compliment.

As it is in the high 90s, we head back to the river. The breeze gives a ten-degree reprieve. The swift current makes up miles delayed while exploring Hannibal. It is a pleasure knowing the river is working as hard as we are.

"Do those Illinois Jet Skiers look like they're headed our way?"

Darrin turns to look back, "Yup! Better stop." Quickly two young men on their trusty steeds are beside us, inquiring about the trip. They have heard of Itasca and know it is the headwaters for "Old Man Miss." Here all this time we thought we were socializing with a young

Miss. We see her as strong, like a Minnesota pioneer woman, sinewy and hardened from the day's labor. They see her as "Old Man Miss," an oxymoron.

Just south of Lock and Dam Twenty-four is a campsite where Rocky Raccoon must have thought he had died and gone to coon heaven. Over thirty turtle eggshells are strewn about. After dinner we give ourselves reminders: Expect Rocky sometime around midnight. Make sure the packs are sealed, the pots and pans stacked. He'll be persistent and destructive. We'll need to meet him head on. As the moon's getting fuller, it'll be easier to spot him.

This campsite is very peaceful and relaxing. There is no mud like yesterday. The temptation, however, is not to bathe. The river is a dirty brown. But I must! The sweat and grime will make sleeping uncomfortable. Besides, river bathing may not be possible much longer.

After I enter the water, the evening's serenity and wilderness feeling are shattered. A train is passing about a quarter mile west on the Missouri side. Like river barges, the trains are carrying a lot of coal to power plants along the river. Perhaps it is the ease with which coal can be loaded and unloaded that makes it an attractive energy source. But the way the coal is distributed doesn't make sense.

Some of the coal trains that rumble by are later stopped on a siding, unloading into a bridge's underbelly. From there the coal travels a quarter mile by conveyer belt to waiting barges. The open hatches swallow it like baby birds, mouths wide open, gobbling freshly disgorged bugs. Water hoses are soaking the coal as it enters the hatches. It is either to keep the dust down or prevent spontaneous combustion in the hold.

A few miles farther downriver, coal barges are being unloaded. The huge jaws of oversized cranes scoop out mouthfuls from the barge's innards, dumping it into a hungry hopper. From there the coal pours evenly onto a conveyor belt leading to a nearby power plant. In other instances, the coal is loaded from barges into waiting rail cars. So here is our question: "Why don't the coal trains travel five miles farther to the power plants before emptying? Why these multiple transactions?" True, it is creating jobs.

After the train passes, a slight breeze picks up. The pleasure it brings, along with birds singing their hearts out, returns the scene to idyllic. Soon, however, an Eckstein towboat, now synonymous with recklessness, enters the picture. It is pushing fifteen barges to the lock.

Our guard goes up. When the Eckstein barges are directly across the river from where we are camped, they stop, waiting to enter the lock. It must be a very heavy load. When the towboat starts up again, it spews out the meanest, foulest streak of black diesel fuel ever seen, ten yards wide and fifty high. It is in stark contrast to bright blue western sky behind it.

Earlier today, as we sat eating lunch, we saw a barge go aground. The whole thing didn't make sense. It was a clear day and the river was quite wide, and the captain was pushing only one barge. He was either a second mate from the Valdez or practicing running aground. How useful is the latter?

COILED TO STRIKE

Because of the heat, early quitting time is now important. We are departing in fog too thick for safe canoeing. Darrin muses, "Aren't we getting close to where Twain's characters Jim and Tom missed the Ohio River by some sixty miles?"

"Are you suggesting something?" Although no verbal response comes, an innocent smirk appears as he turns back to paddling.

The dense fog feels like a storm cloud, thick and gloomy. Its denseness deadens nature's sounds, similar to a newly insulated room before sheet rock is added. The sensory deprivation is multiple. Not only is the sound deadened, there is again the floating sensation, the feeling of a lack of contact with anything solid or liquid. Every now and then we get glimpses of surrounding landscapes, providing moments of attachment. It takes nearly two hours for the fog to burn away. Only one towboat and set of barges passed us. It must have been more stressful for the captain. We can easily maneuver away from approaching objects.

By lunchtime the heat is again upon us in earnest. We need shade. A small jungle island is ahead. A darkened, semi-circle of sandy beach is carved out of the island's center. A canopy of tall, willowy trees shades the forty-by-twenty-yard cavity. Upon landing, the coolness is immediate and refreshing.

Darrin unloads and begins searching for lunch. I check the area for sitting logs or rocks, anything chair height. At the south end is a large downed tree. As I approach, Darrin calls me back. Returning, he dumps lunch into my hands saying, "That's everything."

"I'm headed for the downed tree." The trunk is about three-feet in diameter. Each end is overgrown with vines and bushes. The middle looks like a great place to set up. It is large enough to act as both bench and table. With sunglasses still on, the shade seems particularly dark. As I approach, something doesn't seem right. Setting down my food a few feet from the log, I return to the canoe for regular glasses. While picking up my lunch, I see it again, movement. It is in the darkened shadow under the log. It was just a momentary flick of something. After approaching a couple steps, I bend down to get a closer look, allowing my eyes to adjust.

There is movement no more than four feet away. It stops me abruptly. Staring directly into my eyes, neatly coiled, ready to strike, is a black snake. It is one of the largest snakes I have ever seen. Its body is over three inches thick. The three large coils means it is well over eight feet. The flat head is like a rattler but it isn't, nor does it have features normally equated with poisonous snakes. This is my first totally black snake in the wild before. Since it is ready to strike, I back off.

Snakes have poor eyesight and judge striking distance by ground vibrations. As I crawl backward, it begins to relax. I move only a foot or so before stopping to study it. It is beautiful! Snakes fascinate me. In ninth grade I caught a six-foot Bull Snake behind the gym. I brought it into the game room to show the guys. One saw how nervous I was and asked if he could show me how to handle it.

After taking a hold of it behind the head, he allowed it to wrap around his arm. When the snake became acclimated to his body temperature, he let go of the head. The snake remained calm and began slowly moving up his arm. When it got to his shirtsleeve, it went in. I could see it crawling across his chest as his shirt rippled ever so slightly. When it came out the other sleeve and down his arm, he once again grabbed it behind the head. "Here, you take him."

Once the snake's body temperature reached mine, I could sense it relax. No longer afraid, I let go. Like my friend, it crawled in my t-shirt sleeve and across my chest, giving a light, tickling sensation. After learning snakes react to ground vibrations, I kept the Bull Snake in my gym locker a couple weeks, taking it out periodically to practice being struck. I wanted to break all my fears of snakes. I would put on long pants and hiking boots, lay the snake on the gym floor, watch it slither away, the walk after it. Immediately it would stop, coil, turn, and strike. After a few weeks of feeding it baby rabbits and mice, I returned it to the wild.

I have seen pictures of Black Rat Snakes and know they are similar in lifestyle to Bull snakes. Neither is venomous and both hang out around gardens and dense vegetation, looking for small, furry meals. As I am not interested in snake play today, even a beautiful one, I walk away, leaving him the log.

After a two-hour layover, with the temperature hovering at 100, we move again. The cool morning cloud cover allowed a hard push those first hours. Now the heat saps our energy and causes major water consumption, even at a leisurely pace.

The map and visual approach give no clues for a portage around the upcoming lock. The lockmaster confirms this and reveals that it will be a two-hour wait. The oppressive heat and second two-hour layover equals stress. Where the previous day was a bit of paradise; today is turning into a bit of hell. We are killing each other emotionally, finding fault with everything the other has said or done the past two days. We will never make St. Louis.

"If you didn't need such long lunch breaks, we'd be farther along."

"You're holding me accountable for this delay?" The silence between digs is weighty.

Out of the lock and on the move again, the current seems to be against us. It is deceptive. One moment there is a great boost, moving our canoe along easily, lifting spirits. The next we lay dead in the water as though transported into the middle of a large, calm, flat lake. The only waves moving are heat waves. It is right out of the pages of the Ancient Mariner. Coupled with an earlier hope of making better time, the lack of current is adding disappointment.

Maybe the current will pick up at St. Louis when the Missouri enters. Perhaps at Cairo the current will be swift. This heat and water loss is too much. Light headedness only adds to crazy thoughts. Does Darrin feel this way? I am ready to quit. Again, as if reading my mind, he blurts out, "We should quit." His voice is dead serious. We both want to be relieved of each other and the heat.

As the hours pass, something always snatches away our clear thinking. It can be as absurd as, "We didn't take enough time to explore the river cities above St. Louis." Our big desire now is for the good old days, forty-degree weather. The complaining leads to numerous map checks. As insane as it sounds, we are hoping to be farther along.

The map checks only re-affirm how slow our movement is and how few downriver towns will be within easy walking distance. In frustration, Darrin points out how the levees and flood plains extend farther and farther from the towns. Adding to the stress is heavy boat traffic. The river is crowded, like weekends on Lake Minnetonka. Back in the 1970s and '80s the house rule was: No weekend boating on the Lake. There was too much drinking and too many accidents. The odds of swimmers and canoes being hit were great.

Here the Mississippi is ideal for those same large pleasure boats. The dams form lakes that the locals call pools. Each pool seems to be another Lake Pepin. Today this means endless miles of paddling calm waters with little breeze and plenty of heat.

Both the heat and monotonous paddling is causing my craziness. The only redeeming grace is shady shores, fantastic scenery, and singing birds. The irony is as we experience more civilization, we act crazier. Perhaps our periodic disputes are a show for the boaters.

Eight PM, dinner is over, finds me lying on a wet sleeping bag. Sweat is running off my body as I try to find excuses for today's bad behavior.

Eight hours later, as the sun readies to rise, the day holds all the appearances of crisis-producing. The forecast is for high nineties and headwinds, a perfect match for wilting father/son relationships. Neither of us is making a move to pack up and leave. It is depression. "I can't take any more," says Darrin.

"I can't either." Silence follows until finally I say, "It's important to say I paddled the Mighty Miss with you."

"I'm angry. You're not holding up your end."

"I'm doing the best I can. I don't have your stamina."

"You're slacking off."

"No! The heat's too much for me! Your youth allows you to deal with it better. I'm just too drained."

"Can't you put your negative comments on hold?"

"I'm trying."

"It doesn't sound like it."

"Do you think I feel any different after what you say? We're killing each other."

"What do we do?"

"Keep our mouths shut."

"I agree." He smiles. "How about no name calling?"

"Okay."

The conversation now switches to the story of a father and two sons who started out from Chicago, paddling the Illinois to the Miss and New Orleans. At New Orleans the older son moved on forever, without reconciling.

"I pray it doesn't happen to us," I say.

Darrin agrees and adds, "Maybe their St. Louis solution is the answer."

"Remind me?"

"They purchased a second canoe. The older son soloed to New Orleans."

After a lengthy discussion and an agreement, we stand up and hug. The differences aren't resolved, but we are going the AA way: hour-by-hour, minute-by-minute, whatever it takes. "At St. Louis then we decide whether or not to continue?" I ask.

Darrin's quick and emphatic "Yes!" diminishes the odds of finishing. Not even the beauty, smells, and sounds are enough to lift our spirits this morning. We pack and leave.

Four hours of burning heat later, frustrations again at a boiling point, we pull over. Neither of us knows where to begin the mending. After a few minutes of fruitless tries, I suggest a hotel room. "Let's make a complete break with the river. Maybe cleaned, fed, and rested we'll listen to each other."

Without a word he grabs the map. "Alton, Illinois, is the best bet."

"Fine." We agree not to speak until we have landed.

After arriving at Alton's marina, a hotel reservation is made. "The Holiday Inn is sending a van," I report.

"While you were on the phone I asked the marina owner if we could leave the canoe. It's all set. They have twenty-four-hour security."

Once settled into the Holiday Inn and showered, we head down to the dining room. Dinner is eaten in silence. When dessert arrives, I make the first attempt at conversation. "I don't know where to begin."

"Neither do I." Additional stabs are of no use. Positions are cemented. The problem is the other person.

Sliding out of the booth I growl, "I won't leave St. Louis unless we've worked out our problems. Our relationship is more important than this trip."

Darrin studies me, his face shows genuine concern. "Okay."

We move to payphones for spousal consoling and counseling. Fortunately there are two banks of phones far enough apart we can both have private conversations at the same time. When finished and riding the elevator up, I realize I am no closer to finding a resolution. This does not bode well.

GRANDMA & BILLY

As breakfast is ending, the concierge appears in the dining room doorway, "Your driver's here."

"Thanks!" we call in unison. The hotel stop has done us some good. Our spirits are a bit better. Grabbing an extra roll and orange, we head out. Earlier we placed our bags curbside. They are still sitting and the driver isn't making a move. Picking up a pack I whisper, "I guess I'll save a couple bucks."

After loading and climbing in the van's side door, we are met with stony silence. The driver seems ready to pounce. He squeals away from the curb, throwing me back and fumbling for a seatbelt. Well away from the hotel, he grumbles, "Jesus Christ, I had to get up a half hour early to bring you guys to the —damn marina. Why the —d yah have to start so early?"

He is not a happy camper, but I am sure he got more sleep than me. The air-conditioner's whirling and clicking kept me awake and longing for the soothing chirping of crickets, the buzzing of skeeters and the whining of cicadas. It is marvelous how the abnormal quickly becomes normal. Normal! Now I remember! My towel is hanging behind the bathroom door. That is a switch, a hotel on the receiving end.

The short trip is finished in silence. After unloading, the van squeals recklessly away, bouncing off a curb and swaying side to side. We are happy to see the driver gone.

On the river, very little is said. Decision time will soon confront us. St. Louis is coming up as is the confluence of the Missouri. Warned many times that the Missouri can come bounding in like a herd of crazed cattle, running in every direction and thundering over the waters of the Miss, we are paddling the river's center, intending to hug the eastern shore if the waters are too rough.

They are not. The Missouri turns out to be a gentle giant. Its colliding affects the Miss' current very little. Quickly turning into the heaviest flow, we slide effortlessly past an island.

It seems wherever large rivers join the Mississippi, islands form less than a hundred yards from the mouth. Somehow, over the years, silt from two colliding waters give birth to an island. Now, quite large, this island has a swift channel running alongside it. The momentarily heavier current is enjoyable, but the lazy Missouri makes it short lived. We go back to pondering the trip's fate. It weighs heavily. Noon and the Arch are coming up.

The shoreline below and the bank leading up to the Arch is a typical tourist trap. There are small kiosks and mobile peddlers out in force. The merchants appear to be drooling over the milling crowds. Hawkers' eyes glint like digger machine operators at the county fair. Truly these merchants are more like melodrama villains gently twisting a moustache end while peering into tourist pocketbooks. The price of worthless jewelry just went up.

Despite our problems, this landing, a completion of more than half the Mississippi, feels like a creditable accomplishment. Our comments and voice tones indicate we are both happy. Drifting across the water are sounds from a nearby paddle wheel's calliope. The laughter of children from vacationing families also helps lifts our spirits. With the canoe secured and lunch unpacked, we head up several flights of stairs to Arch's National Park.

As we leave the underground visitor's center, a hub of activity, Darrin grabs my arm, "Wait, I wanna patch." In an instant he returns to the hive, the tourist frenzy, enriching his patch collection by one.

His goal is to visit every national park before he dies. Not such a bad idea since America has so many magnificent ones.

Taking up seats at a shaded picnic table overlooking the river, we see the canoe secure but bouncing and sliding on the cobblestone riprap. River traffic has picked up considerably. We leave our lunch and hurry back down.

The cobblestone shoreline actually begins about sixty feet before the water's edge. This erosion prevention also doubles as a summer parking lot. How far into the murky waters the cobblestones actually extend, we cannot tell. But the wave action, bouncing the canoe against the riprap, has already caused deep scarring on one side of the canoe. After quickly unloading it, the canoe is dry-docked some five feet up from the water's edge.

Returning to the picnic table, we begin a relaxing meal. The plastic food bags holding sandwich makings, fruit, and condiments are undisturbed. Around us are freshly scrubbed and perfumed tourists. In spite of the hotel stay, we are again looking and smelling grubby. Unshaven, with dirty, sweat stained hats and shirts, sun-faded shorts, and sandy, wet water-shoes, we look more like street people than river rats. The use of plastic bread bags only adds to the picture.

Below us, near the river's edge, a street runs just above the cobblestone riprap. A second street, about halfway up the bank, is ten feet behind us. Both carry bumper-to-bumper traffic.

After lunch, we lie down on two empty park benches, another mark of a good street person. So far we have avoided the inevitable discussion. A large Winnebago is parked on the street directly behind the benches. It has been quiet up to now. Without notice, the side door flies open and out bounds a young boy of eight or nine. Close behind but stopping on the top step is Grandma. "Now, Billy, don't go too far," she calls. He listens about as well as I did at that age. Then, for some unknown reason, Grandma wants Billy to return. "Billy, come back here!"

"Oh, Grandma, do I have to? Can't you come over here and see the river?" He is standing on the lower bar of the sidewalk's railing, leaning over as far as he can to get a good view of the river stretching out north and south. Grandma does not move. She calls a second time. This time she is more insistent.

Dutifully, Billy dismounts and begins returning slowly, like a reluctant learner. Grandma must see a teachable moment, perhaps a geography or science lesson. She comes off her lofty perch to meet him halfway. Stopping five feet to my immediate left, Billy's head is bowed subserviently, giving her the attention she has demanded.

"Billy, go back over there and take another look at the river. Tell me what you see." Her voice is shrill and nagging. Her spoken attitude captures my attention. I sit up. She throws an irreverent, sideways glance at me, but only for a moment. Then, with snobbery few can pull off, she lifts herself up to full height and crosses fattened arms under abundant bosoms before giving me a second dismissive glance. Done, she devotes full attention to Billy. He is back looking at the Mighty Miss, but no longer with enthusiasm. Most of all he seems to be avoiding Grandma's stare. His actions speak volumes.

"Now Billy, tell me what you see." Grandma wants some sort of scholarly report, even though she is not giving Billy a clue.

Begrudgingly he again climbs onto the lower bar of the railing and scans the river. He is obviously in a quandary. After a long quiet period, he steps off. With head bowed, he turns to face her. Shrugging his shoulders and extending his arms and hands out, with palms up, he meekly replies, "I don't see nuttin' different."

In the meantime Grandma has moved into a position directly behind my bench. For some reason she feels it necessary to shout instructions over me, as though she wishes to involve me or ignore me. Whichever, she has made me a part of the event. Sadly for Billy, he is not getting the point of Grandmother's insight. His frowning plea shows she will not give up until he answers correctly.

"Well, what'd yah see?" A reproving tone if ever there was one.

"Water?"

Good answer, Billy, but I will bet it is not what Grandma wants. Intrigued, I turn to look directly at her. She avoids eye contact by looking more pointedly at Billy and moving sideways around the bench and forward a couple feet. With her back to me she says, "What color is the water?"

Billy turns and looks. Without looking back he says questioningly, "Kinda muddy?"

Billy has answered correctly for Grandma proceeds. "Yes! It's called the Muddy Mississippi because the waters are brown from its source in Minnesota all the way to New Orleans."

Oh, no Gary, keep your mouth shut, comes my intuitive sense. But the rogue in me can't stand by in silence. I turn to Billy. "Billy, your grandmother is mistaken." Oh, no, Grandma's face has dropped and gone rigid. The opportunity to give her the respect and tactfulness due her position has now passed. She is furious.

Quickly I turn back to Billy to complete my lesson before he is called away. "Over one fourth of the Mississippi lies in Minnesota. The first section, except for a small stretch running through Minneapolis and St. Paul, is a beautiful blue. It is not muddy at all. In fact you can even drink straight out of the river in some northern spots. I know your grandmother is trying to be helpful and instructive, but I want you to know it's not always this muddy. There are many great places to fish and swim on the Mississippi."

"Well, I never!" is Grandma's retort as she stomps back to the camper. Climbing again to her lofty perch, she yells, "Billy, you get your ##%&*## ass over here right now and into this camper. You'll wait inside." So Grandma has a potty mouth.

After Billy enters the camper, she comes back down off the steps, moving to within five feet of me. She appears to want to salvage something from the mess she is in. In short, staccato commands, she questions me about canoeing and camping, testing my knowledge and Mississippi credibility. She concludes with a loud, "Humph!" followed by, "What kind of canoeist carries food in bags used by street people?"

My reply has no small amount of sarcasm, "The kind that wants to eat dry food even when the pack gets wet." If looks could kill, I am definitely dead meat. As a grandfather four times over, and one who continues to make his share of mistakes, I can attest that this grandmother's wrath equals her glare. She again turns and stomps away, this time into the recesses of the camper.

In college I acquired the habit of directly challenging fabled facts. It began with a professor intent on pawning off opinions as facts. His bias is now a constant companion as I, too, love story telling and find exaggerating far too easy.

A couple has stopped after overhearing part of our conversation. They are curious about safety. "Don't you fear those big boats?" "Yes, we do."

After their interest is satisfied and they wonder away, Darrin turns and optimistically says, "Our two-month goal is still doable." All right, you have my attention. "How badly do you want to finish?" Before I can respond, he adds, "I still don't think you respect my decisions. I'm not some teenager."

Whoa. I need to collect my thought. Don't screw up, Gary. "If I've treated you that way, it was not intentional and I'm sorry. But it sometimes feels like you see me as someone who no longer has the where-with-all to lead. You know I won't go quietly in the night." When he says nothing, I continue, "I thought you knew how much I respected your judgment. I trust my very life in your hands."

I thought this might impact him on a gut level. It doesn't. "Then allow me fifty percent of the leadership."

"I thought I was…maybe I'm scared. You are young and can easily take over. I still want to lead."

"Well I do too…at least fifty percent. I am your son. You taught me that."

Touché! We go quiet. Have I shown so little respect for his leadership? "What do you want from me? I know I screwed up on the water containers. I know you've read more than me in preparing. I know you're in better shape. What am I not acknowledging? I know I have the experience and wherewithal to do this trip."

"Maybe that's it. What you're not acknowledging. I don't know. Maybe it's the angry tones. I just want to be listened to, especially on portages and camping spots."

After much more discussion we end with what can only be described as an I-wanna-continue hug. Perhaps I have compromised. I am not sure. I know our needs and desires are still about as clear as the Mississippi mud, yet we are turning toward the canoe, intent on continuing, even though we haven't said so. This little park and our hour and a half in its shade must have been more relaxing than I thought. We are now wistfully hoping the current will be of greater assistance.

Drifting aimlessly out of St. Louis, we pass permanently parked, rusting, and sinking barges. Their fates were sealed long ago. Partnered close by is a fleet of mothballed towboats bobbing gently in the wakes of passing boats. Due to a lack of spring rains and summer run off, sunken barge hulks, many with gaping holes, are emerging from an island's river shallows. A few bows stick straight up. Others are at forty-five-degree angles. The shore looks like a war zone.

As the afternoon wears on, heavy cloud formations gather. "Let's stop and check the weather," I suggest. Darrin turns on the marine radio. Within moments we learn severe weather is headed our way. "We'll need to be prepared to get off."

"Yeah, but if the rain comes it will be a relief," he adds.

When the storm hits, relief comes, but with a price. The heat, motivated by revenge, sends an angry, oppressive humidity. When the north wind tries to counter with coolness, the collision sends more lightning shooting in every direction, driving us once again to land. After unloading and tipping the canoe over, the rains pour down. While running up the bank for tree cover, we realize the foolishness. Stopping, we pull off dirty t-shirts. Using them as washcloths, we scrub away the day's grime. Putting them back on brings instant coolness. A second rain-burst hits. These drops are larger and heavier, more like a massage showerhead. Not wanting to pass up the benefits, off come the shorts and shirts a second time. The only thing missing is a bar of soap.

The last time I had this much fun was standing under a two-story Victorian. The roof's valleys channeled the rain into a cascading avalanche, charging down and pounding off the roof. Like that water, today's rain is cleansing, cooling, and refreshing for body, mind, and spirit. It all ends too quickly. Within moments the north wind is no longer able to compete with the more aggressive southern heat. The humidity becomes oppressive, reminding me of the alternative to eternal glory.

As evening nears, we are approaching Crystal City's Co-op Marina. The collective was formed to maintain a flood plain landing. A dozen owners welcome us as they finish six hours of rehabilitation, clearing hardened flood silt from the marina parking lot and boat landing. They also installed two fifty-foot docks—one on each side of a launching ramp. The mud scraped off the road and parking lot has been pushed over the embankment to reshape what the Miss washed away. The marina is simple and utilitarian. There are no buildings, just a parking lot, launching ramp, two long docks, and a picnic shelter with tables.

"Hi, I'm Bill." A warm, tanned, and hardened hand envelopes mine.

"Thanks for inviting us in." Each new handshake brings more warmth and feelings of genuine love. We need this. The heat, humidity and arguments have again taken a toll.

"You guys want to stay the night, you're welcome." Bill says. We accept. Together we head up some fifty feet to the top of the present riverbank. The marina consists of a few acres of flat land, a long driveway leading to a city dike, a crushed rock parking lot, and a thirty-by-forty foot picnic shelter overlooking the river.

The co-op owners are proud and contented people. They talk exuberantly about their marina and their friendships. Theirs is a special bond with each other and the land. "You guys want to eat with us?" a young woman asks. The others nod approval. We are being offered friendship, food, drink, and shelter. Thank you God for good people!

Another adds, "We're really just caretakers, the present stewards. This land belongs to the people who need it." Didn't I tell you Mississippi people were great? The delight in their smiles tells us we have only to ask, and the shirts off their backs are ours.

This group even comes with its own grouch. He has been less than enthusiastic about our coming ashore. Up to this point he has stayed on the periphery, pacing back and forth behind the others. Now he steps forward, breaking between them. He has got a challenge, "What the hell do you guys want coming here?" Perhaps he is the group's black sheep. If he is, they are laid back about it. They are more accepting of this grouch than any group I have ever met. They make no excuses for his behavior, nor do they make fun of or condemn him.

I feel a bit intoxicated with the peacefulness of it all. It is hard to explain the tingling in my body and spirit. Although they don't accept this man's attitude, they show genuine respect for him by their gentle disagreement. "Hey, —, they're just on a vacation. We invited them in. They'll be gone by tomorrow." Another man comes up and puts his arm around the grouch's shoulder. If only I were always so tolerant. We thank them for the bar-b-que offer, but decline. We sense it will still be another hour or more before they eat. We need to be in bed by then.

Our guess is correct. By the time they pack up, we are done eating. We say our good-byes and watch them drive down the road to their early summer celebration. We look at each other with a deep longing for our friendship to once again be like theirs.

No doubt about it, the most important part of a Mississippi trip is the people—those we meet and each other. Mississippi books should warn travelers to set aside more time for people. Our goal of two months doesn't allow time to truly know God's greatest natural resource in the valley: river-people. Aiding this evening's euphoria is a gentle breeze rolling over the body, caressing aching muscles and wearied emotions.

CAPE GIRARDEAU

It has been over twenty-four hours since Crystal City. The morning's fog is light and moist. A Great Blue Heron squawks at me for infringing upon her early morning fishing haunt, a rocky point and backwater pool not ten feet from where I exited the tent. The current is slowed to a crawl in her pool. Standing in the middle, she is plucking out small fish. Her head moves back and forth between watching the quiet area and me. The smaller fish cutting into this pool are expecting a momentary respite but finding eternal.

The Miss feels like a river again. Her banks are narrow, the water deep and the current swift. It is what the Mighty Miss should be but hasn't been for most of the time. Once on the river, Darrin begins flipping map pages. "Yesterday we did twenty miles before the incident and forty after." He is referring to a disagreement we had. His statement is intended to be filled with irony. However, he is right. Those last forty came from releasing frustrations by paddling rather than having a physical fight.

Our nose-to-nose confrontation and clenched fists ended when we turned away and spent a half hour walking in opposite directions, pondering a resolution to our tensions. When we returned, we apologized. Our tension peaked over a large map being left behind on the beach where we ate lunch. We blamed each other.

As communications are once again moving in the right direction, I ask, "Do you think we can do seventy?" His "fine with me" indicates I shouldn't push it.

As Cape Girardeau nears, Darrin is spending an inordinate amount of time reviewing map pages. "Let's stop for water." After more discussion, his real motive comes to the fore: calling Schalleen. I will call her mother-in-law to find out what Schalleen is thinking. Darrin has been tight-lipped of late.

As we approach Cape Girardeau's landing, we both say, "Looks like a prison."

Darrin laughs, "We've been together too long." I take his response as a positive.

Cape Girardeau's fathers and mothers have erected a fortress wall to keep out spring floods. In front of the wall are eight rolls of concrete stadium seating. The cement shoreline in front of the seats is a docking area for larger boats, perhaps showboats. Remembering the canoe's scaring from St. Louis' rip-rap and wave action, we dry dock Golden Wings on the first roll of stadium seating.

Before visiting Cape Girardeau, we stop to stare at the great wall and wonder what lies beyond. The old river sections of towns are usually a good distance from the new malls and neighborhoods. It is now the asphalt-way, not the water-way, that determines placement of river city homes and businesses. The result: canoe visits always feel more historical than contemporary. What life was rather than what it is.

A block and a half into town are two pool halls nearly across the street from each other. Many towns this size don't even have one. Upon entering the nearest, the air conditioning brings instant relief. A pay phone hangs on a post near the center of the bar. It is convenient for calling the Missus, letting her know you will be working late.

Our Missus are home. Before updating me on the grandchildren, Jacqui highlights the latest leg of our journey. She has a three and a half foot Mississippi map on the wall nearest our bed. It is a comforting reminder of how far we have gone, what is left, and we are still safe.

After leaving the pool-hall/bar haze, we do a walk-about of old Cape Girardeau. Even though the city initially looked like a walled prison, it turns out to be a friendly, relaxing place. Most of the homes and businesses in the old section are still from another era. The open first-story sitting porches and second-story screened, sleeping enclosures, give a quiet, peaceful feeling. In stark contrast to the older store fronts are two, new, sanitized, box-like structures housing a subway shop and ice-cream parlor. After double-dip, chocolate fudge-nut cones, we head back to the river.

Approaching the flood wall from the city side gives a whole new perspective. The twenty-foot high levee walls are huge murals of Cape Girardeau's history. The scenes form a grand entrance to the river's summer-stock theater. The stage, however, has yet to appear. The cement shoreline's huge metal moorings are perfect for a showboat play, a concert and oratorio production or a prayer meetin' by some paddle wheel evangelist.

An elderly couple approaches. "That your canoe?" the husband asks.

"Yes!" we respond.

His wife then asks, "I see it says Red Lake. Did you start there?" After I explain the endowment campaign, she reveals seventy years of their lives are invested in Cape Girardeau. I want to ask for details on the theater, but she abruptly takes her husband's arm, wishes us good luck, and leaves. In a way they were friendly, but cutting off the conversation with no explanation leaves us both scratching our heads.

"Hi, guys! Where yah headed?" A biker has stopped behind Darrin. After introductions, he volunteers, "I'm a kayaker and biker... pretty familiar with the river and surrounding thirty miles." He is friendly and interesting and wants to talk. If he is a salesman, his pitch is well underway. Because he and Darrin appear to have more in common, I leave to find a place in the middle of the stadium seating. I want to meditate on the river's fast current and the day's events.

A woman in her thirties is entering the theater from the northernmost opening of the sea wall. After seeing the canoe and finding me sitting alone, she heads directly over. Without hesitation or introductions, she sits down two body spaces away. She is attractive and modestly dressed in a full-length, flower-patterned, cotton summer dress. Her dark blonde hair frames her face.

Looking straight ahead she says, "I come to the river often. It provides me with some healing." Her tone is businesslike and tells me not to interrupt. As she talks it becomes obvious she is working out issues. "I'm in counseling due to a recent event in my life." Except for parishioners who purposefully set up appointments, I have never experienced someone quite so forward in choosing me, a grubby stranger at that, for listening. What does she see that allows her to be so forward? Perhaps it is the fact I am just passing through?

"In my last session I was asked to use the river to help wash away some pain. I've written down the painful experiences I'm trying to let go of. In a moment I'll tear up my problems and throw them into the river." This method makes sense for river city folk. I must have been chosen as an impartial notary.

On the plains of Minnesota and the Dakotas, counselors offer a similar two-step process in detachment, particularly from difficult situations. The counselee is asked to write out, in full, all of the pain and suffering he is going through and needs to let go of. Next the written words are taken to an evening's campfire. In the warmth and pleasantness of that surrounding, the written words are cast into the fire, visualizing a purging and the problems going up in smoke. For some counselees it helps them to both acknowledge and begin letting go of deep pains.

This woman's counselor advised her to use the river, another element with the power to purge. Tonight the Miss' broad shoulders will be called upon to carry her burden to the gulf or bury it under a ton of silt. Thankfully there are places and people who have the power to help us cut free of diseased thinking. Tightly clutched in her hands are several handwritten pages. The Miss' swift current will be the hand of God, carrying off her pain. She seems anxious to tear them up but something is preventing her, holding her back.

"What's your name?" she asks.

"Gary. My son is Darrin. We've been on the river about a month."

She now shares her name and turns the discussion to canoeing and children. Having established a safe environment, she begins tearing up the pages. Standing, she purposefully moves toward the river's edge. After a couple steps she stops, turns back and smiles, "Don't worry, Gary, my pain will be far ahead of yours and Darrin's."

When she sees the startled look on my face, I hadn't shared any of our problems, she says, "I'm sure there must be moments when the two of you have differences." As she turns back to the river, I silently pray for her healing. She does not move until each piece has disappeared beneath the water's surface.

When she returns, she shares more. "My troubles began when my husband became involved with a girl fifteen years younger." So he chose a chickie over the hen. Although I hear only one side of the story, it does seem lust won out over common sense. If my judgment of this woman is halfway accurate, he has let a good woman go.

Today this mother of two seems determined to resolve her problems and those thrust upon her children. As I am just a drifter, I was allowed to witness part of her letting go. Knowing she has several good friends walking beside her and the children, and that she has a caring counselor putting her back, fully in charge of her life, leads me to believe she will be okay.

Her image of being able to throw the emotional refuse into the current and see it drowned, washed to the gulf, diluted by an ocean, is very poignant. It inspires me to look at the Miss in a new light, personal healer. Perhaps this is why adult river baptisms have such impact. The newly baptized see their sins being washed away, dispersed by millions of molecules of baptismal waters, diluted and absorbed by something far larger than their imagination and the unfathomable love of their God. What a marvelous source Mississippi river people have at their fingertips.

The experience has left me feeling I am in the middle of a romance novel. Not romance in the sense of male/female love, but romance in its literary terms. Is Cape Girardeau comparable to Thomas Hardy's Egdon Heath in *The Return of the Native?* We have the marriage problems and the pre-occupation with a younger woman. We have the biker traveling about the area, meeting and greeting people. What will I learn about him from Darrin?

After leaving Cape Girardeau, we share bits and pieces of new found information. Once again we realize how minor our differences are in the grand scheme of things. We forgive and forget. The good people of Cape Girardeau have temporarily given us a reprieve from our pain, guilt, and sin. How will we use this opportunity?

Soon another wing dam comes into sight. Each time we now run one, it feels like we are tempting fate. They are becoming more powerful. Our approach is always slow at first, looking for a dark-water "V." These indicate an opening torn in the top of the dam, a place where, in all likelihood, the canoe will pass through without scraping. Mostly we enjoy the downside of wing dams where calm spots boil up. Rising an inch or two higher than the surrounding surface waters, the calm spot's smooth waters rush outward from the center. Riding one means the canoe will get a quick scoot out the other side. Originally Darrin wanted to approach them slowly, but speed is necessary to overcome the initial outward thrust.

This wing dam is like all the others. After finding the dark water "V," we paddle at nearly full speed. On passing through we relax a bit and head onto a calm spot. This one is larger than others we have seen, perhaps thirty feet in diameter. As we begin moving through, the bubble slowly moves left. I lean forward and dig the paddle deeper, wanting more control. I am about to ask Darrin to do the same when he yells, "What is happening?"

I look up. The calm spot is gone. In its place is a huge whirlpool grabbing at the bow and pulling it inward. Darrin shouts again, "What's happening? Are we capsizing?"

I wished I knew. Finally, I yell, "Paddle harder!"

I have no idea what is going to happen. Capsizing is certainly a possibility. If we go down, the whirlpool will take our belongings and suck them into oblivion, tumbling them along the bottom to only God knows where. As the undercurrent seems far greater than the surface's, I don't want to find out. Quickly the bow pulls out, but the stern now struggles to break free. It is clear why Darrin was in near panic a moment ago.

Away and shaken, we float to let the river soothe us. When our heart rates return to normal, we talk about it. The swirling vortex had threatened to suck us down just like bathtub whirlpools do scum. After wondering what might have happened if the calm spot had moved right rather than left, we pledge never to take wing dam short cuts again. I also vow to wear my life jacket at all times. What would have happened had we capsized? In today's heat, I was foolishly paddling without a life vest. Also, none of our bags were tied to the thwarts.

With adrenalin levels at normal, we joke about the dumb things people have done on Lake Minnetonka. Darrin then wonders out loud what kind of turbulence we will hit when the Ohio enters.

Not wanting to leave the whirlpool discussion, I switch back, "We should be thinking about warning others. Survival is more than cooking, tenting, and wielding paddles." Darrin doesn't respond so I prattle on, "I suspect we've just experienced one of those whirlpools my Uncle

Hank talked about…said they'd suck a boy into oblivion. I always believed his stories were to keep me out of his men's fishing excursions on the Miss. I still do, but now I know at least part of his story is true.

Next I recall an incident from two days earlier. Darrin asked me to throw him the field glasses. Our policy is to avoid passing objects on our short paddles. They don't reach far enough and bodily movement destabilize the canoe. We throw objects, landing them on the soft top of a pack. This prevents fumbling in the canoe's narrow confines. A soft pack will stop an object in place. On this occasion Darrin waited patiently to retrieve the glasses.

My aim was perfect. Unfortunately the binoculars hit something hard and bounced directly into the river. The current acted like a purse thief: snatch and run. Quickly out of reach, the glasses joined the hundreds of wrecks that line the bottom of the Mississippi. Perhaps they will wash into the gulf and reappear on the southwestern shores of Padre Island, off the Texas coast. Shoes, toys, and other household items often wash ashore during gulf storms. On one occasion my daughter found a bottle with a note from a young girl in Wisconsin.

As day thirty-three ends, we are somewhere north of where the Ohio joins the Miss. The cool evening breeze is keeping the campsite insect free. It is a special pleasure to lie on the warm sand, pampered by a breeze and the day's whirlpool incident safely behind. It may not be incident free long. Thunderstorms are brewing in the west. Two fronts are colliding. Is the canoe secured well enough? Before I can answer my own question, the swift current grabs my attention. "Hey, Darrin, remember the brat cook in Girardeau, the one who thought we'd be in New Orleans in two days?"

"Yeah, what a laugh. Nine hundred miles! Maybe by motorboat!"

"Just getting food and water slows us down. I should've told him I left my superman outfit at the office. We'll be lucky to arrive by the (July) 15th." Now other bits and pieces of recent events sally forth into my consciousness. "Hey, remember the guy at the marina last Sunday, the one driving the three-hundred-thousand-dollar houseboat?"

"Yeah, why?"

"I don't know…it was something he said after talking about his dad being a dentist at the White Earth Rez."

"What?"

"He was marveling at where life had taken him. I knew he was bragging when something happened...'tax loopholes for the rich'."

"What'd he say?"

"We were in the middle of a conversation on White Earth when his girlfriend handed him a receipt."

"How'd you know it was a girlfriend?"

"He treated her more like a girlfriend. Anyway, he stops in mid-sentence, as if we'd never been talking about the Rez, holds up the receipt and says, 'One hundred and seventy-five dollars. No problem. I'll write it off as a business expense, just like this boat.' When I looked for some type of advertising or company name, he sensed my thinking and abruptly said, 'Good-bye.' I never did find out his line of work."

"Maybe he thought he'd said too much."

OUTA SHAPE

Another beautiful day for a well-fed and exercised body to do what it loves: canoeing and endless swimming. Singing birds are preparing themselves for another day in paradise. They have no apparent enemies or problems finding food on Mother Nature's river flats, only peace and tranquility.

Some 10,000 years ago a tribe of Indians made this area their summer home. Traveling north along the Mississippi, they would bypass the Cape Girardeau/St. Louis area in favor of the Illinois River. Their summer encampments were someplace north on the Illinois, between the Miss and Peoria. I believe they were called the Cahokia. I now understand why they were so excited to be traveling north along "The River." Perhaps they called it, "Tranquility."

I feel a sense of freedom with the early morning's pleasantly warm breeze. Unfortunately it is a harbinger of heat waiting to overtake paradise. The river has, however, again narrowed, making the current swift. My moment of perfect contentment is over. It is time to pack and get on the river.

Peeking out from the first downriver bend is a contingent of barges. The massiveness of this flotilla looms huge as it rounds the bend: six wide and seven long. How long and wide is that? As each barge is about 195 feet long and 35 feet wide, this towboat's charges are the equivalent landmass of forty city homes on half-acre lots. It's a good reminder of how our canoe is merely a small intruder. The barges have enough sheer size and muscle power to prove it.

A few barges mean the captain needs only a single engine towboat. Forty-two barges need at least a twin-engine. If the captain is lucky, he has got a big "three banger," as we are fond of calling the monster engine houses of five decks and three stacks. The larger towboats carry two captains working twelve-hour shifts. Do they each have their own suite? How would Mark Twain's writings be affected by the size of those wheelhouses?

The barges speak volumes about the food, fuel, and other goods needed to satiate the appetite of Middle America. They are a convoy of goods ordered by the gods of the cities to keep the inhabitants happily serving the culture of the moment.

The temperature rose to the mid-seventies within the first half hour and has not stopped climbing. Presently cloudy, it is in the eighties with a slight breeze. The shaded shorelines boil with carp. "Hey, did I ever tell you about the frozen carp stuffed in a school closet?"

"No…give me the short version."

"Okay."

The story gives us some good laughs and a non-confrontational topic to beat upon, easing the heat and work tensions. We twist and turn every Iowa and Minnesota carp story ever told. Then silence ensues.

Like the Missouri, the Ohio River comes in gentle as a lamb, not at all what the book learning taught. Those authors must have come through during high water. Its peacefulness allows us to soak in the scenery while floating and eating a leisurely lunch.

Sometime after resuming paddling I ask, "Who do you suppose erected that cross?" Darrin looks up. On the Kentucky side of the river, high atop a hill, is a huge cross. From here the cross appears to be well over fifty feet high. It could be of polished metal. As Darrin is cogitating something and doesn't respond, I continue, "Maybe it's a good omen." Still no comment.

The irony is the cross has always represented the best for me: salvation. Now it signals a cross to bear. Since lunch, the dreaded southern head winds have become more challenging. Twice as much effort is needed for half the distance. The heavy barge traffic only adds to the fracas by making more pronounced waves.

"I want off," I say.

Although his swift "No" is backed up by a stiffened glance, there is a twinkle in his eye for he continues, "Sometimes the going just gets tough!" The words ooze sarcasm. However, it is short lived. Within quick succession, we are nearly capsized twice by smashing, two-foot white caps.

The combination of wind-driven whitecaps opposing a fast current, while being plowed up by numerous barges, has brought about a dangerous situation. Any one of these factors alone would be no hassle. Together they are causing us to make many corrective maneuvers. Something else is new. Darrin is barking drill-sergeant orders. They are not for corrective action, but rather to correct a problem: me. In printable language, "I am to straighten up and quit screwing around."

I love it. The whitecaps and crosscurrents are within my power to control. If Jesus could calm the seas, apparently one of his deacons can rile them up. I want to laugh but the timing and effort needed to turn toward shore does not allow it. Despite his momentary belief that I know absolutely nothing about canoeing, Darrin is thankful. He mutters something to that effect, then adds, "If you'd read the same books I had, you'd know better." As we approach the shoreline he relaxes while insisting we stay on the river.

"Come on," I say. "Look at what we're experiencing! We're paddling downstream and the waves are smashing over the bow as though we're going up a rapids. We're hardly moving. The wind's fighting us every inch. I am burning up far too much energy."

"Okay, I'll look for a landing." Immediately he indicates a shady shoreline. The embankment is steep.

After dragging the packs halfway up, we turn over the canoe. "Oh, no!" I wince.

Darrin looks up. "Did you say something?"

I turn my face away and sit down. My position is mostly hidden behind the other end of the canoe. I don't dare respond. I thought for sure he heard it, the crack. It sounded like a shot heard round the world. It feels like someone shot an arrow straight through my upper right-hand chest and shoulder muscles. The pain is excruciating, racing down the right arm and shooting straight out the middle three fingers, like tiny lightning bolts. My right front chest muscles, arm, and middle fingers have gone numb. I can't move them. "Oh, God," I moan to myself and rock ever so slightly.

The heated arguments and physical stress must finally be taking their toll. As Darrin climbs the hill, I slowly lie back. If I say anything, I will incur wrath for being out of shape. I have never wrenched my back or chest muscles before. I am assuming that's what it is. If this is a heart attack, I am too far from anyplace for help. I'll lie here and move into the shade later. Pulling my hat well over my face, I hide tears of pain. It feels like the end.

Not only has the struggle on this muddy bank left me in pain, it has left me thoroughly dirty. The farther south we go, the more rank the Mississippi mud and I become. There must be a lot of decaying matter in it. My present state of affairs leaves me wanting to laugh rather than cry. It is a joke. Look at me! A bedraggled river rat in the most elegant of terms: dirty, smelly, sweaty, spent of energy, wrenched back and chest muscles, limp arm, and numb fingers.

The sun is too hot. I need to get out of it. Rolling over onto my knees, the crouched position makes it hard to breath. I need the shade. Darrin is laying comfortably, hat pulled over his eyes. He will wonder soon. After struggling to stand, I slowly climb to a spot fifteen yards to his right.

The swiftness and short bursts of pain continue to pierce my chest and run down my arm. After lying down the pain is still excruciating. Finally I scream, "I need a shower!" It takes my mind off the pain.

Darrin is cool, "You got no towel." His chuckle is followed by a serious, light-hearted comment. "If you'd get your lazy butt in gear, we could be on our way." I turn my head enough to look at him through an air hole in my baseball hat. He is wearing a self-satisfied smirk, as though he had been waiting for just the right moment to say it.

I've got to take my mind off this pain. The heat, humidity, and headwinds lend themselves to thoughts of writing a great murder story. The opening line could be, "Heat, humidity, and wind create a witches brew bubbling incessantly in the mind of a haggard, insane canoeist. Nearby and innocent sleeps his son...." I've got to think of something else. There is a towboat passing, another forty-two barges. I can't get rid of the pain.

Struggling to keep a prone position on this forty-degree slant only adds to my misery. Relaxing brings a slow slide down the slippery slope. I dig in my heels. What was that? Oh, no! My water bottle has begun a slow roll to the river. The loose cap is spilling water into curious teardrop designs similar to those used by 1970s hippies in copper jewelry making. Angrily I ask, "Is this how people feel before they snap?" I know I have said it to get Darrin's attention. I need help. Darrin sits up and stares at me.

"Thud!" The water bottle takes another quirky turn, hits a small log and stops. I lay my head back while Darrin stares. Good, maybe he will think I have snapped and allow a longer rest. The low-lying cottonwood branch providing shade is an irritating distraction. The crazy swaying periodically scratches my bristled face, causing an itch. Please, God, don't let this be a heart attack! With dug in heels, I lie immobile.

After an hour and a half Darrin stands, "I want back on the river." Although subsided, the pain is still present and I don't dare speak of it. After turning the canoe over, he grabs the first pack and loads it. I grab the second with my good arm and drag it to him. He says nothing.

On the river the pain comes in waves. The numbness and tightness in my upper chest and arm return in full force. Bursts of pain still travel down my right arm and out the three middle fingers like electrical impulses. Paddling on my right is all but impossible. I am forced to paddle exclusively on the left. My right arm has no strength to pull back on the paddle. I can only push forward.

Even though the Ohio has joined the Miss, the current is slowed to a trickle. The river has widened by a mile. Years of flooding have allowed it to dissipate over ever widening plains. As my pain increases, so do my negative thoughts. I need a distraction. People, that's it. I will think of people.

Some river people are similar to the blind men sent to India to discover what an elephant is like. Each reported what he found. One knew it to be a snake after feeling its tail. Another knew it was a tree after touching its leg. River people are like that. They know the Miss from their experience. They report it as reality. Unfortunately their reality is usually only good for the ten to twenty miles near them.

Darrin loves to quote a particular book written by two canoeists who paddled the Mississippi during high water. Their explicit warning of no sandbars or sandy shores below Cairo caused Darrin needless anxiety. I tried to tell him the sandy camp sites of Iowa were an indication of what lay ahead. But, no, if you have read it in a book, it must be true.

Oh, God, what is happening to me? These are the thoughts of someone whose dream is ending. Sure, in flood times expect no beaches south of Cairo. But this is a normal summer. There are beaches everywhere. When it is hot and dry, the river falls rapidly. We marked the shore one night with a stick. By morning the level appeared to have dropped over an inch. Is that possible?

Now twenty miles below Cairo, a large sandbar lies dead ahead. Darrin wants to camp. As I have been struggling, paddling exclusively on my left, and nothing has changed, I have got to tell him.

After hitting shore, I remain seated, immovable. Darrin knows something is up so I just blurt it out. "I need help." My tone forewarns him. He is silent, listening, waiting.

"I don't know if I can go on. This afternoon when we unloaded at the hill, something happened. My right arm has shooting pains. I can barely stroke. I can push but not pull. I'm sorry."

"Why didn't you tell me?"

"I didn't want you angrier with me than you already are."

"It's come to that? I'm sorry"

"It's not your fault. I'm outa shape! I'm not sure what's happened."

"You need a doctor!"

"No! I mean...I don't know. For a little while the numbness and pain were going away. I just don't want to quit." He says nothing and gets out, setting up camp and preparing dinner. I know he wants to think about it before saying any more. I lie down.

CHAPTER 6

CAIRO TO NEW ORLEANS VIGNETTES

MAP THREE, 860 MILES

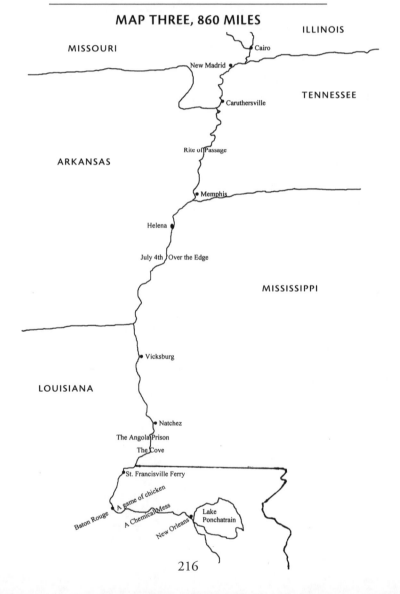

ILLINOIS

MISSOURI

Cairo

New Madrid

TENNESSEE

Caruthersville

Rite of Passage

ARKANSAS

Memphis

Helena

July 4th / Over the Edge

MISSISSIPPI

Vicksburg

LOUISIANA

Natchez

The Angola Prison

The Cove

St. Francisville Ferry

A game of chicken

A Chemical Mess

Baton Rouge

Lake Ponchatrain

New Orleans

CATS FOR SALE

With no new complications, we decide to continue while monitoring my progress hour by hour. It is dark and cool as we push off. The afternoon will be too hot for travel. Moisture is now everywhere, in the tent, the backpacks, and clothes and on all of the dishes. A layer of sand sticks to every item like a slab of fruit rollup, unfortunately it cannot be peeled. Brushing only drives the fine sand deeper into the fabric's weave, sweat pores, and metal crevices. Heat, moisture, and sand are now Mother Nature's gods of hardship, misery, and suffering. Stress is taking a much bigger toll than ever imagined.

The current is not nearly as fast as before the Ohio. More water, less current! Go figure! Wider channels, slower currents, sandier beaches, and more numerous wing dams channeling greater amounts of water into shipping lanes, sending swells of one to two feet rushing headlong toward the main channel. These swells shoot across the main channel, hitting the far bank hard, forcing surface water upstream ten to twenty yards before being rolled over and under by a stronger, downstream current.

When we get too close to that mixing, the over-tow pulls the canoe north. It is eerie. It is as if the water has been plotting, waiting for some unsuspecting soul. It snarls after hitting the bank, like some German Shepherd guard dog just before it attacks, that moment when it is still trying to intimidate. The water, in those instances, is anxious to sink its teeth into objects. Already two of those currents have felt like a game of, "Got yah." For a split second, as we rode the bumpy water, the canoe twisted and strained as though being shaken in clenched jaws.

The Miss continues to play fast and loose. She is a trickster, soothing with peaceful swimming in her gentle currents and plying us with caressing breezes. She is like a beautiful woman giving emotional and physical comfort via a gentle back rubs by sitting in her rapids. Her affectionate hugs and kisses, cooling winds, and shady banks are a siren's call learned long ago. Now it softly whispers, "Come, take a free, easy ride to Natchez."

Believing she has us at her beck and call, she disappears around a bend, leaving us on a placid lake, wondering if she will ever return. Does she even care anymore? Has she just been teasing? Today, as on other days of late, I yearn for her to hold me in her arms and carry me quickly and quietly to New Orleans.

She sends out come-on invitations via scents. Her show of natural beauty leaves me feeling I am the only one she loves. But her heat, her slow steamy currents, shows another side: sullen anger. Why does she act this way? She knows I love her. She has awakened in me a new sense of being—only to leave me feeling duped, trapped.

See this? I'm wearing my life jacket. I've grown leery of you. You've plied me one too many times. I'll not fall prey today. This trip is my one chance. I'll never get a second date. Even if you promise, you'll probably send your ugly stepsister.

Oh, God, what is happening to me? It has only been three hours in the heat. Darrin is being patient. My fingers and arm are still numb. The muscles in my right arm won't work.

"Let's stop for fruit and water." The out-of-the-blue comment shocks me back to reality. "New Madrid is just ahead. It'll be a good break." He is being accommodating. I will not complain. My thinking needs redirecting.

The town's levee is much higher than any other we have encountered. Atop we see nearby homes where we might get water. "That looks like a store," I say pointing to a small white building a half block away. The sign indicates fresh fish for sale.

Inside we find three people crowded into a small service area. Larry, the proud owner of this twenty-by-forty-foot shop, is a wiry man my age. He exudes energy. Catching catfish is his love. After the customers leave, we introduce ourselves. He has owned this store for twenty years. It is an abandoned house he moved as part of his dream—being an independent fisherman and fish monger.

"The community doesn't seem large enough to support you," I remark.

"It isn't. Not enough demand to fish more lines. I do other part-time jobs." He mentions postal clerk and security guard. "On a good day I catch a hundred and fifty pounds. Lately it's been around seventy-five."

"What do cats (catfish) sell for?"

"Two dollars a pound." This seems a decent price for bottom feeders on the lower Miss. Today most people prefer farm fed, although a recent article in the *Wall Street Journal* left me wondering.

Testing has shown mercury and other toxin levels to be nearly equal in the farm-bred cousins.

"I go out about five thirty in the afternoon to lay out three lines. Each has a hundred hooks. Here, let me show you." Larry takes us into his backroom. On the workbench are two-foot square, three-inch high, wooden boxes without lids. "I buy two fishing tags for each box…ten dollars for fifty hooks." He points to some Hilex bottles. "I attach tags to those and tie 'em to the line. They're within easy reach for the game warden and tell me where to begin pulling out. I bait each hook with a night crawler and press the point lightly into the top edge of the boxes." He demonstrates.

"I start in a corner. Here's a finished box." Each hook is neatly set next to the previous while the length of line between each hook is looped and laid in the box so as not to tangle with the previous loops or hooks. The neatly framed box of writhing worms resembles those weaving frames children use for making hot-pads.

"I gotta be precise. It's important the hooks pop off as I motor downriver. Done right, they fly off like toy soldiers being knocked off a sandbox wall." We don't ask about the "what if they don't." Larry doesn't seem to want to discuss that option. "It takes me about an hour to bait and set a hundred hooks. I work it while waitin' for customers."

Larry now reaches under his workbench and pulls up a flat piece of metal. "Here's the weight I use to set lines and keeps them in place after the fish are caught." The ten-inch square metal plate once secured train tracks to oak ties. When I was a boy I watched Gandy men drive spikes through the holes of those plates, always pounding from opposite sides of the rail. I wondered if a hammerhead ever came flying off. Before pile drivers came along, their rippling muscles, pumped from the workout and glistening with sweat, made me envious. The pleasure of watching spikes being driven faded with the new put-put car hammering machines.

"What's the test?"

"Five hundred and thirty-five pounds. It's got to support the weight of fish and withstand mud sucking."

"Mud sucking?"

"Yeah. During the night two to three feet of silt settle in. I don't care for pulling 'em out. After retrieving 'em, I gut, peel and toss 'em on ice. I get a variety of sizes. Suits my customers. I just freeze what's left."

Larry's down-home friendliness is enjoyable. We want to linger both from a desire for different company and my recovery. Larry's lack of pretenses makes staying easy. We get what we see. He isn't asking for anything. He is offering: beverages, conversation, and comfortable chairs. As usual, he is surprised the kid drinks beer and the old man doesn't. After telling him beer doesn't agree with my stomach, he keeps the cold Pepsi flowing.

As neither Darrin nor I smoke, Larry's habit is one we would prefer to avoid. I am trying not to keep track of the number of cigarettes he is smoking. He is a special gift in our lives right now. I would prefer he live a long, healthy life.

"We need to go grocery shopping."

"Leave your water jugs here."

As we finish shopping and head to the checkout lane, Darrin says, "Does that sound like Larry?" We round the last aisle and spot his broad smile. He and the checkout lady are laughing over something. Obviously he shut down the store to pick us up. How long has he been waiting? His quiet, unobtrusive way leaves us feeling even more grateful.

Back at the fish shop he says, "You guys come in for a while. I still got a few more beers."

Once settled, iceman stories begin. Larry and I both remember the occupation, but for different reasons. The iceman quit coming when I was about six or seven years old. Prior to that, the iceman always parked mid-block on the side street nearest our home and cut through a neighbor's backyard. As he did several home deliveries from one stop, the neighborhood kids quickly knew of his presence.

While the truck stood unattended, we would make a beeline for the backend and the loose chips. If none were in sight, we would grab the pick jammed into the side rail. Today OSHA would fine the iceman for leaving such a dangerous tool unsheathed and in the open. Funny, except for murder mysteries, I never heard of any ice chipping deaths. A couple of good whacks on the nearest block had chips flying and kids scrambling to get in and get out.

Larry's experience was a bit different. "My grandfather was the iceman. I began helping in late elementary. Sometimes Grandpa sent me out alone. I wasn't very tall so a couple pillows helped me see over the steering wheel. A twenty-five-pound block was as much as I could carry. Customers helped me with the fifties."

Today it is almost too hard to imagine the hard work Larry and others did at such a young age. Imagine asking an elementary age grandchild to drive your business route. The truth is humans always rise to what survival dictates.

The door flies open! "Hi, Larry." Her voice is warm and powerful, just like her presence. She is in her early thirties, a regular. She greets us before ordering.

"What size cats yah got?" She means freshly caught. He shows her three different sizes. She chooses an eight and a half-pounder.

"Want it cut into steaks?"

"Yes." Chopped is more like it. The backbone on an eight-pound catfish can be a half inch or thicker. Larry makes several horizontal slices along the back. Each shows the thickness of her steaks. When she nods approval, Larry takes up cleaver and hammer. Carefully placing the blade in a slice mark, he comes down hard with the hammer. After each clink on the cleaver, a thud cuts through bone and flesh. The steaks look inviting.

"Havin' company?" Larry poses the question because of the quantity.

"No, I jus love fresh catfish."

As she is being served, Darrin and I discuss a picture above an ice chest holding the day's catch. It is a huge catfish, 105 pounds, held by a proud fisherman. When the woman leaves, I ask Larry for the story.

I should have a tape recorder. What I thought would be an easy answer turns into a long and involved story. Essentially the fisherman struggled for eight hours. Immediately he brought it to town for pictures and admiration. Soon remorse set in for the grand old fish was dying. Returning to the river, he released it. Too late! He then brought it back to town.

Larry's voice now takes on a tone reserved for the elderly who have fallen prey to flu or pneumonia. "A younger, healthier fish might have recovered, but age took its toll. He brought it back for cleaning. It had a ka-zillion eggs!"

The afternoon is been relaxing, but we need to leave. "Thanks for everything, Larry. It's been great."

As I take hold of the door knob, Larry says, "Don't turn the wrong way on the river." I look back expecting a smile, but get not even a glimmer. He is serious and quick to see my expression. "Oh, no, that wasn't a joke. Downstream is an island with a rock dam between it and the shore. The DNR recently punched a hole in it. There are some dangerous whirlpools on the downside."

Once on the river, we decide to paddle as late as possible to make up time. I won't call it lost time. Life with Larry was definitely a gain. Although my arm, chest muscles, and three fingers are still numb and good only for pushing, I am rested and can paddle on the left. The pain is no longer as persistent and sharp as yesterday.

The map shows no sandbars in the area we would like to camp. There are a few river parks along the way. Most are located high on banks to prevent major damage in spring flooding. We have now passed up two such sites as they are perched atop steep, muddy banks. With nightfall nearing, we will take whatever we can get. The next county park is also perched atop a steep embankment. At nearly thirty feet straight up, it will be a major assault. The shoreline is a quagmire. Summer rains and receding waters are oozing knee-deep mud. There is a ten-foot wade to solid ground. In the midst of unloading, I tell Darrin of a nightmare from two nights ago.

"I stepped into some muck that began sucking me down. I was about to suffocate when I awoke…reminded me of the old Tarzan movies at the Rivoli. Quicksand was always quick karma for the bad guys. Seen backing away, gun in hand, they would fall into a pit. Screaming and trashing, while being sucked down, brought an ignoble death."

Darrin smiles. "Maybe your dream is prophetic." He, too, knows nightmares deal with anxieties. Perhaps the un-dealt with slings and arrows are suffocating me. The stress has certainly found my body's weakest link.

Dragging gear and canoe up the slope leaves us laughing. We are now a dirty mess. Only the picnic tables and level tenting area portend some saving grace. As the park has no running water, precious drinking water is used for cleaning up. A posted sign explains that the main bridge is out and being replaced. The chasm between us and town is deep, muddy, and running a trickle of water. The nearest bridge is a two-mile trek.

The picnic table provides some eating luxury on this warm evening. The breeze blowing up the embankment, encircling us, is almost sweet tasting. With dinner over, Darrin heads out, flashlight in hand. Earlier he found a narrow spot in the chasm and threw down logs to create a crude crossing. He wants to provide Schalleen with some love and comfort. Perhaps he also needs it. I am just too sore and tired to move.

In spite of the three-hour visit with Larry and my numbness and pain, we did sixty miles. It is a testament to the current. In our haste to make up lost ground, we passed up a long sandy island. It beckoned us to stop. Now instead of freshly washed sand, we are at a mud spa!

METH LABS

Another idyllic morning: a slight breeze, no insects, temps in the low seventies, and clear skies. From our hilltop vantage point, the current continues to run pell-mell, tumbling over itself to reach New Orleans. It conjures notions of an easy paddle. If only!

Darrin is sleeping in. During the night I briefly wondered whether he might meet some unexpected fate in the dark, along his deserted path. Due to flooding, river flats are notoriously abandoned areas. With the additional isolation of the bridge being out, his walk must have been an extreme example. The positive here was no traffic or partying teens.

Just as my nightmare of being sucked into the mud did not deter me from unloading yesterday, so I dismissed concerns for my partner's fate. If not, I would have gotten little sleep. There are too many things that go bump in the night. I accept the adage that a coward dies a thousand deaths, a hero dies but once. As Darrin is saying nothing about his conversation with Schalleen and the walk into town, I don't ask.

Today will be a half day, stopping in a town large enough for a Catholic church. Besides church and shower, there is a need for fresh fruit, veggies, and meat. The half day will also allow me more time to regain strength in my right hand and arm. The constant movement is helping. The periodic, stabbing chest pain still feels like a spike is being driven through, front to back.

Yesterday's sand beaches are minor compared to the one we are presently passing. It has been about an hour and still more beach lies ahead. This continuing evidence of what the river is like fascinates me. How many scientific discoveries still await questioning Mississippi minds?

As business manager for Camp Cayuna, thirty miles northeast of Brainerd, Minnesota, I once ran into a college biology professor who was under the impression all scientific information had been catalogued.

During those years it was a gift to harvest the dark meat from snapping turtles. This particular incident began while tooling down the dusty road leading back to camp. I had just left one of those over-stuffed, small town hardware stores: a handyman's piece of heaven, a place to search for hidden treasures.

The old, rusty, donated pickup was leaving billowing clouds of dust on that calm summer day. The radio was blaring one of those great hits of the early '60s, a truly sweet moment in life. As I flew around a curve, I came screeching to a halt. Crossing the road was a big, old turtle. It resembled a snapper in color, size, and shape, but I knew it wasn't. Still, it might have a good muscle structure. I decided to harvest it.

Later I was disappointed. She lacked any significant meat. Filled with guilt for killing an animal I couldn't eat, I planted her eggs in warm, sandy soil. Hoping to relieve more guilt, I placed the shell, with its unique shape and depth, atop my camp trailer home. The summer's heat and insects would clean away the nasty smells; later I would make something worthwhile from the shell. But the more I thought about the shell, the more I wondered. We had plenty of bird identification books but nothing for turtles. Curiosity got the best of me. I took the shell to the biology department of the Brainerd Community College as no one at camp could identify it.

The biology teacher held the shell as I explained how much I enjoyed turtle meat. I said I knew it wasn't a snapper, but killed it thinking there might be a lot of great meat. He just stared at me. After what seemed an eternity, he asked, "Where'd you get it?"

I explained how Camp Cuyuna's road runs between two small lakes previously inaccessible. "It must have been in pursuit of a nesting…"

"Liar!" he shouted, thrusting the shell back at me. His word spat out a second time, "Liar!"

I was dumbfounded. "Why…why, why'd you say that?"

Punctuated with a stabbing pointer finger, he said, "Buddy, you think you can waltz in here and pull a fast one on me. I'm not falling for it."

"How…how… can you say such a thing?" In those days stammering was not my typical reaction. A snowplow hitting a drift at sixty miles per hour would be more descriptive of me: words flying everywhere.

With me looking like a fool, he sneered, "This turtle's never been farther north than Iowa. It couldn't survive our winters." His sarcastic tone let me know I wasn't to challenge him anymore. I remember backing off.

I did regain enough confidence to speak again, but his mind was made up. He believed that I had gotten the turtle in Iowa and brought it north as a ruse. He wasn't going to be anyone's fool. Now curious, I wondered who had fooled him, students?

On the return trip to camp I salvaged some pride by imagining this was how Galileo felt when his truth was confronted. For the first time in my young life, I had met someone truly close-minded. Today I laugh over his missed opportunity for fifteen minutes of fleeting fame.

Why is the Mighty Miss causing these musings, daydreams from a younger, more innocent time? Dear God, take me away from these thoughts. Let me enjoy the stillness, the tranquility, the opportunity for the Miss to wash over and rest me.

Perhaps this thinking got its start from the book that claimed there were no sand beaches beyond St. Louis. Were these last six miles a mirage? It is a little like the afternoon a couple days back when Darrin tried to convince me there were no bears along the southern Mississippi. Our discussion started with his finding a large paw print and sketching it.

"That's a bear," I said.

"No, it's more like a large cat. Besides, what would a bear be doing this far south?"

"Living in the wilderness…maybe you should read some of Faulkner and others who talk about hunting in the South. The next time we meet a park naturalist, show it to him." As Darrin has such a keen interest in nature and does such a terrific job drawing things, I keep telling him to become a naturalist.

"Scientific observation is just fun," he says. Well, duh, what should work be? Darrin likes analyzing the out-of-doors. I like experiencing it. I hope I am proven wrong on this one. He can walk circles around me with book knowledge. Besides, we don't need another thing for the old man to be right about.

I have got to change my thinking and move on. It is too beautiful a day to spoil. Besides, Caruthersville, a hotel, and church are coming up.

The hotel clerk gives directions to the Grizzly Jig, a sporting goods store within walking distance. We need cook-stove gas. The Grizzly Jig is a modern, well laid out sportsman's paradise, living up to its great name and providing a wide variety of hunting and camping equipment. The people are friendly.

"Let me introduce you to our staff," an elderly woman offers. It turns out she is the matriarch of the family. Okay, this is unique. Within moments we understand the store is a family tradition. Walking in has made us a part of the family. Unfortunately they don't have what we need. But instead of sending us on our way, they offer help. Chad, in his twenties, volunteers to drive us to another store. First it is Wal-Mart. They, too, do not have the stove gas canisters we need.

By now our quest is secondary. Chad and Darrin are talking army. I listen to modern war stories. It is a special moment. Chad was an M.P. involved in Desert Storm and Desert Shield. Along the way he was stationed in Panama and Germany. Everywhere he went he searched out local fisherman and hunters to guide him. It took stress out of his army career. He is now returning some of their generosity by acting as a great guide for us. His gregariousness warms the heart. He is an instant friend.

We learn how population demographics, housing developments, and traffic patterns, mainly a new bridge over the Mississippi, altered the shopping center from downtown to the bridge area. The stores in the old section, like Grizzly Jig, have fallen on hard times. Many of these family-owned businesses and fortunes have taken a big hit, including Chad's. They, too, wonder what the future holds.

Chad has now taken us to several places. No one carries the gas canisters we need. Camping rule number 555: purchase only portable stoves with commonly used canisters. Thanking Chad, we return to the hotel and prepare for church.

After Mass and introductions at Sacred Heart, we find Father Joe is on loan from the Fargo Diocese. Immediately we begin exchanging names and places. It turns out he is a friend of Father Jerry Noesen and knows that Father Jerry's love for canoeing led to starting "Lake Trails Canoe Base" on Lake-of-the-Woods. This little known canoe base can only be reached by driving to the most northerly point of Minnesota, that protrusion at its top, the Northwest Angle. Once there, a six-mile paddle lies ahead. The canoe base is on an island.

Father Joe seems a little scattered. Perhaps it is the sick calls he needs to make. He is happy to accept the Red Lake Mission fliers, but as he cannot help out with transportation, he flags down a sheriff's officer who graciously agrees to take us to a supermarket.

As the deputy can't stay, he stops a city police officer and asks if he can bring us back. Rather than a tangled web, it is a labyrinth of support. God is good! With a ride back we really load up. The officer is very patient, never wavering from his commitment even though it has become an inconvenience.

On the way back we discuss the local drug business. The police are doing a sting on local meth labs. It is fascinating. A small town like Caruthersville is doing such great detective work. Particularly enjoyable is information on a hot tub that lures in the bad guys. As we leave, he promises to keep an eye on the canoe during the night.

Before heading to an all-you-can-eat buffet, Darrin packs away our purchases. I shower again. The massaging of chest, arm, and finger muscles, plus our downtime, seems to be helping. Once at the casino's buffet, the smell and density of smoke is unbelievable. Clouds of smoke, laced with tar and nicotine, hang heavy in the air. The chairs and tables are stained, as if varnished by it. Cigarette burns, gum globs, and a multitude of stains shade every foot of carpeting.

One cloud of stale, heavy smoke hangs at the three-foot level. At six feet there is a lighter, bluer cloud. This fresher smoke emanates from a multitude of one-armed bandit players. They are trying to clear a view for sevens and oranges by blowing smoke at the screen. Even during my smoking years, I never experienced such a nicotine high. Already the tar clings to my pants and slickens my skin. I will need a third bath. Our waitress appears and disappears into clouds of smoke, heightening the surreal experience. When the food arrives, its color fades while being placed on the table. We eat quickly before too much sludge can settle on it.

RITE OF PASSAGE

It is barely dawn as the shuttle pulls alongside the hotel's back stairs. As our hotel room is so dirty, it feels like we are sneaking out. Dirt and sand from the packs seemed to be everywhere when we packed up this morning. The bath tub is coated with black scum. Little piles of sand give a feeling ants have been hard at work burrowing homes.

"Hi, guys! Am I really taking you to the river?"

"Yeah!" We both smile.

"Never dropped anyone there…what's the transportation?"

Darrin holds up a paddle. This is hard for the driver to grasp. "I've never known anyone who enjoyed canoeing more than a half hour." We laugh and share information about our trip. At the river he asks, "Why in God's name would you want to do that?" Without enough time to explain a lifetime dream, we smile, thank him, and grab our gear.

The canoe has not had a peaceful night. "Someone's been here!" Darrin says. "I didn't think the police could watch it all night." The initial shock is disconcerting. My tied-down seat pad is hanging out. Darrin's is missing. It looks like a hit and run. Perhaps a squad car did keep the thieves from taking more.

As Darrin's seat cushion doubled as a sleeping pad, he will now be sleeping on the ground. It is a small price to pay for the canoe being intact. In a sense the thieves were generous. They took only the cushion and left behind life jackets and the extra paddle. Everything else we portaged to the hotel.

Within an hour of being on the river, Darrin's excitement is evident. "This is great!" he says. Once again we are using wing dams as short cuts. Coming in quick succession, with much greater rapids, we are shooting them more for enjoyment than shortcuts. However, when water enters the canoe, Darrin reminds me I really do not know what I am doing "back there." I have listened to it so much I know it is just part of the routine. As my back and chest muscles are still sore, I keep my mouth shut, grateful we are only six hundred and eighty miles from New Orleans. I may yet make it.

Due to the heat, our morning and noon breaks are each an hour and half. Nearing mid-afternoon a small john boat approaches. Moving up slowly the driver says, "Hi. you guys been on the river since Minnesota?"

"Yeah, Itasca."

"I'm Mike. I come out weekends to photograph interesting people and objects." He views himself as a keeper of Mississippi history. "You guys mind if I take a couple pictures?" We appreciate his asking and friendliness. Perhaps someday his collection will be a significant contribution to an understanding of the Mississippi. He, too, sees her as a mighty animal, a fascinating creature. "I can feel her strength and changing moods," he says. After a few posed action shots, we wish each other good luck.

As evening approaches, two john boats are drifting together in the middle of the river. Each holds three men and lots of fishing equipment. Their eyes are upon us, awaiting our arrival. As we draw near Darrin greets them, "been fishing?"

"We have!" Without pausing, one man lifts a stringer of cats. "Would you like some?" He's my age and fishing with his son and grandson.

Before we can answer, his grandson grabs another stringer. After pulling it up, he points to a particularly large cat. "I caught this one!" His father beams with pride. "This is my first trip with Dad and Grandpa." He must have passed a rite of manhood. I remember feeling the same satisfaction when seeing pride for me on my father's face.

The fish are beautiful and tempting, but we have neither the time nor equipment to cook them. In truth, Darrin and I fear eating fish raised this far south in the Miss' waters. In the end, one boat gives its stringers to the other. Both sets of men and boys are contented and at peace. Life is good! The Mighty Miss has produced another cherished memory. As my body is ready to crash, we thank them and move on.

As we set up camp, there is a near perfect sunset along with a gentle, cool breeze and waves lapping quietly, meditatively, on golden sands. We are so pleased with this site we are again taking a chance and camping on the river's edge. After erecting the tent and laying out my sleeping bag, I gaze out the door. Seeing only water, I feel as though I and the tent are floating.

Paranoia tries to sabotage the moment, What will happen if the Corps decides to open the dam gates and raise the channel water a couple inches? How close is the summer runoff from recent heavy rains in Minnesota and Iowa? We will definitely be floating if either catches us. It would take less than three inches to inundate this site. Finally, if a barge grounds here, we will be leveled.

Since losing his sleeping pad, Darrin maintains the soft, warm sands add extra pleasure to his sleep. I am not sure who he is trying to convince. I do know the hot sun keeps the mosquitoes away. In a moment that will be different. The feeding frenzy will begin. The sun is setting.

RAIN FOREST RICK

The beautiful, clear sunrise promises another hot day. The numbness in my fingers and chest are still there. I get no sympathy from Darrin. In fact he is presently saying, "Yer pain is comparable to what I felt in training for war."

"War? I'm not preparing for war." Okay, that was stupid. The sergeant in him re-surfaces.

"I am not interested in bellyaching from someone who didn't spend time getting in shape."

What will the final toll be for being out of shape and stressed? The negativity, disrespect, heat, humidity, eight to ten hours of daily paddling, sun exposure, all seem to be conspiring against my health.

Mid-morning finds us taking another floating break, discussing the hurt we still cause each other. It ends with another truce that includes not speaking, this time until we arrive in Memphis.

Several hours later finds us turning up an inlet beside Mud Island. We are headed for the Memphis Yacht Club. The marina store doesn't sell much in the line of food, just chips, dips, and soda. However, it is giving away something far more valuable: friendship. Pat is the gentleman's name. The nicest counterman anyone could hope to meet.

"I'm really more of a drifter. Came here a couple winters back looking for a boat slip. The marina offered free rental in exchange for clerking one day a week. I am getting restless…put my houseboat up for sale."

With business slow, we move out and under the canopied deck. It juts out some thirty feet over the inlet waters and beside the marina docks. The slight breeze adds to the comfort of shaded tables. With a soda, good company, and a cheap cigar to celebrate the moment, it is a pleasant place to be. My body goes limp from sinking into the cushioned patio chair. After Pat gets comfortable with us, Darrin looks at me, wanting me to pop the question, "Any possibility of camping on the deck tonight? We're usually gone by sunrise."

Pat's face lights up. He is eager to have new company and conversation. "I can't make a commitment, but I'll be happy to introduce you to the admiral. I can vouch for you. You guys seem all right." That is the opening we wanted. We are tired of each other's polemics. Besides, a marina this size must have showers. At the present time their whereabouts eludes me. This marina is spread out over a few acres of water and land. None of the buildings within sight appear large enough to house showers. Maybe they are on the north end, under the large metal canopy housing over 50 percent of the boats. This canopy covers over a half acre of docks. Then again, most of these boats are large enough to have their own showers.

The ensuing discussion on possible places to pitch a tent sheds no light on showers. "I'll lock up and take you to meet the Admiral." The walk marches us past endless aisles of boats, all neatly tied and stowed in case of a storm.

When Pat originally mentioned the admiral, Darrin and I gave each other quick, questioning glances. We have never met a real admiral. "So, what's the admiral like?" I ask in between a few dozen other questions. I am beginning to babble. Perhaps I am nervous or just plain tired silly. Before Pat can answer my first question, I throw out two more: "How long's he been admiral, and what did he have to do to become an admiral?"

Pat smiles. "First of all, the admiral is the title given the marina manager. Secondly, Sal isn't a he." Pat's smile says he is waiting for a reaction. Okay, so Sal the admiral is a she. So far I have only seen men on the docks. What type of woman keeps the boys and their toys in line?

A friend is leaving her boat as we walk up. We nod and greet him as he passes. Sal stands graciously at the door listening to Pat's introductions. He is being too generous; he is trying too hard.

In her thirties, Sal is good looking and a born manager. More cautious than Pat, she talks informally, asking about the trip, where we are from, how we happened to land there, etc. She is sizing us up, listening for what is not being said. Once her concerns are allayed, she gives approval but with one stipulation, "The tent needs to be on an out-of-the-way landing." She makes it clear the night security will need to know when we are leaving.

Convinced we are not going to be an imposition, her voice changes from manager to friend. "By the way, the mosquitoes are horrendous here." Although the warning sounds ominous, we already know. Those bloodthirsty suckers have gotten more than their pint of blood from us. In the calm of this backwater marina they will be worse than the sandy shores.

I am about to inquire on showers when Pat reads my mind, "Do you suppose they could use the showers in the restaurant?"

The restaurant turns out to be a building some forty to fifty yards straight up the riverbank's 45-degree angle. That dry land building didn't seem remotely connected to the marina when we arrived. There are no steps, only six-foot long, six-inch wide, cement vehicle traction pads. The upper building contains not only the restaurant and showers but also the main office. At this time the complex is closed for remodeling.

"Are the showers still working?" Pat is certainly asking all the right questions.

"I'm not sure. You'll need to ask Ray." Ray is the general manager. Pat leads the way.

As is true with everyone we have met, Ray is friendly and supportive. "Sure! Go round back to the loading dock...door's unlocked. If I lock it while you're inside, you can still get out. Don't bother looking for a switch in the hallway, you won't find any. Turn right after entering and go down to the "T." Turn right again. You'll find a window in that hallway. Go down the right-hand side. The shower is about halfway down and should be unlocked. There's a light switch in there. The hot water is still on."

Pat takes us the long way back. He wants to show us his house-boat. As boat slips go, he is in the back forty, the farthest corner of the marina, away from any action, an ideal year-round living nook. For a single guy, Pat's houseboat is perfect. It has all the amenities: a double bed, shower, washer, drier, refrig, microwave, and dining area. The large "For Sale" sign hanging on the front door reiterates Pat's itch to hit the road, but in a simpler mode of transportation.

My curiosity is peaked, "So whata yah want?"

It is the question Pat has been waiting for. His grin is ear-to-ear. "You'll appreciate this. It's the real reason I brought you here. Go out that side-door." Darrin looks at me as if to say, "What's the big deal?"

On the back deck of the houseboat is an old, aluminum, guide canoe. These canoes are nearly two feet wider and three feet longer than regular aluminum canoes. Rather than a curved up stern, it has a square back for mounting a one to two-horsepower outboard. It is Pat's dream. I smile appreciatively. The wheels begin turning.

The floor of Pat's canoe is topped with a one-inch square, wooden lattice. "Keeps my feet and packs dry during those unexpected mo-ments. I built in saddlebags for stowing gear." These are fore and aft the bow seat. "It gives ballast when I am sitting stern." Other ameni-ties are a comfortable, high-backed, captain's chair in place of the nor-mal, flat, stern seat. "The running lights are solar powered. When fully charged, they last two nights."

The coup de grace is a canopy. "I made the frame from electrical conduit. Designed it to set up with one easy pull, like the old fifties convertibles. Additionally canvas sides pieces convert it into a floating tent." During the heat of the day or in a rainstorm, this canoe will keep its occupants cool or dry. With a five-gallon gas tank, he can mo-tor along for a number of days.

It is an ideal mode of transportation for a river rat—plenty of space for coolers and dry food storage, a decent cook stove, and much more. It can be docked just about anywhere. As a floating tent, there is plenty of room for stretching out a sleeping bag. Jacqui would be nervous if she knew how I envy this exquisite mode of transportation. My greatest fear, should I own one, would be motoring off into the sunset, like a monk walking off into the desert. Pat's mode of trans-portation provides the solitary life or easy access to any marina. The cost is pennies a day.

With excitement in his voice, Pat says, "I've steered her from Minneapolis to New Orleans, down the Texas coast, east to Florida and up the eastern seaboard. Now it's time to get moving again. I'm tired of houseboat living, too confining. I'm thinking of going to Cuba." I don't ask why. It just sounds good, any adventure does. Ninety miles in a motorized canoe would be an easy day's travel. I'd do that!

Pat's wanderlust is far more intense than mine. I am better at burying desires beneath layers of work challenges and domestic tranquility. He continues. "I once long hauled (trucking), but it was too confining. The water is where I wanted to be. I quit and hired on with a husband-and-wife team sailing the world. One week out killed it for me. Their constant quarrelling was too much. I jumped ship at the nearest port...been that way ever since."

"Quarreling?" Darrin looks at me. We smile and seal our lips a little tighter. Needless to say, Pat is not married. He tried it once but the wayward wind eroded the edges. The marriage needed more attention than he was willing to give. Did he love his wife? The answer seems to be yes, but not as much as the water. Pat's lesson is not too hard to fathom, finish the trip and head home with friendships and marriages intact.

Like the biblical symbolism for the number forty (the average life span of someone living in ancient times) our forty-day journey is definitely a life-changing experience. So much so that in recent days, we have both felt a strong desire to chuck it all and return to real life, home, and job, where life is always rosy and idyllic...right? "Let's call home before showering," I suggest.

"Hi, Love!"

"You're at the Memphis Marina?" she says. The audible pause is my bewilderment. How did she know? We don't have caller ID. "Gary, you still there?"

"Yes...how'd you know?"

"Schalleen and I were concerned when we didn't hear from you for three days. I did what you said...called the Coast Guard. They put out an all-call to the barges. Within minutes a captain said you were turning up the southern tip of Mud Island, thought you might be headed to the Memphis Marina."

I pause again. There is no sanctuary left for a river rat. The barge operators, from their lofty perches, act like the minor gods of Mt.

Olympus, watching every movement. Brushing aside the gods, Jacqui and I have a great talk.

Everything in the restaurant complex is as Ray said it would be with the exception of the obstacle course. The hallways are packed with an odd assortment of desks, filing cabinets, dining chairs, and tables. In the dark, we bang into them more than a few times.

Showered and refreshed, we walk the upper bank more relaxed than we have felt in days. "What did you think of Pat's story about the quarreling couple?" Darrin asks. Since he is reaching out, I consider carefully before responding.

"Our quarreling is making the trip harder. It could tear us apart."

"I agree. How do we prevent that?"

As this is too serious, too quick, I joke, "If one of us doesn't jump ship and the quarreling continues the stronger will drag the weaker one into the flood plain, never to be seen again. I don't want that to happen to you." He groans and we agree to continue talking over pizza.

Before our order arrives, Darrin begins, "I know I need to listen more…I've said some dumb things."

"You're right though about me being outa shape. I let you down." Thus begins a meal conversation that ends with enough issues resolved to continue the journey. After dinner we stand, hug, and head out to make a quick purchase of fruit, cheese, and meat. We do not want to miss Mud Island's Museum.

Mud Island, despite its name, is really a pleasant place. There is no muddiness. The name must be from a bygone era. It is really a well-groomed piece of land with paved river walks. Couples are strolling hand-in-hand or walking dogs. Their umbrellas pop out as a warm mist begins.

The Memphis Belle, the storied WWII bomber, is our first stop. It is located in a special, open-air hangar near the museum entrance. To see and touch her is an unexpected thrill.

Darrin pulls me along, "The museum's going to close in forty-five minutes. Let's go. We can return later." I agree.

The museum's main focus is a replica of the Mississippi. It begins with a tributary wall showing the entire Mississippi water shed. Flowing down the wall and through the scale model replica is the comparative amount of water presently descending the Mississippi Valley. The long replica walk is made more meaningful by historical markers describing towns, steamboat sinkings, prisons, cotton landings, civil war events, Army Corp projects, etc. It is all very detailed and accurate.

Because of the wealth of historical information and limited time, we split up, hopping back and forth across the model, each gathering data on every other sign. It is impressive how the locks and dams and bends are all positioned so accurately. Time runs out just as we reach the delta/gulf area. There is a huge reflecting pool showing the backwaters and main channels leading into the gulf. The museum hosts shoo us out. We return to the Memphis Belle.

Thirty minutes later finds us descending the steep landing to the marina docks. With food packed, we head back to the marina store and more conversations with Pat. Under the canopy we are protected from a light rain while enjoying an evening breeze. As the rain ceases, an antique Chris Craft pulls up. Pat tells us the two occupants make the marina a regular stop. After introductions we believe the two men to be river lovers in more ways than one. They are friendly and gregarious, leading to much small talk.

My eyes keep going back to a huge neon guitar a few blocks downriver. I am trying to figure out how the guitar logo fits the hotel. It has nothing in common with the hotel's name. Finally I turn to one of the guys who joined us, "I just can't figure out the logo on that hotel. What could it possibly have to do with the chain?"

I turn back to look at it, adding one more intelligent thought, "Maybe it's something to do with the city." With no answer forthcoming, and silence in which a pin drop could be heard, I turn to Darrin for enlightenment. He, too, is looking at me in disbelief. I look around, hoping to find some clues. Am I totally out of it? Then it dawns on me, but too late. Even though I often ask leading questions with a straight face, Darrin and the others know my question is no joke. If it had been a joke, I would have laughed sooner. I feel a little foolish and get a well-deserved razing.

"We haven't had any Elvis sightings in a long time."

"Maybe you'll see him tonight," Pat chimes in.

The younger boater advises, "Perhaps Elvis will turn over in his grave tonight."

Okay, I deserve those. They have a good laugh, but surely I am not the first to come to Memphis and forget it is the home of the King! I reassure myself that I am still normal by remembering that Elvis is not the King I follow.

I am being rescued by a new arrival. "Guys, this is Rain Forest Rick," Pat says. Rick immediately sits down and acts as though he has been here all night. He begins by turning the conversation to himself, bragging about starting the Rain Forest Restaurant chain. He claims to have sold it a few years back, retiring to do other things. As he talks, I feel I am being "had."

I look around the table like a gambler, trying to get a read on the others' faces. They seem to indicate he is for real. I am not so sure. The stories of the Rain Forest founder that float around the Twin Cities say he started by rigging up his home to look like a rain forest, animals and the like. His dinner guests in Brooklyn Park encouraged him to go public with the idea. Maybe Rick is that man, but he is offering no such information. Besides, I thought it was a Steve somebody who created the concept.

Rick now jumps back in time. He has a different version of how he got started in the food business. "I opened my first pizza place at seventeen. Left home at age fifteen, jaw wired shut from the old man's left. I never looked back." His story feels real. There is definite pain coming from his words. Either he is a good actor or this is a part of his past.

"I'd taken all the abuse I was going to. It was the late sixties and I became a hippie." His descriptions are as I remember. In some ways I believe him, for he is talking with disdain about the wealth he has accumulated. He speaks of stewardship for the land, animals, and people of planet earth. He speaks of a manatee rescue and release project in south Florida, and several other Rain Forest projects in South America.

Is Rick for real? Although his stories sound complete, the start-up details bother me as do the bragging. Sure I ate at the Rain Forest restaurant in the Mall of America, but that hardly qualifies me to judge the worth of what he is saying. What I remember about its décor and ambiance is my grandchildren loved it. Not me! We sat under a loudspeaker blaring jungle birdcalls and an air-conditioning vent blasting freezing air. The latter is one of Murphy's Restaurant Laws: "Keep it cold in the summer and hot in the winter, customers will eat quickly and give up their seating."

Rain Forest Rick is one of about a dozen boaters who live year-round at the Memphis Marina. While some residents leave for Florida in the winter, Rick doesn't or at least has not for the past two years. "So, Rick, why do you live here all year around?" Darrin asks. "With all your money, you could live anywhere. Why pick Memphis?" Now that is getting up close and personal. Darrin must also have reservations.

Rick takes it in stride. "A friend was starting a restaurant, needed a hand and asked me to help. I just stayed around a little longer than anticipated."

Marina people seem that way, an independent breed, rejoicing in their solitude yet needing action nearby. Interesting is the docks and water seem like more rigid divides than fences and sidewalks. "Keep your distance," they warn. Earlier a house-boater backed out his slip and motored two slips down. Dropping anchor, the two families visited deck to deck. It felt friendly, but somehow it was distant. No one left the safety of home.

Boat life is a curious oddity. Take boat cruising. It is akin to the late 1940s to early '50s when people walked around town on Sunday afternoons, or drove their cars to visit people out and around the lake and at city parks. In those years homeowners sat on their porches to keep cool, waiting for passersby. It seemed the picnickers and beach people were also waiting for visitors. This was certainly true at the drive-in eating establishments.

House-boaters cruise the river and marinas for much the same reason, visiting. They are looking to pull alongside another boat or up to a sandy stretch populated by other boaters swimming and picnicking. There is also a similarity between houseboat owners and present day travel campers. They both use the same bric-a-brac to decorate their decks and small lawn areas.

It is now clear why Rick and the others have joined us. We are new mail, new ideas and stories from the outside world; once we are gone it will provide plenty of fodder to fill several evenings of conversation. They can wonder where we are, if we are safe, and what new things are happening to us, spending hours tweaking our idiosyncrasies as we will theirs. Besides Rick, Pat, and Sal, there are other singles living on the boats. One apparently is in the doghouse. Most owners are married couples.

Rain Forest Rick, as he likes to be called, has a forty-foot boat. My question about the size of his boat opens up the floodgates on a story about a fifty-five-footer he gave away to the manatee rescue people. "We're a part of Jacque Cousteau's organization. I gave them the "Ribbit V." It had been sunk in a storm. Salvaged it for six thousand…invited some of my old hippie friends from Minnesota to help clean it. Gave 'em room and board during the restoration."

Later, when I stand up to say goodnight, Rick insists Darrin and I join him on his boat. His offer of comfort sounds too good. Darrin gives me the "yes" look. He is not interested in setting up the tent. I agree, but only if Rick is going to bed now. We need a few hours of sleep. Immediately we are greeted with a chorus of "No, don't leave that soon." "Stay a few days." "Hang around…relax." "Memphis has great fireworks." "We'll show you the town." Their generosity is tempting, but we gotta be drifting along; jobs and spouses are waiting.

"We can't take that much time. Besides, the trip's length is already becoming a challenge for us."

Darrin nods agreement and adds, "We gotta move on!" I know he's thinking of Schalleen. She is quite anxious to have him home.

Grabbing our sleeping bags and personal packs, we follow Rick. Once on his deck he makes a revelation, "Got a sick nephew in the cabin…can't invite you in." Well, that's a novel excuse. Okay, what's his plan? "You guys can sleep on the pilot's deck."

Now he tells us! "What about mosquitoes?" Darrin asks.

"Don't worry…got covers for the deck openings."

"Won't that be hot?" I ask.

"Naw, I got a fan." We climb the ladder to the pilot's deck. It is much more cramped than Rick's description. He is right about one thing; the couch seating is comfortable. What he failed to note is the comfort is offset by the "L" shape in which we must twist our bodies. Rick disappears below.

"I don't like this," Darrin grumbles.

"Maybe we should go back and set up?"

"Too late!" Darrin says.

Rick reappears with a fan. It moves the air but doesn't cool. Our body heat quickly raises the temperature in the enclosed area. Foul dispositions rise as endless streams of mosquitoes enter through breaches in the window seams. This is the first night we are being bitten with impunity. Awake, frustrated, and dozing in and out causes more fatigued. How will it end?

It is 3:32 AM. I am calling it quits. The mosquitoes have slowed their buzzing. "Darrin, let's move out." We broke our number one camping rule: follow survival instincts. We sacrificed a good night's sleep for what was billed as comfort. I am sure Rick and his companion are comfortable. We dress, pack, and push off without breakfast. On the calm water, we move effortlessly down the side of Mud Island and back into the Miss' main current. Breathing in the morning's coolness is relaxing.

By midday the temperature is over a hundred. The heat and humidity are draining. We have pulled over to sleep in the shade and wait, conserving strength and sanity.

The river has a new, steady rhythm. Every mile of flood plain and riverbank comes from the same mold—flat and wide with tall, lush green grasses mingling around skinny trees. Nothing seems to stand out in the peacefulness of the thick vegetation except an enormous insect population. The birds are in paradise.

Animal prints continue to dot the sandy beaches. Wild boar and something the size of a bobcat are common. Some tracks are definitely bear. Earlier today, in the midst of enjoying the serenity and wild setting, a castle protruded above the river grasses. Too gaudy and incongruent for the muddy floodplains, it could only have been a casino.

Lying in the shade now has brought on a very technical discussion on the differences between southern and northern mosquitoes. Darrin is absolutely convinced the southern variety is faster than its northern counterpart. As proof he details how easy it is to kill a northern mosquito. "Perhaps," I muse, "these southern brethren interbred with the fly."

One thing we both agree on is the southern stinger. It is longer and sharper than the northerner's. Darrin equates it to a vampire's bite because these mosquitoes draw blood painlessly. We never feel the mosquito until its soft belly is full and the stinger is being pulled out. I am encouraging this erudite conversation because at previous rests Darrin has taken verbal jabs at my soft underbelly.

It is a fascinating eve to the Fourth of July. For the first time I am on a huge river, mostly alone, and mostly in the wilderness. Earlier there were cool breezes from the northwest. Not so now. We are fortunate though. The dreaded southern headwinds have still only come in short spurts, more cooling than confrontational. We will make New Orleans by July 13th. My strained right shoulder muscles and numb middle fingers are still evident, but the current and knowledge we will be done in less than two months has brought a more relaxed pace.

After returning to the river, we soon find ourselves approaching the dike protecting Helena. "Let's climb it," Darrin says.

Once atop we find a backwater area separating it from the town. "Whata yah think?" I ask.

"The map doesn't show this road." The dike we are on doubles as a road. Darrin's statement is really a question. He is wondering how long the walk for food and water will be.

"Here comes a car. Let's ask," I suggest.

The car is a late model, blue sedan. It is the type salesmen drive. "Hi, I'm Jason Cox." He is an agent for Transamerica.

"We're trying to determine the distance to town."

"More than you want in this heat. Jump in. I'll take you."

As Darrin wants to shop and visit, I stay with the canoe. By the time they return, they are discussing Jason's love: hunting. He speaks with passion about his trips. I look at Darrin knowingly before asking Jason, "You ever meet Wade from the Grizzly Jig in Caruthersville?" He shakes his head no. "You guys are brothers under the skin. Wade loves hunting and fishing as much as you. You guys gotta be about the same age, probably soul mates." I suspect if these guys ever begin swapping stories, there will be no turning back. "Next time you're in Caruthersville, look him up."

At 7 PM the breeze tempts us to consider evening travel. However, we know it is plagued by horrendous mosquito patrols. The dark nights also make river navigation more difficult. Although skilled canoeists do it regularly, we are not interested in any more experiential learning, especially since barge traffic is non-stop most nights. Perhaps the captains figure they are safe when we are off the water. More realistically, they are doing what we should be doing, avoiding the heat of the day.

Although the weather makes camping at the water's edge perfect on this deep sandy beach, the flip side is we are far too exposed to sudden winds, rains, and lightning. We are over a half mile from the high water shore. The few storms we have experienced indicate tenting here is hazardous. The only thing holding down the tent is body weight.

Stranded logs and five-gallon water jugs anchor the canoe. It wouldn't fair much better in a storm. The wind would sail it, anchors and all, for the canoe would catch the wind like a sail. The weatherman says there will be lightning and scattered showers tonight. Too bad this cloud cover couldn't come during the day. We now lather on number fifty baby sunscreen three to four times a day. Adult sunscreen, especially around the eyes and mouth, brings burning and redness.

Something new started happening today. Whenever I sit or lie down for a rest, dizziness immediately sets in. It is worse if I close my eyes. The nausea, akin to seasickness, lasts a minute or two. The sensation is like a fast ride on a tilt-a-whirl. On the positive side, I am regaining feeling in the three middle fingers. The chest muscles only hurt when I cough or laugh.

OVER THE EDGE

It doesn't seem like the fourth weekend. Our thoughts are only about survival. The days all run together. It must have felt this way crossing the prairies and oceans two hundred years ago. The early morning breeze carries a heavy humidity intensified by the seventy-seven degrees and rising heat. The sun's rays, invading starched clouds, are hues ranging from magenta to pink. The trees on both sides of the river sway gently and are filled to capacity with cheery parents singing in a new day while nestlings demand to be fed.

Again a Blue Heron's fishing hole is adjacent to our tent. After bringing the morning water to a boil and sitting down with tea, I find myself in a staring match. While I eye the heron with contentment, he eyes me with what seems to be daggers. His squawking reminds me of my dad when I was a youngster. If I talked too much in the fishing boat, Dad would say, "Quiet, you're scaring the fish." The heron seems to be saying I loused up his chances for successful fishing.

To stay on track and finish our journey by July 13th, we are not stopping today. I find myself dwelling on that, as well as calling home before Jacqui calls the Coast Guard again. Darrin has got a contented look as he crawls out of the tent. "I really slept well. The sand's warmth kept away the dampness." I find this hard to believe but say nothing. He has never said how he feels about the theft of his sleeping pad.

Shortly after we push off, a set of barges appear from behind. "What'd yah think? Do we want the left?"

"Yeah." As the barges are still over a mile away, it is an easy turn.

Three quarters of an hour later the barges near us and the captain's loud speaker crackles to life. Sarcasm floats over the waves. "You guys cut too close in front of me. You need to be careful."

Darrin quits paddling to look at me. Although his face says it all, he asks anyway, "Is that guy having a bad day? What's with the attitude?"

By mid-afternoon we are wallowing in the high nineties and consuming large amounts of water. This moves Darrin to ask, "You use your pee can?

"No." He was right in demanding two water jugs. Between cooking and drinking, we now consume nearly ten gallons a day. Judging from the last map check, we will be out of water an hour or more before landing.

The Mississippi has turned broad and lazy again; it is a mile and a half across. We are paddling the shipping lane, approaching a bend that swings the channel an extra half mile to the right. Because of the heat and humidity, we are not enthusiastic about this wide turn. However, there is a shortcut to our left, a wing dam.

"Wanna run it?" I ask. "It's got some rapids." As more mobility has returned to my right arm, I can paddle on that side longer. Nodding agreement, Darrin digs his paddle deep on the right. Quickly and silently the canoe responds, turning toward a dark-water "V" in the wind dam. The opening is less than forty feet off the left bank.

Within moments the strong current grabs the canoe, pulling it into more turbulence than expected. Over the water's roar, I shout, "This has gotta be our last. They're getting too unpredictable."

With ambivalent agreement, Darrin again nods languidly. The heat has slowed not only our energy output, but also our thinking. Perhaps exhilaration from a swift current will arouse us. "Let's move farther left; there's a heavier flow!" Before we push downriver, I want to catch the current hitting that bank. As we enter the "V," the swift current portends a fantastic ride.

The thrust in the narrow gap is exhilarating, both pushing and pulling us toward a calm spot. This particular bubble is higher and larger than any we have yet encountered. Our speed quickly propels us onto it. The rise and outward flow are twice anything we have yet experienced. As the bubble begins moving left, there is an odd sensation in my body tingle. It is not so much excitement as fear.

Oomph!

The bubble has burst! For a moment we hang in mid-air, but only for a second. Dropping hard, we are immediately sucked into the vortex.

"Oh, my God," I pray silently, "save us." The smooth bubble is now a whirlpool. In one fell swoop the entire canoe has dropped two feet into a swirling mass. It has taken less than a split second. We are listing toward the whirlpool's three to four-foot open eye. We are so close I can see into its bottomless and foreboding pit. The pull on the canoe is relentless. The bow is bending downward while the rest lies flat in the whirlpool. How much stress can it take?

My pounding heart feels like it is in a vice-grip. The canoe is dwarfed by the maelstrom. At over forty feet in diameter, we are half its size, descending out of control, out of hope. Its destructive force has silenced us.

Fright is an understatement. I have shot plenty of rapids and experienced numerous pulls trying to re-route my canoe. That power doesn't bother me anymore. I understand it. But the suddenness and the unexpectedness of this is something else. I don't think I have the knowledge and experience to handle it.

In the rapids there is always a warning of obstructions or current changes. If a rock or log is under the water, haystacks and other signs of turbulence give warning to presence and depth. From hours of experience, instinct says what to do. The power created by thousands of gallons of water rushing through a narrow opening or bounding over and around immovable objects leaves a signature. The reads are somewhat predictable. Adjustments can be made in a split-second.

But being dropped into a whirlpool, without warning, being sucked toward the core, is something new. No experience has prepared me for this moment. It is straight out of a Freddie Krueger nightmare: the scare, the adrenaline rush, being dropped and pulled sideways. It is terrifying. Neither of us blames the other. When Darrin finds his voice, it is almost calm. "How do we get out?" He is neither pleading nor whining. He is seeking a maneuver that will bring us to safety. The moment is demanding every ounce of strength as we paddle on the left to prevent capsizing into the core opening. "Are we going to die?"

"Don't think it. Your life jacket is on. Larry said we'd be held up until the whirlpool dies."

The swirling wall rushes past in layered, tight ringlets. If anything is caught in it, like a doll or binoculars, it will stand out like a sore thumb. Why do we appear to sit in one place while the water rushes round and round? It has got to be an optical illusion created by speed and imagination. There has got to be a way out.

Although we are paddling with the circular flow, the illusion is of moving in reverse. It cannot be. Are we paddling just to stay out of the center hole. The powerful movement is now beginning to bend the stern downward. The crease is just in the front of my feet, as if to bend the back half completely under the front half of the canoe. This must be what Darrin felt a moment ago.

The noise is like water rushing over a dam and dropping forty feet, pounding on the surf below. It is deafening. The bow is now headed up the side and countering the stern suction. Two forces are tugging for control, pulling us in two directions as though the canoe could be stretched. Something must give.

Oh, God, what now? We are being catapulted. The canoe is being lifted out of the water after hitting the opposite rim. We fly out. Is this really happening? Within seconds the canoe leaps a full length, slung by the whirling force. I am in shock. God is good! We have momentum and are not looking back. Faster and faster we paddle. If the hand of God plucked us out of hell, we have no intention of going back.

Quickly out of the white water and into the river's calm, paddles drop to catch a breath. Neither speaks. We are too stunned. Pent up emotions rise, "You're responsible! You almost got us killed!"

I would be stupid to answer, but I, too, need release. The adrenaline is rushing pell-mell. I cannot speak. Fear will not release its grip. My heart will not slow. The pounding hurts my chest. Yoga…I need yoga… breathe deep and rhythmic…in…out…relax…breathe deeply…exhale slowly…envision the heart relaxing.

Over and over I repeat the mantra until breathing and heartbeat come into alignment. Still I can't speak. Fear won't leave me. I have never encountered a terror so great, so swift. Not even the night as a sixth grader, when I ran through a darkened alley to scare a high school neighbor, did my adrenaline rush like it does now.

That summer night was so peaceful. Both Jerry and I were returning from a triple-A, double header. He was about a block ahead. Why I was alone, I cannot say. But I knew he wouldn't expect someone to jump out from behind a shadowed corner, particularly someone growling like a werewolf. When he didn't take the darkened alley as a shortcut, I did. I ran like crazy to get to the edge of the lumberyard building that abutted the sidewalk he would turn onto.

Jerry would walk right past this spot. There in plenty of time, I lay quietly, crouched, prepared for a midair leap. His instincts were as quick and automatic as my spring. Grabbing me in midair by a nap of shirt material directly under my chin, he lifted me up and slammed me against the wall of the building. I remember the thud and his huge fist headed straight for my mouth and nose; the heat of his panicked breath and white knuckled fist stopping just short of smashing into my face was punctuated with, "Damn you, Hoffman! You scared the shit outa me!" He let me fall limp to the ground.

Now I can't stop wondering, "What would've happened if we'd capsized? We would have been sucked down, perhaps headfirst. We could have broken our necks on impact with the bottom!"

Once, while visiting a river park as a young married man with two children, I met some nineteen year olds diving into the downside of rapids. They were giddy with excitement. "What's so great?" I asked.

"The power…pulls you down…bounces you over a sandy bottom before spitting you out."

I remember thinking, "I'd enjoy that." Looking down the shoreline at Jacqui playing with the children and back at the guys, I decided it couldn't be that dangerous…they were doing it…they're okay.

I went for it. Just before I dove in, one of the guys yelled, "Jump first…it'll give you a feel."

I was grateful. The rapids had more power than was apparent. After a couple jumps, I dove in. Immediately the water grabbed me in a new way. Over and over across the sandy bottom I rolled, bumping and sliding, the sand giving way ever so slightly, forming clouds that swirled around my face and body. Thankfully there were no boulders.

The first dive seemed like an eternity. How long would I be down? The question was answered as quickly as I thought it. Spit back to the surface with a few new scrapes, I quickly went back for more dives. As river levels can vary so much from day to day, I knew I might never have a second chance. I haven't!

How long would Darrin and I have been kept down in the whirlpool before being spit up? Uncle Hank, wherever you are, I believe you! Until now I had thought your stories of huge whirlpools below Mississippi dams to be urban legends. Now I believe a wing dam is why Chase and Marc's red ice chest floated by.

Darrin is no longer blaming me. After nearly half an hour of floating and silence, I can no longer restrain relief. Tears flow. "We've grown careless again," my words choke. Darrin hears the sadness and we exchange one and two-word statements. The event is dissected and ends with a renewed agreement: "That is our last warning…no more wing dams."

"If we can't read the writing on the wall, we don't deserve to make New Orleans," is Darrin's assessment. The Miss has been more than generous with warnings. Still, I have this ominous feeling.

As the day progresses, the heated winds no longer soothe. They dry and dehydrate. The humidity is no longer velvety soft, but sweaty and gritty. The drying winds and sweat leached with sun-lotion burns my eyes. To top it off, the main channel current is stolen by barges. It is a witch's brew. What will it take to stay sane for eight more days, to actually arrive in New Orleans in one piece?

Evening finds us on another pleasant stretch of sandy beach, but it is hard to consider sleeping. Clothes and bodies reek while the water appears too dirty for bathing. "Let's go swimming," Darrin encourages.

"I'm not sure I wanna risk it."

"There were a lot of people swimming today. Anyway, what's worse, your smell or the river's?" His humor doesn't move me.

The size of boats has changed. They are no longer large pleasure craft, mostly small, flat-bottomed johnboats and regular fishing boats. A few larger johnboats have house-like structures built over their hulls. Canopies are common. That is what we need.

Earlier in the day thirty-some boats were beached on a sandy stretch. One left the rest and came out to greet us. The driver asked about our trip before revealing his motive. "The last canoeist claimed he designed the Pennsylvania quarter. What's your claim?"

"Just trying to canoe fifty to sixty miles a day and stay sane. By the way, how can you play in this heat all day? We've pulled over twice."

He shrugged his shoulders. "Don't know…maybe we're used to it."

For two days the heat has caused our body salts to leave faster than replacement. Never having experienced this, we didn't pack salt tablets or salt.

"Come and look at this." Darrin's request jolts me back. While looking for a place to bathe, he has dug a washbowl in the sand. Clear, cold water has filled it. "Must be filtering down from the banks. I'm digging in my water bottle," he says.

It is a good idea. The water is twenty to thirty degrees cooler than the river's. The holes re-fill with sand too quickly for bathing, so Darrin is again eyeing the river. "I think I'll chance it," he says. After further discussion, I pledge to join him.

Emerging, our bodies smell a bit better, but are neither cooled nor refreshed. Returning to the water bottles, we dig elongated trenches for our legs, feet, and butt. This emersion begins a cool-down. Trying to hurry the process, I drink my cooled water in a quick second. It provides little added relief. Resting in the mornings and afternoons just isn't doing it. Our vacation is now an endurance test.

A fifty-mile day in the Boundary Waters is considered significant. Here, out of shape, doing fifty-plus miles a day is crazy. Sure there is current, but it is not substantial enough to change the daily workload. Darrin is right; I am crazy to be doing this trip.

He is staring at me. He must have a pronouncement. "I've been thinking about what you said, when we'd end." His tone is ominous. "I don't want to end on the thirteenth. We'll need to layover a day or you'll need to paddle faster."

Is he serious? Does he think I don't have enough garbage messing with my mind? If I respond, we will argue. As he is standing, I stay sitting, staring at the river. Turning away he says, "I'm going to recalculate the miles."

He knows I can't paddle faster. If I had thought it was hot earlier, no more. I am steamed. "I'm going to start dinner." Immediately after dinner I head for bed to avoid further discussions.

In the morning, I head out the tent door before Darrin awakens. I don't need a thirteenth discussion to begin this day.

At the river's edge a cool breeze comforts me, stroking like soft hands. The addict in me needs this emotional, spiritual fix to begin each day. The grace from the pastoral serenity, joyful birds, and morning prayers help me to ward off some of the daily grind and heat. What's that you say Lord? You want me to forget challenging the thirteenth! I can try.

With breakfast over, a second routine kicks in: the daily dump. My body now functions like a well oiled machine. Daily exercise is cleaning out years of accumulated waste, breaking it loose from joints and muscles, flushing it out, scrubbing arteries clean. While the body sleeps, the accumulation is compacted and made ready. The release is refreshing and constantly reminds me of two Outward Bound experiences.

The first involved a person who had never been camping. Everything was new, up close and personal, especially relieving herself in the bush. One morning she reentered camp exhilarated, "This is so great." Her face danced with delight. "I love it, but I'm wondering what's going to happen when I return to New York and get the urge to use Central Park?" No one had a comeback. I finally understand her feelings.

The second experience was not so great. It involved a brigade member who wouldn't eat fruit, dried or fresh. After several days with no bowel movement, her pain made evacuation to the nearest hospital a necessity.

We have been on the river for about three hours now and are approaching the Greenville City Park, Greenville, Arkansas. A tall, smiling ranger is coming down to greet us. "Hi, I'm Lonnie. Isn't this a marvelous day?"

"It is now!" I respond. His attitude, warm handshake, and genuine caring are infectious. He loves working here and treats the park and his work as a personal gift from God.

"Let me introduce you to the other rangers. I'll see if you can use the showers." "Free" is what he means. At the ranger station, the others are as friendly and gracious as Lonnie. They talk about "their" park, the one they keep immaculate.

"Hey, you guys missed being on TV."

"Really?"

"Yeah, the local station comes down on the Fourth to interview boaters." He is making the point because I just told them about the endowment campaign.

As the rangers and we explore a variety of topics, one in his late thirties says, "I admire a father/son team taking on the Mississippi. I'd do something like that with my son but we'd just argue." Darrin and I sit up, reticent to respond. The rangers notice our sheepishness and wait.

"Our trip isn't always a bed of roses. We have our share of arguments. I usually explain our differences this way. 'When one of us wants to go east, the other insists on west, even though we're headed south.'" Their laughter and appreciation of our ability to admit failings helps break the ice more.

"Try a short trip first," Darrin advises.

After relaxing for some time, we head for the pay phones. Neither wife is home. Messages will ease their worries that we have abandoned them or each other. Next we shower and shave.

"You use any hot water?"

"No."

"Me neither."

After returning to the river, we make good time in the main channel. There are fewer barges. The terminals must be busy loading and unloading. So far we have been able to stave off temptations to use wing dams.

After several more hours of canoeing, we encounter a two-mile stretch of sand. "Want to call it a day?" Darrin asks. He doesn't have to ask twice. Soon the water is boiling and beef stroganoff with mushrooms is ready. Hillshire Farms' no refrigeration beef is added to make it a tasty delight.

"What kind of havoc do you suppose the preservatives play with our innards?" I comment.

"Don't ask! Just enjoy." He turns back to eating and watching the river. I am still astounded by the beauty and power of the lower Miss. I try to imagine it twenty feet higher and a mile wider, as it is during flooding. It must have a tremendous speed then. I like this lower, narrower current. Darrin and I both believe we are experiencing near perfect water levels.

After a restful night, the harbinger of another hot day confronts us: thick fog. I have never experienced so much fog in such hot weather. With the water temperature approaching the nineties and scum lines on every shore, the river feels and looks like reheated, twice-used, winter bath water. Yet, in relationship to the air, it is cool. Right now the air is not stirring and water is running down my face and arms. It is not sweat. As I move about, I am collecting moisture from the air. My clothing is soaked from fifteen minutes of preparing breakfast. It is what I had imagine walking through a rain cloud might be like. The humidity also makes breathing harder.

The heat and humidity have actually made this beautiful campsite unbearable. Even when the fog burns off, the heat of the day will create volumes of humidity. I will be wet all day again as the baking sun won't dry me off fast enough. It may not be raining, but the humidity is 100 percent. Even lying naked on my sleeping bag last night did not help. I collected water at a constant rate, like heavy sweating. My bag clung to me. Every time I rolled over, I felt like a stick 'em label or peeled fruit rollup.

There is a real oddity to my frustration. The days are glorious because of the birds, greenery, and people! No matter where we go, people are great. Every day someone gives us a kindness or generosity that seems to make the entire trip worthwhile. And the lush green floodplains are always uplifting.

After getting on the river, we begin encountering many licensed line fishermen bringing in their morning catch. They each stop us, wanting to talk. As New Orleans is now a higher priority, our conversations are short. Our facial expressions and body gestures encourage people to let us move on, even though they have more questions. We are both losing a precious gift: a better sense of people's zest for life. The present pace means missed opportunities, but there is no stopping us now!

The camping and canoeing are a military campaign; we wish to return to normal life. Our daydreams are now the drug of choice. We constantly talk of cold sodas, dishes of ice cream, café au'lait, cool showers, clean sheets, and dry clothing. We dream of pontoons as the better way to ride the river. Not only would we have more time to visit, we could carry enough water and food for several days.

It is still amazing to watch people's jaws literally drop after meeting us. We are an odd couple: an old, bald-headed guy and his tall, physically fit son, enjoying daily canoeing and camping on the Mississippi. Most seem to feel we are from a mythical place, like Lake Woebegone. Some ask about Minnesota as though it were a foreign country. Not one person we have met camping, fishing, or leisure boating in these southern states has ever visited Minnesota. Some can't imagine the cold we endure, as though it were the North Pole. Others believe our northernmost lakes are frozen year around.

The small business entrepreneurs along the river are the most interested in worlds outside of their own. They are the quickest to invite us into their lives and inquire about our world, a place they have yet to visit. Their depth of yearning gives us a strong desire for staying longer and learning more about why the river holds them so fast.

We are now about seventy miles north of Vicksburg and in need of food, water, and medicine. This morning Darrin looked at my left eye. He said it was okay, but I know something is seriously wrong. I have felt it before. I even had some pus and matter crusted in the corners this morning. The pain grows worse with each passing hour. I carry a prescription. Little good it does out here.

This virus has flared up three times before. When not treated, cornea scarring begins quickly. How much damage will occur in the next twenty-four hours? The shooting pains grow more intense with each passing hour.

At age four the only eye doctor in town struggled to cure what he called an eye ulcer. When a new eye doctor came to town, my parents took me to him. He had the infection under control and latent within two weeks. The first eye doctor turned out to be an alcoholic.

It flared up again in my thirties after a work-related accident, but was under control within a day. Sixteen years later, while on a business trip to Brownsville, Texas, it returned. I was traveling by car with a missionary who had spent twenty years in South America. As he was hacking most of the time, I asked him, "Bill, are you sick?"

"Nah... fourteen years ago I acquired this weird cough in Venezuela. Doctors can't find anything wrong." By the time we hit Brownsville, I was sick. I thought it psychosomatic and spent the next five days working, figuring to rest on Padre Island after the assignment. The recuperation was slow. The stress reactivated the virus.

Upon returning to Crookston, I went to the only eye doctor in town and explained the virus. He prescribed a medication. Worse the next day, I went back. He got angry. "Why the hell didn't you tell me about your history? I'd have taken care of it." The more he talked the more belligerent he became. He reminded me of drug users in my support groups. He kept saying he would claim no responsibility for his actions. I walked out in the middle of his yelling and went directly to an eye clinic in Grand Forks, to a doctor with his head screwed on straight.

So here I am, ten years later, paddling toward Vicksburg, faced with another flare up. No doubt the constant physical stress, the grime, the sweat, and sun block trickling into my eye have all done their best to reignite the problem.

In spite of this knowledge, the heat and humidity are worse than my eye problem. It weights oppressively, causing us to feel as though we are wearing wrist weights while paddling. The day is a burden, a test. The breaking point is not far away. Did Job feel this bad when the devil inflicted his many tests? Surely Tennessee Williams felt some of this kind of "heat pain" to have written his celebrated, *Cat on a Hot Tin Roof.*

Camped now, lying perfectly still, tent flaps wide open, the sweat pours off. I chose this tent because the entire front and rear have screened windows, the ultimate tent for catching a breeze. Little good it does when there is no wind. The sleeping bags are near worthless. Wet when unrolled and getting wetter.

The pleasantry of camping on sand beaches is now outweighed by the humidity and sand in our tent, sleeping bags, clothing, pots and pans, and food. It sticks to clothing and body even when brushed off. It is impossible to shake. The moisture holds the fine sand in the clothing's weave and the body's pores. The ensuing clay clogs all bodily cooling vents. The evening's heat continues to deteriorate my mind. I must think happy thoughts.

The day's current was great: consistent and easily accessible. We paddled sixty miles. Tomorrow Vicksburg will be ours by mid-morning. Darrin wanted to push farther today, but the heat was too much for me. I smile. He must appreciate his built-in excuse for not having to work too hard. Four breaks today: mid-morning, noon, mid-afternoon, and late mid-afternoon. To bolster my rest requests,

I reminded him, "We didn't set out to prove our manhood. We've already accomplished that. This is supposed to be a relaxing trek down the Mississippi."

A light snack accompanied each break, mostly to replace lost salts. The heat and humidity also mean no more sodas, beer, or coffee. They all feel good going down but sap the body's endurance. The quick rush is followed by sweat oozing out as sugar and caffeine burn off. The pause that refreshes is not worth the after-burn.

Most of the day lent itself to daydreaming. Peering down the river to the next bend, three to four miles away, gave way to imagining crossing Lake Superior. That would be an easy jaunt. Its width along the north shore can't be more than twenty to thirty miles: a day's paddle in coolness.

Ah, northern Minnesota with its extended summer daylight hours and cool evenings. Daylight is noticeably shorter on the lower Miss, so is our workday. We turn in early to avoid mosquitoes. If they don't zap us the barge operators do.

Right now one is doing so. His spotlight must be two to three thousand lumens. The way he moves it around our camp, slowly searching every corner, silently zeroing in on packs and the tent door, leaves the impression our privacy is being invaded. Perhaps we are an evening distraction from the river's routine. We know they are not searching for channel markers; there are none on shore. Maybe he is hoping for a peepshow. Perhaps he is inventorying our supplies. Could life on the river be so dull?

$356 AN OUNCE

"Expect a high of one hundred and three, breezes and scattered thunderstorms out of the southwest...the present temperature is seventy." Darrin turns off the marine radio and sits up. "I was thinking about what you said."

"What'd I say?"

"You know...about your eye...what caused the flare up."

"Okay, I'll bite." I can hear playfulness in his voice.

"Well, you said it was physical exertion…that doesn't make sense."

"Really!"

Now the twinkle comes, "Yeah, you haven't worked that hard."

"Thanks for your sympathy."

He smiles appreciatively and gets serious. "You're right, though. The sunscreen and sweat seem toxic. Are you ready to get up?"

"Yup." A distant rumbling brings immediate notice of the promised scattered thunderstorms. We will need to track its movements. The rumble is different here. Minnesota's is milder and more continuous. "Let's pack and head for Vicksburg. There's no protection here."

Darrin agrees and the three hours to Vicksburg go quickly. By 11 AM we have found a drugstore. I feel fortunate. They close at noon.

"Sorry, we're out of that medication. You want me to call around?" The sympathetic druggist can see my problem. He calls a store four blocks east. "They've got it."

By the time we arrive, the medication is ready. The druggist holds it close to his chest. "That'll be eighty-nine dollars."

I hand him my Blue Cross card. "I have co-pay."

He shakes his head. "Sorry, you didn't go to the emergency room." My questioning look brings a quick response. "If you go to the emergency room, co-pay will cover."

"Really?"

"Yeah. Your insurance only covers prescriptions from a recent visit. This prescription is over six years old."

I pause and consider my choices: go to the emergency room (a couple hundred dollars for the insurance company) and pay fifteen dollars, or pay eighty-nine dollars now. "Forget it. Here's my credit card."

I sign off as he says, "You'll need to take it for at least a week. Did you say you're on the river?"

"Yes."

"This medication needs refrigeration. It'll go bad quickly in this heat." Another twist!

We stop at the nearest grocery store. "We don't carry block ice. Don't know anybody that does." After purchasing a couple bags of cubes and a cheap Styrofoam cooler, we call a taxi.

While packing the ice Darrin asks, "How long will it last?"

I shrug my shoulders and place the quarter ounce bottle, sealed in a plastic pouch, atop the ice. "A day, day and a half." I look up to see him grinning. The irony of a two-by-three-foot ice chest to carry a quarter-ounce bottle is not lost.

The day turns hotter and more humid than predicted. The good news, even though Vicksburg slowed us down and the heat is messing with our minds, Darrin is patient. Today he saw the red lightning rods emanating from the center of my eye and heard the druggist's concern.

The trip's length and summer heat back home must also be affecting Schalleen. When I talked to Jacqui, she told me Shalleen is not planning to fly down and celebrate our arrival. As Jacqui is uncomfortable coming alone, our dream of a flag waving, band playing, tickertape parade will not be.

It is 5 AM. Last night we pitched the tent adjacent to a natural, high water shoreline, a quarter mile from the river. Here the trees grow tall and willowy. Nearer the river we would have been the highest point during the lightning storm.

Even though the scattered thunderstorms missed us, it rained inside the tent. Caught in the middle of the storm's muggy periphery, the fog drifted through the screens all night. Trying to escape through the tent's waterproof fabric, the fog shifted into droplets that slid down the ceiling, cheerfully joining others. This is the fifth time I have been awakened by water splashing on my mouth and cheeks. It does no good to sleep on my stomach, I always roll over. Moments earlier I was dreaming of lying on my back in the grass, arms outstretched, as a warm summer rain fell softly on my body. It was pleasant.

Now fully awake, it isn't. Shadowy, early lights glisten on droplets racing each other down the tent ceiling. Happily conjoining with others, they rocket off when full. Their willful pleasure is both fascinating and frustrating. Pools of water have gathered in the tent's corners. Not only is my body wet, the bottom of my sleeping bag is soaked.

As Darrin, too, cannot sleep, he turns on the marine radio. "Hey, listen to this." He turns it up. A cheery voice predicts "…scattered thunderstorms throughout the day and early evening."

"You ever hear anyone so happy to be predicting thunderstorms?" He laughs.

I shake my head and open the ice chest. "We lost half the ice." Since less than twenty hours have passed, we will be looking for more.

This is the fourth straight morning a cloud cover has enveloped us. Today's thickness deadens sounds and allows only a few feet of sight. "I'd always imagined the cloud separating Moses from his enemies to be like this," I tell Darrin.

With a bit of sarcasm and twisted irony, he retorts, "Fortunately, we don't have any enemy pursuing us."

The wet sleeping bag and dripping tent are too much. "Let's push off and eat later." Darrin agrees.

The sensation is weird. The fog is lapping up river water like a thirsty dog. Hovering inches over the surface, it is visibly thickening. Not only is the cloud sucking up moisture, humidity is rising from the shore's greenery and sands. We are getting wetter.

As the fog makes it impossible to see barges, we stay close to shore. Barges coming downstream are like Stephen King's *It*. Suddenly they appear, without a sound. One moment they aren't; the next moment we see a mass of steel plowing away the fog. The downstream tows are silent and deadly. Slow travel requires little need for engine power. We are constantly looking over our shoulder.

Even on a nice day, with a full sun, when we have been lollygagging along, the shrill whistle from a rapidly approaching barge awakens every nerve. A lumbering mass of steel bearing down is scary. Although wanting to make headway before the heat hits, we go slowly. We have no desire to be steamrolled into the depths of the Miss' belly. Right now I see only a silhouette of Darrin as he sits in the bow. But hey, who cares, we are headed for Natchez.

Ah, Natchez! I love that name. It has got a ring to it. Distant towns with interesting names make them sound like legends. In Minnesota, Twin City folk speak in hushed tones of Greenbush and Warroad's macho hockey players. Claims are made these hockey stars come from crossing strong Norwegian women with powerful German mine workers.

The parents from these northern towns work their fingers to the bone so their sons and daughters can practice bone-crushing checks. It is claimed that a child's first set of shoes in Warroad are hockey skates, bronzed for bragging rights. Those worn thinnest from ankle bends and crawling on the ice are coveted.

But Natchez is truly legendary! It conjures up a more civilized game. Here parents put chips and cards in their children's hands, teaching them to stay away from the dead man's hand: aces and eights. A child's first math lesson uses Texas Hold 'em and Five Card Draw. The children are taught never to draw to an inside straight, but always to count their chips while sittin' at the table.

Ah, Yes! Why wasn't I born in the South? I never could skate worth a darn. My only claim to skating fame was going through thin ice on a cold New Year's Day. My best friend Danny lay down on the thin ice and grabbed my hand as I was about to go under. I could have been frozen clear through like Sam McGee from Tennessee. Instead, here I am, dripping sweat.

After arriving in Natchez, my first order of business is to call Jacqui. While talking I ask about Pete. "He's planning to arrive in New Orleans the day before you," she says. My brother Pete promised to drive from Denver to meet us. "He'll be at the Café de Monde at 1 PM." Pete's the second oldest of my seven brothers. Now retired, he is doing his first love: carving and painting. He has always been generous and self-giving. I am thankful! "He wants to know how you can be so sure you'll be there at one."

"Tell him to spend forty days doing the same thing, day in and day out, and he will have a fair idea of what to expect the next." As there is little room in Pete's compact truck for three adult men, Darrin has decided to fly home. That's best! His young bride is anxiously waiting, and his long separation has caused a burning desire. I can't blame him. We have had more than our share of disagreements. I tell him it is good training for married life. He doesn't appreciate the humor. I'll give him a couple years.

"Pete's okay with staying in New Orleans a day or two." Something in Jacqui's voice leaves me feeling there is skepticism on Pete's part. He may be coming to verify my canoeing claim.

After hanging up, I survey Natchez's waterfront. What is left of it: a cement parking lot for maybe twenty cars, a couple docks, a boat launching ramp, and the backside of a few decaying buildings. Is this all that is left from the glory days of steamboats? As I will never get into Natchez proper today, I may never know.

A short distance away is the Capri gambling boat. The security is most inhospitable. In truth they are the only casino security people who have not been friendly. Maybe it is the heat. Maybe it is the way they were trained. Management's attitude has such a major impact on worker bees.

Perhaps our appearance looks like the criminal element they have been trained to detect. No doubt we look the part of Big Jim Gerty's band of cutthroats who once inhabited the caves under the bluffs of Natchez. But that shouldn't make a difference. Annie Christmas cleaned out those ruffians a long time ago. Maybe it is because we are not as neat and crisp-looking as the rest of the Capri's patrons.

At the casino bar I ask a waitress, "What do you think it is: the heat or losing at gambling?"

"Sorry, I don't know what you're talking about."

"This is the first casino we've been to where no one has taken an interest in two river rats. Are we that out of place?" She smiles as though to say, "The sooner you boys get on your way, the better off Natchez will be."

My eye is definitely getting better. As we leave the casino I ask Darrin, "Do you suppose the free ice was just to get us out faster?"

Darrin hesitates but finally says, "Do you expect me to answer a rhetorical question?"

These little social challenges make me yearn for Jacqui's love, the stability of a home and office, daily Mass and parishioners. Darrin and I now begin another discussion on relationships. The marriage image continues to seem appropriate. We have gone beyond each other's shortcomings and are working with each other's strengths and abilities.

Much later, again settled in at an evening campsite and low on emotional and physical energy, we are grateful for the morning talk. We now believe our low emotional energy may be due to the dirty river water. It smells more acrid and rotting the farther south of Vicksburg we move. It is now quite pungent, a prime motivator for quickly ending the trip. If river water splashes on my body, particularly my face, I immediately wipe it off. If it hits my lips, I spit and rinse with drinking water. More than once today we mused, "Whadda yah suppose this is doing to our immune system?"

THE COVE

I wake up to Darrin's chuckle. "Okay, what gives?"

"Come over here," he motions me to the tent door. "See the top of that wall?" Over the tops of some trees, a distance away, is what appears to be a cement wall.

"Yes!"

"That's the Angola Prison."

"You knew we were in the backyard of the Angola Prison and didn't bother to tell me?" His smile does not abate. "Maybe that's why you were so remorseful last night." Actually, I am thankful for the heart-to-heart talk we had. Once again, as we near the end, we are emphasizing the importance of our friendship being intact when we finish the trip. The heat of any given moment does not always recognize our love for each other. It is rather humbling to seek forgiveness so often for the same sin, against the same person.

Before shoving off near the Angola prison, we agree not to pick up any river hitchhikers or talk to strangers coming to the river's edge. The morning paddle begins by just getting on the river and allowing a gentle float. We would like to get a better look at the prison. Unfortunately we cannot see too much of it from the river, just a bit of a wall.

It is nearing mid-morning. We are pulling ashore to wait out a heavy downpour rolling in from the southwest. After we unload and place the canoe over the gear, the downpour begins in earnest. We stand in it, once again acting like five year olds, whipping off soaked t-shirts and using them as washrags. The clouds are heavy with water and the downpour is cool. Back home the temperature of this rain would be considered tepid and a humidity raiser. Here it is cool and refreshing.

Darrin must think me crazy for wanting to squish my toes in the mud and the sand so often. He has watched me do it every day. It is an aspect I never tire of. As this major storm beats upon my body with large, cooling drops, it is also massages aching muscles. Best of all, there is no loving wife to ask, "What do you suppose the parishioners would think?" At this moment I could care less. My childhood freedom is re-birthed.

We have spent forty-some days playing in the water, sand, and mud. Although tired of it, I wouldn't miss this moment. Not since childhood have I been so shoeless and free to stomp in mud puddles and rushing streams. No one is yelling to come in out of the rain.

When the rain stops and the clouds pass, the brilliant blue sky again allows the sun to cook the earth and give muscle to humidity. It is suffocating. It changes our paddling pace to slow. Adequate oxygen only comes with heavy breathing. This must be what fish feel like when out of water.

A few hours after getting back on the river, two guys wave us over to their fishing hole. After grabbing their Johnboat we hear the usual, "You guys want a beer?" Darrin rolls the cool one over his forehead, going for double pleasure. Even though I do not drink beer, my mouth waters for its coolness.

These guys are in their early twenties, enjoying quiet fishing on a hot summer's day. Actually their main activity is not fishing, it is lounging. Fishing was never really the name of their game. The river is just a pleasant way to relax. As the heat has caused our ice to deteriorate more rapidly than yesterday, they offer to refill it. They have only two beers left. We thank them and push off.

As evening approaches, a great camping spot appears where the current is rushing headlong past a sandy, shady, circular cove. The walls were carved during high water times. We will need to turn ninety-degrees and allow the swirling water near the shore to hit us broadside. The resulting 180 will slide us up against the shore. It always feels good to accept a water challenge and reach a treasured spot. This is such a moment.

It is quiet, peaceful, and cool in the hollowed out cove. High, black, earthen walls soundproof it. Life continues on around us, but we can barely hear water and bird sounds. It is a new camping experience. The sandy floor, perfectly flat and circular, also helps deaden the sounds. The distance from the shore to the back of the cove is about twenty-five yards. The high, straight-up walls tower some thirty feet. Atop are mature trees standing guard, shoulder to shoulder, encircling the rim of the upper embankment. Their height and shade only add to the seclusion. A claustrophobic person might feel a bit cramped here.

As I prepare dinner, Darrin lies down to read. This will be our first meal cooked on coals. We ran out of gas even though we have searched every town since Caruthersville. The positive side is that meal preparations are now more leisurely. Waiting for the wood to burn down allows me to turn to journaling.

Out of the corner of my eye I believe I see movement. Because of nature's soundproofing, I heard nothing and am unsure. Still I have this nagging feeling something is moving up behind me. As Darrin is not moving, I dismiss it as imagination. No, wait! I hear it, a faint rustling. It is moving closer. Whatever it is, it must be fairly large.

Wanting neither to scare it nor to be attacked, my senses go on full alert. It is approaching behind and to my left. I judge it to be about fifteen feet away, moving slowly and methodically, as though stalking. Survival instincts kick in. I cannot recall any logs or hiding places in the cove. Upon landing I surveyed the campsite like an old gunfighter not wanting to be caught off guard.

Slowly I turn my head and come face to face with it. Immediately it stops dead, ears and nose perk up. We stare at each other. I want to call out to Darrin, but I know it will run. I have never been this close to a huge beaver. We have a stare down.

Finally I can stand it no longer and whisper, "Darrin." He looks up. Although the beaver is halfway to the water's edge, Darrin's sudden movement scares it. It turns and goes lumbering back to a den located in the side of the cove's black earth, about ten feet off the floor. A hillside ramp leads from the sandy bottom to the den opening. Both the pathway and dark opening blend into the rich, dark earth. The late afternoon shade provides additional camouflage.

In high water his entrance would be well below the surface—a perfect spot for such a magnificent swimmer to enter the current and begin fishing or seeking vegetation. In this low water, when vegetation abounds everywhere along the riverbanks, he must first travel by land.

"Stay alert. He'll be back. He hesitated long enough before entering the den that it is obvious he wants to get to the water." Darrin nods. We adjust our sitting positions to prevent any movement once he returns.

Sure enough, within five minutes, he wants out again. He pokes his head out of the cliff and stares at us, sniffing the air. He is almost comical, feigning nonchalance. Soon he is waddling down the runway to freedom. He might lumber on land, but in the water he is smooth as silk.

Now about ten feet away, he pauses to look at us with some curious discernment. He seems larger this time and far less fearful. His movements are almost regal, with the ease of someone poised and confident. As we sit nearly atop his normal path to the water's edge, he is not going to skirt us by much. The force of old habits is strong. Perhaps our position has baffled or upset his routine. Maybe he now realizes we are going to be sharing this space for the night.

At the water's edge he stops and turns, intentionally looking us over more carefully. He must feel safe knowing the intruders can't get him. His posture almost shouts, "You boys should excuse yourselves now and be moving on." Of course he can look at us with disdain; he is safe. Still, he refuses to take his eyes off us as he steps into the water. His body is so big and round that when his head moves sideways he appears to be a bobble-head toy. It is a personal moment in history for him and us. Our two sides have reached a truce; we will share the area. Once gone, Darrin and I chatter like young school girls thrilled by a new band.

As dusk begins, thousands of cicadas unleash a deafening peal from the trees overhead. It is far too thunderous for the earthen walls to absorb. Our quiet womb has erupted into the full battle cry of an invading insect population, advancing, intent on bringing us to our knees. Sleep will be impossible. As the roar grows, it is as though they are teetering on the edges of the surrounding cliff, leaning over to give full effect. Their sounds are ten times louder than spectators screaming in an echoing gym during the final seconds of a basketball, sudden-death overtime.

But that is not our greatest concern, dinner is. Will we get a chance to eat before the mosquitoes descend? The cool darkness will encourage their voracious appetites. This cove will fill with a frenzied buzzing, anticipation of fresh blood. Supper is eaten quickly because the setting sun is causing a hasty tent retreat. Again we try to cool off by lying naked atop wet sleeping bags.

A GAME OF CHICKEN

Today, Baton Rouge! Less than 200 miles left. The mosquitoes did come out in force last night, competing with the cicadas, trying to drown them out. Now sitting next to the shore, enjoying a cup of breakfast tea in near peace and quiet, the few mosquitoes that failed to retreat from the coming heat are competing to see who can draw the most blood from me. The ensuing game has left bloody splotches on my arms and face. Darrin says it looks like chickenpox.

He is packed and waiting to leave. It used to be me who packed first. It is not fatigue or laziness. I just want to linger, tarry longer. My carefree days are coming to an end. Although Darrin can also sense it, he is anxious to move on to the next step in his life. I am grateful to have a son who cared enough to make an old man's dream come true. The swift current beckons us. Hopefully it will hold up all day.

As noon approaches, the cooler's ice is nearly gone. My eye is healing rapidly, but the infection will come back without continued medication. It must be made dormant and kept that way for several days. We are approaching the Morganza Silo area and the St. Francisville Ferry landing. There must be ice on a ferry. "Let's pull in on the west bank," I suggest. "It looks more inviting for lunch and a visit to the ferry."

When the ferry arrives and begins docking, I set down lunch and head over. The cars begin unloading immediately. I am up the ferry's ramp before the last one rolls off. A wheelhouse worker is coming out. His facial expression shows skepticism.

"Hi, I'm Gary. My son and I are canoeing the Mississippi and carrying medication that needs refrigeration." His eyes seem to say, "Then why yah so dumb to be on the river on such a hot day?" I explain my predicament further.

"Wait here." He goes to speak with someone in the wheelhouse. They huddle in air-conditioned comfort. I can see them gesticulating through the door's window. My gut level says they think I am playing a con game. I have seen that look before. He returns.

"Sorry, we can't help. Got no extra ice. The state won't provide it. We buy our own."

"Thanks! I appreciate your asking." I turn and walk away, dejected. I believe my appearance has affected their decision. Trying to persuade them would be fruitless; they have a schedule to keep. I also know from door-to-door sales, if I truly believe in what I am asking for, I will get it by asking enough people. I have plenty of motivation. I won't quit. Silently I pray for guidance. My facial hair, my stench, my dirty clothes and general unkemptness will not help. I will ask drivers waiting for the ferry's return. Someone will believe me.

Actually someone does. As the rejection left me feeling abandoned, my return walk down the ferry's ramp may have seemed like a condemned sailor walking the gangplank. Perhaps I am subconsciously putting on a poor-me act. "Hey, man, wait a minute. I'll give you some ice." I turn and look at the ferryman. "Hurry, I only got a couple minutes. I'll throw it in a plastic bag." He hurries into the wheelhouse.

I am not sure what changed his mind, but I am grateful. I know God has given me a quick answer. As I head back up, his partner rejoins him just inside the doorway. I can't hear them but I can see their conversation is animated. My new friend steps out the door and hands me a bag. His buddy turns his back on me. I reach for my billfold. "Can I pay you?"

"No, sir, it's yours. You need it."

"Thanks!" is all I can say. Humans! Don't you just love them? To the employee on the ferry that tenth day of July, 2002, thank you! You are my hero.

Since the ferry, we have been paddling straight through. It is 4:30. Baton Rouge appears on the eastern shore. Boat traffic is heavy. To avoid it, we are passing about ten feet out from a fleet of docked barges. Each section of parked barges is seven wide and fifteen long. We spot a downriver casino. A hotel can't be far away. "What say we celebrate your birthday with a hotel room?" I ask.

Darrin wheels around, "You serious?"

"Yes."

"Let's do it."

There are twenty-yard openings between each set of parked barges. According to the map, a towboat re-fueling station is between us and the casino. A towboat is now seen pulling out from behind the parked barges, probably coming from that re-fueling station. Unfortunately it appears the captain wants to move up alongside the parked barges.

"Do you think he sees us?"

"I'm not sure. Let's stop and see if he's going to pull out."

"I don't think we should. He's headed straight up." Darrin's right. Quickly we dig in left and turn toward the middle of the river. Twenty yards later I look over my shoulder, "He's turned and headed our way. He wants the main channel." Because this is a collision course, we immediately turn and head back toward the parked barges. Once turned, the captain turns again.

"If he's planning to run us over, we're trapped!" Darrin shouts.

Darrin is right. The towboat operator has trapped us, boxed us in! The parked barge openings are behind him and behind us. The one behind us is too far back to attempt. This is crazy. He knows we are here. If he wants to play chicken, we are outgunned.

Not since the last Eckstein boat has anyone been so brazen. Even though we are quite capable of maneuvering our twenty-foot canoe, we are just too tired and emotionally spent for this kind of foolishness. As we do not want to face him in deeper waters, we stop and allow him to come dead on.

"We won't have much time. Don't panic. Just do as I ask!" It is a command. "We'll turn at the last minute. Paddle hard backward on your right when I yell." I can hear pleading in my voice. Darrin knows I am scared and says nothing, nodding assent. "We can't paddle too soon," I add. Again he nods. We both realize we are sitting ducks.

This time, however, because of previous dangers and near catastrophes, we are as prepared as we will ever be. Darrin's anxiety is beginning to show in body posture and agitated movements. He keeps re-positioning himself.

Neither of us wants to be pinned against the docked barges when the backwash hits. We are about fifteen feet out from them, dead in the water. Only the current moves us. The towboat operator is moving in at full throttle, picking up speed, coming head on, literally face-to-face. I do not understand his thinking. He can't be dumb enough to run us over. It would be premeditated murder. He must have something else in mind.

It was obvious we tried to avoid him, we flinched first. We know we don't stand a chance. My mind is running a hundred different scenarios. Has he been drinking? Is anyone dumb enough to deliberately hit us?

He is now twenty feet away, bearing down at top speed. I still can't believe he'll run us over. Suddenly, at the last possible moment, within ten feet of our bow, he turns to parallel us. Our anger and anxiety are full blown. I cannot even imagine the fear that must be going though Darrin's mind as he sits face to face with a thousand tons of steel, nearly twenty feet closer than me. His adrenalin must really be pumping. We will need it.

"When are you going to turn? We'll get sucked under!" he shouts.

"Patience. He must believe we won't react." Why is the towboat captain so bent on being this close? It doesn't make sense. Darrin is right. In a moment we will be pulled under by his draft. What am I not seeing? He really can't believe his wake will capsize us. There has got to be more to it. He has to know his present speed and position will pull us under, into his prop. He is so much closer then I believed he would dare come. I was counting on more room. His bow now parallels ours, five feet away. Its bluntness is enormous. In a moment we are going down.

"Now! Now!" I shout.

At the very moment we begin our turn, the towboat captain shuts down both engines. His strategy is out. He wants to catch us in the wake coming off his stern, created by his sudden stop. He maneuvered well. The effect is a huge wake now rushing up the side of his boat, even rolling over his rear deck. If we continue our turn, we will be both broad sided and hit by recoiling waves off the parked barges. He is planning on rough waters taking us down. But what happens if he throttles back up, riling the waters a third time?

"Darrin, continue back paddling hard!" I am thankful for his strength. I hit forward just as hard. It is Winni all over, but only for a moment. We are going to be caught between two sets of waves. We will be bounced back and forth as if on a Colorado rapids. To keep from capsizing, the canoe must not take on more than a small amount of water.

The first set of waves rushes up our bow. By stopping our turn, we slowed the broadside hit but not the rising, curling wave. It is seemingly in slow motion as it rise up and over the bow. Ever upwardly and along our gunwales it rolls, spilling over at will just aft of Darrin. The power and sheer size of his boat has generated some awesome rapids. Our movements are now those of navigating rapids, but from a standstill position. In these first few seconds we take on nearly three inches of water. We will be lucky to prevent a capsizing.

For a split second we are safe. I look up to the wheelhouse. The captain's face is pressed against the window, peering down, contorted and laughing, pointing with what appears to be a can of beer in his hand. In the moment our eyes meet, he senses we may not capsize. I am straining to identify him.

Once, in my child rearing years, I discovered a window-peeker outside my daughter's window. I remember how the police questioned me. "How could you be so sure it was him? You only got a glimpse."

"No" I shot back, "I got a good look!"

"How could that be?" They were skeptical. People normally panic and scare an intruder off before getting a good look. I told them how I had watched him for over a minute, motioning my wife to come over and help identify him. The man was a major mover and shaker in the community. I didn't want to be alone in identifying him. Also, he was wearing a beard. I wanted to be positive. Jacqui whispered who she thought it was. Once agreed, I yanked open the patio door and watched horror come over his face as I called out his name. They questioned me no further but went to arrest him.

Again I want to remain calm if I can. I want to be able to identify this maniac. I now see the same horror in his eyes that I saw in the window peeker's. The barge captain's laughter has turned to terror. He realizes I am trying to identify him. He hits full throttle and turns away. As he does so I realize I am so badly shaken I have failed to note his boat's name. However, that shouldn't be too hard for the Coast Guard. He just left the first refueling station upstream from the casino. It is 4:30 in the afternoon.

His original waves are now bouncing off the parked barges and hitting us from all sides. More water comes in, but still not enough to swamp us. We are barely afloat and there is more to come. "Hard forward!" I yell. We head directly into the rapids created by his sudden hurry to leave. The rebounding waves picking up speed in the artificial rapids are actually helping propel us into calmer waters just as the wing dam's whirlpool did when it spit us out. We have taken on over four inches of water. The canoe is nearly full. If we don't work on staying stable, we will capsize.

Badly shaken and angry, adrenalin will not allow me to remain calm. We and the bags are floating. "We've got to pull over and unload before everything gets soaked," I say.

We say nothing more, simply going through the motions of docking, thankful to be alive and with all of our gear. However, I am once again trying to slow a speeding heart. I had hoped the trip's physical challenges would add years, not take them away.

After emptying the water, we paddle to the casino. Its shoreline is comprised of silky mud, the consistency of my mother's chocolate pies. We slide onto it and are held in place. Neither of us wants to get out. I stare mindlessly at the dirt on my arms. It intrigues me. I run a fingernail through the black, greasy substance. It is thick and stains like heavy weight oil.

"Darrin, I don't care what it costs; we're staying at a good hotel. Our lives are just too damn fragile on this river. We must get as far away as possible." He nods. His exhaustion is showing in slumped shoulders.

Eventually we step onto Baton Rouge. Darrin volunteers to stay with the canoe. The nearest good hotel is the Sheraton connected with the casino. I arrange for the hotel's van to pick us up. They will park atop the dike. I have just enough time to return and help unpack the canoe before stowing it.

The casino security is friendly and happy to allow us to store our canoe under their dock. Even before the van arrives, Darrin and I are feeling sorry for the mess we will leave in the hotel room. We and our equipment are just plain filthy. Ringlets of sand and mud slough off the packs when we set them down. As my clothes are dirtier than me, there will again be no need to undress for showering.

After two hours of clean up, we push open the Casino's front doors, heading for a quick meal.

Quick it will be. The smoke can be cut with the proverbial knife. If I die of lung cancer, this place can be named in the lawsuit. The slick and sticky carpeting reminds me of walking across a tar pit. With each lifting of my foot, there is a momentary sucking sound. Although we order what sounds like great food, we lose our appetites.

Back at the hotel, we shower again.

THE ALEXANDER

Even though we turned off the A/C during the night, our clothing stayed damp and cool. Normally this would feel good, but not after sleeping in a Deepfreeze. Everything is so relative. Cold? Was it really cold last night? After a few weeks of ninety-plus degrees and humidity, it seemed so. Before we can finish breakfast we are told, "Your shuttle's here."

I head over to the reservation desk and hand the receptionist some money. "Sorry for the room. Give this to the housekeeper."

The casino's tight security kept the canoe intact. This morning, at the river's edge, I am presently glorying in my cleanliness. "This should be a relaxing fifty miles," I say. "We'll stop just north of New Orleans and arrive rested around noon. Bands will be playing, crowds will be shouting."

"Dream on."

Last night the front desk clerk gave me the name of a local TV newscaster. I spoke with him in hopes of an interview. He said he would rendezvous at seven if a camera crew were available. Now overlooking the canoe, there is no crew in sight. We will be gone in fifteen minutes.

Yesterday we found a fairly solid path where the silt had settled from the baking summer heat. With packs in tow, we carefully retrace those steps, zigzagging across the rubber-like flats. The cushion in each step is equivalent to those two-inch foam mats laid under playground's trapezes and slides. Here, however, beneath these springy footholds, is a gooey mud made up of the oiliest, grimiest compound I have ever seen. Its odor is a cross between rotting fish and moldy vegetables, topped with fertilizers and petro chemicals. Each step causes it to wiggle like Jello.

With the canoe parallel to the water and resting lightly on shore, Darrin steps in and steadies it from sliding sideways. After placing two Duluth packs in, I return to fetch the water jugs. With over forty pounds in each hand, I pick my way gingerly across the flats. One wrong step and the mud will have me. Carefully placing the first jug behind Darrin, I turn to place the second behind the middle seat. What I failed to reckon with was how the first jug's forty pounds would drop the bow lower in the water and raising the stern. As the second forty pounds comes to rest on the canoe's bottom, its momentum slides the canoe away from the slippery flat.

Off balance, I grab for a gunwale to adjust and stabilize. I do this by moving my left foot. Too late! The slide continues. My foot does not find solid ground. With a sickening thud, followed by a sucking sound, my leg is swallowed up, hip deep. My dream of traveling clean collapses.

Darrin loves it. It is one of those instances where a non-threatening accident happens in a flash. I want to swear, but it'll do no good. I could cry, but Darrin's grin and laughter is growing ever brighter, ever louder. My stance is beyond awkward. One, clean, lily-white leg is bent at the knee and lying atop the mud, the other is hip deep in slime. I can only imagine how ridiculous I look. Mother Nature and the Miss just cut my cleanliness pride a good dose of humility.

Have I learned nothing in the past forty days and nights? Holding onto the canoe, I slowly transition my stuck leg to the surface. I do not want to lose my water sock in the ooze hole. Once out and standing, I turn butt first and ease myself backward into the canoe seat. After pushing into deeper waters, one clean leg in the canoe, one dirty one dangling over the side, I begin the task of washing off the grime and stench.

From beauty queen to hobo king, it took but a moment. Trying to divert attention, I say, "I hope this isn't a prelude to the next fifty miles." As this does little to contain Darrin's laughter, I continue, "What type of toxic waste do you suppose I was exposed to?" As he won't let go of the slapstick image and laughter, I say, "All right, enough's enough!" He turns around.

We merge into the main current. It does not take long before we encounter our first boat, an older Chris Craft. It is downriver about a half mile, zigzagging from the eastern shore out into the main channel and back. As we head for the west bank, it suddenly stops zigzagging and turns. Revving up to full throttle, it heads directly toward us, as though wanting the space we occupy.

As with the towboat operator yesterday, we immediately turn and head away from the intersect point. No good. He turns again, keeping a direct heading toward the middle of the canoe. As with the barge captain, we move again, trying to evade his path. He turns, again. Out of options I say, "Let's stop!"

"What the heck is going on?" Darrin is both disgusted and disheartened.

"I wish I knew." We turn and face directly into the oncoming boat, waving our paddles and pointing with our arms, pleading with him to move further away. It doesn't faze him. He keeps coming.

I stand up and try to motion him off. Nothing! It only seems to anger him. He speeds up more, now roaring directly at our bow. I sit back down and brace for the inevitable. At the last minute he slows and abruptly turns, stopping parallel and ten feet off starboard. This sends a large wave and cuts us off from moving into shore.

There is no need to shout instructions now; we do the instinctive and ride out his wakes. The boat is the Alexander. I cannot tell if it is a reflection from the sun or if his windows are tinted. Whichever, we cannot see who is operating the boat. Moving slowly, he pulls alongside, very much like a big truck or mirrored limo pulling alongside a small car at a stoplight. We are being observed without knowing who is looking or why. Slowly and silently the boat begins moving around us. Nothing is said. We turn our heads to follow the catlike movements.

As we are at a disadvantage and the tension is getting to me, I call out a friendly, "Good morning." The lack of reply, the heat of the morning, the quiet circling; it is ominous.

After some silence, his P.A. system comes to life. From behind closed windows comes what sounds like a threat, "I'm watching you. I am going to be taking care of you today!" There is no warmth in this mixed message.

Darrin turns, "Is he threatening us?"

The operator's voice is that of an older man who seems to want us to believe that he is either threatening us or warning us of danger ahead. As we have traveled 2,400 miles and have not needed much help, why will we now? What is going to change? I decide to act as though his message is friendly. If he is hostile, I am not interested in irritating him further. "Can you come out? We'd love to meet you." That irritates him. He begins revving up and circling faster.

As we turn and follow his menacing actions, I am reminded of when I drove my father's '57 Desoto to a stoplight, looking for a drag. His bow rears up out of the water, plunging back and tightening the circle. I feel like prey that will be pounced upon at any moment. Is that what he wants? It is creepy, especially after yesterday's episode.

Darrin's expression is both fear and disbelief. Turning back to the Alexander I give a fake smile and wave. "Thanks for your concern!" To Darrin, "Let's begin paddling…slowly." Once moving, I turn us toward shore. The captain roars away, churning up a wake and forcing us into a quick maneuver. There is no good-bye, but we are glad to be rid of him.

Unfortunately he doesn't go far enough. He waits at the next bend. As we approach, he roars down to the next. Again and again this happens. This cat and mouse action goes on for nearly two hours. He always stays about a half mile ahead, never letting us out of sight, leaving us with the feeling we are being stalked. Why?

"Let's pull over and take a break…see if he leaves," I suggest.

Darrin's "Fine with me," comes as much from emotional exhaustion as anything else.

Once on shore, the Alexander moves downstream and around the next bend, out of sight. "Let's wait awhile…see if he comes back." Darrin is in agreement.

After a half hour, Darrin says, "Let's go."

As we hit mid-stream Darrin shouts, "He is roaring out from behind the bend." Before we can make shore, he reaches us and begins zigzagging both in front and behind us, seemingly intent on keeping us boxed into the main shipping channel. We should have treated him more like a wild animal and kept our backside clear by staying closer to shore.

He is pressing his luck, seeing how near the bow and stern he can pass without hitting us. He must be looking for a reaction. We are slowly moving closer and closer to shore. This is angering him and he is tightening his circle more and more by moving faster and faster. The more we edge toward shore, the more erratic he becomes. He swoops in and out, slowing our movements to a crawl.

After nearly forty-five minutes of drifting and turning, we get close enough to shore to prevent him from passing between shore and us. Quickly we paddle the last fifteen yards, floating within inches of shore. He roars off at full throttle. I believe we have not seen the last of him.

We haven't. He has turned around and returning at full throttle. His boat's draft will keep him at least fifteen yards away. He swoops in, turning suddenly to send a heavy wake our way. He does this time and time again. It is almost comical as his waves have so little effect. The shoreline here is flat. The waves just wash up without rebounding. We just sit and watch his antics. Finally, having enough of it, we head down-shore to a rocky area where we can step out without sinking in the mud. We will eat lunch and try to wait him out.

As we eat, the Chris Craft takes up a position about thirty yards out, bow pointed directly at us. "You got any idea what he is up to?" Darrin asks. Almost instantly his question is answered. The driver motors downstream about a hundred and fifty yards. After doing a u-turn, he is returning at full throttle. By the time he passes us he will be doing top speed and running as close to shore as possible.

We are so busy watching him, we have forgotten our canoe. It is half on the rocks and half in the water. His waves quickly send our light canoe bouncing and scraping against the cement pieces lain to prevent erosion. We are up and running for our lifeline. Quickly we snatch our canoe out of the water, but not before the damage is done. There are new gouges.

That's enough. Retrieving our food bags, we get back on the water. There are some tall pilings and catwalk a couple blocks down-river, probably part of a docking site. We will park behind them, where his waves can do no harm.

Our move incenses him. He is now roaring back and forth in front of the pilings, as close as he dares, causing many sets of waves to come at us. The pilings just break them up. Some workmen, about a hundred feet down and atop the pilings, have been watching the action since our arrival. "Darrin, let's paddle down and ask them if they have a cell phone."

When we get within earshot, we ask, "Do you guys have a cell phone?"

They seem genuinely concerned, but perplexed. Instead of responding, they question us as to how this got started. Finally one of the workers yells down, "It won't do you any good to call the Coast Guard!"

"Why not?"

"That's a Corps boat. He's a Corps surveyor." We are dumbfounded! The workman just lifts his hat, scratches his head, and shrugs his shoulders. He does not know what to advise.

Darrin says, "I say we stay here 'til we're sure he's gone." I agree.

As the waves subside, the Corps boat once again takes up a position directly in front of us, bow pointed dead on as if we are in a stare-down. His mirrored windows continue to make this something straight out of a horror flick. A half hour passes. He must finally sense we will not leave our protected position. As he moves away, we pray it is his quitting time. He is heading upstream. The guys on the piling structure have continued to watch the entire event. They, too, must have been wondering how this standoff would end. Once the Alexander moves out of sight, we wait another ten minutes before beginning a slow paddle down the inside of the remaining pilings. We sit at the opposite end, staring in the direction the Alexander disappeared.

After an hour of waiting, Darrin says, "Let's get going. If he returns, we can pull into shore and take everything out." In relationship to the whole of the Miss' humanity, there are still only a small handful of God's people who turn out to be total jerks. This guy must have a terrible anger raging inside, or am I just still too naïve about life on the river? We will probably never know why this happened…only that it wasted a lot of ours and the Corps' time.

"Do you suppose his working for the Corps will have any effect on the rest of the trip?" Darrin asks.

"I hope not. We don't have much time left…we will need to be suspicious of any approaching boats." We remain quiet and watchful for the remaining hours of paddling.

As dusk approaches, we are again settled emotionally. The only good in this incident, like the others, is a cementing of a working relationship. Still, it is unfortunate that only a common enemy can unite us so fully.

We have yet to find a suitable campsite. The river frontage now is all low-lying marshland and mud flats. A barge-loading/unloading site is coming up on the east bank. On the west shore is a level, sandy spot of dredging materials, probably from the docking site. With about a half hour of light, we set up camp on the dredging sand, praying the skeeters hold off until supper is finished. Darkness comes, but only a few mosquitoes. "Where do you suppose they are?" I ask.

"Come on, you can smell the chemicals? Look at that cloud hanging over the barges. If it weren't so dark I'd demand we leave."

The chemical smells continue to hang heavily in the early morning fog. We leave without breakfast. The tradeoff is cleaner air.

"Hey, Darrin, remember yesterday's cat and mouse game?"

"Yer tryin' to be funny?"

"No, no. I was thinking…perhaps we showed fear in the beginning…maybe that enabled him."

"Come on, who you kidding?"

"Seriously…in our fear we forgot about our marine radio. We coulda called the Coast Guard."

"If he'd really meant to be helpful, he's one of the dumbest boaters I ever met. Let's drop it."

At mid-morning we are still discussing barges and boat operators when a towboat and some barges approach from the rear. Before we can comment on him, his speaker comes to life. It is the Kelly O. She has been running silently and is now about a quarter mile off port. We hold our breath wondering what will be said. "Hey, guys! Great going! You did sixty miles yesterday. My hat's off to you!" I nearly fall out of the canoe. His compliment and friendliness are just what we needed.

About a half hour after the Kelly O passes out of sight, we meet our second towboat of the morning. This one is crossing the river to meet us. Will he be as friendly as the Kelly O? I doubt it. He has already traveled well over a mile, making several course changes, to keep on an intercept course with us. We are taking no chances and are nearing shore. When he is as close to us as the river depth will allow, he makes a sudden turn and sends a big wake our way.

Darrin shakes his head in disgust. "What the hell is it with these guys?"

By late afternoon the winds have picked up, bringing thunder, lightning, and a sprinkle. I suggest, "What say we camp early?" Darrin agrees.

Again the only feasible spot for tenting is a sandy mudflat opposite an unloading facility. The practice must be to dump dredging materials on the opposite shore. It is the only reason we can fathom these small, sandy areas. Neither of us cares what they are unloading, we are too near the end and weary from recent experiences. With my part of the evening chores done, I retreat to the tent. Darrin is carrying on a running conversation with mosquitoes. It isn't exactly what I call friendly communing.

Winni-The Day After

One of 28 Locks

The Glory of Natchez

Jackson Square Landing

9/11 TERRORISTS

Either Darrin has forgotten or he is saying nothing about arriving on the thirteenth. Perhaps he feels as I do: enough's enough. It is cloudy and cool with lots of oceangoing vessels, tugs, and towboats. The cargo ships are all headed north. Their wakes are gentle, like a child's roller coaster; the bigger the vessel, the calmer the wakes. Paddling close to anchored ships is a bit awesome. Canoeing next to ocean going vessels gives a whole new perspective on miniscule. Two tugs, three-quarters of a mile away on the west bank, are headed north, apparently to assist an oceangoing vessel slowing near a docking site. Moments later, Darrin groans, "Those tugs are heading our way?"

"Sure looks like it. Let stay our course until we're positive."

Within moments Darrin is irritated. "Come on! Turn us in! They're on a collision course."

"I know. I just can't believe it."

Now lined up, one behind the other, moving at full throttle, they continue charging across the river. We will never make shore. It seems the harder we paddle, the faster they move to intercept.

"It's no good! We stand a better chance facing them." Darrin agrees with my assessment.

Our initial excitement in riding rollers and canoeing past anchored cargo ships has faded. This last day is not going to be a piece of cake. The inevitable seems to be a one-two knockout punch. Traveling tandem, the two tugs are twenty yards apart. We turn to face "the music." After the first one comes as close as possible without hitting us, he revs his engines and makes a hard left. Paddling like crazy to keep balanced, I search for the eyes of the second captain. Our gazes lock. He is seeing a grizzled, tired, bald-headed man. Our eyes do not part. He quits the game. Slowing to a crawl, he turns early. Perhaps my pain caused him regret. Darrin and I cannot be mistaken for the father/son team we are. Does he have a wife and children? Maybe he wanted to leave with some pride. "Darrin, did we just see repentance?"

"Not funny." There isn't even a hint of lilt in Darrin's voice, only sadness.

"Sorry, it's either that or scream." As the tugs move back across the river to the waiting cargo ship, it is apparent they went over two miles out of their way to swamp us. We float and watch until they begin pushing the ocean-going vessel sideways into its unloading position. "When will it end?" I ask.

"Not soon enough!" Although I agree with Darrin, I wonder.

As the morning passes, towboats and tugs no longer challenge us, but Mother Nature does. She is sending quite a storm. The heavy winds are kicking up plenty of wave action. The lightning strikes are still downriver. Darrin is demanding we hug the shoreline but stay on the river.

"We need to get off."

"No, I want this trip over."

"Fine!" I'm angry because there are new and more spectacular strikes downriver. Finally I plead, "Let's get off!"

"No! I'm not getting off 'til Jackson Square."

"It's too damn risky."

"The lightning's plenty far away."

As Darrin's prognostication fades in the wind, a huge bolt of lightning strikes with an instantaneous thunderclap. My skin tingles ever so slightly as the hairs on my arms rise. I clearly feel the air and water vibrations. I can taste what seems like battery acid. The flash comes straight down over the river, less than a half mile in front of us. Splitting about two hundred yards above the river, it shoots fire east and west. Once above land, the two concurrent parts simultaneously bolt straight down.

This is not a quick bolt of lightning. It accentuates its power by coming down for several seconds. It looks like a huge divining rod, all lit up and pointing to God. I have never seen nor felt a strike of such prolonged performance, nor have I ever seen a strike split over a river. I wonder out loud, "How common do you suppose that is?"

Darrin is not curious. He wants off the river. It takes all of thirty seconds. Mother Nature's message is clear.

The storm lasts about thirty minutes. We are not on the river long when another moves in. This time there is no discussion; we are off. The system passes quickly, and once again we are headed for New Orleans.

Passing the old wharf section lets us know exactly where we are. There is no need to hurry. Paddling past these abandoned docks and buildings is relaxing, allowing us to admire and regale each other with images of past glories. We are excited to know that workers, big, burly stevedores, family men with job security, voices ringing with laughter and jokes, sweating and toiling in the heat and humidity, made history here. These musings are brought on by dilapidated, sagging buildings, leaning precariously on pilings, awaiting destruction in the next hurricane. Suddenly our joy turns to pain. Jobs have been lost; families have suffered. The discussion becomes too hard. We go silent.

After rounding the next corner we are greeted by a huge sign: "New Orleans Police Water Patrol Headquarters." Standing under it and four abreast on the dock are three policemen and a policewoman. In front of them lies their trusty steed, a swift-looking police boat, ready to move out at a moment's notice. They are waving to us. We wave back. The silence is broken by the shrill wail of a police siren screaming across the water. We wave again, thinking they are giving us a friendly hello. It is not so! "This is the New Orleans water patrol. You are ordered to immediately dock at this station!"

"Say, again! Are they kidding?" I ask Darrin.

"I don't think so, Dad."

I call out, "Are you referring to us?"

"Yes," comes the terse reply. I am incredulous. Now what? Did we violate some boating regulation? The officer certainly doesn't sound friendly. So much for a grand welcome! We turn and paddle over. It is obvious they mean business. Their hands are gripping holstered revolvers.

There is no "Hi, hello, welcome to New Orleans." Instead the officer in charge says, "Where you guys from?"

"We've been on the river since Memorial Day…started at Lake Itasca in Minnesota. We're canoeing to Jackson Square. It's not too far up, is it?" I add the question trying to be friendly and deflect what might be coming.

"Never mind that! We're asking the questions. What's in your packs?" Their hands have yet to leave their pistol grips.

"Food and clothing."

"Are you U.S. citizens?"

"Yes!"

"Do you have identification?"

"Yes!"

"Can you show it?"

"Yes!" Is this a joke? I dare not ask or move too fast in opening my pack. I am sure he is not interested in any of my smart aleck, off-the-cuff remarks. I know I am not interested in landing on the deck of this police station.

"A barge captain called in…said you boys were dark-skinned Arabs…probably loaded with explosives and headed for the Corps offices."

I can't resist. In my most innocent voice I ask, "Where are the Corps offices?" I am hoping to defuse and relax the situation as we are only moments from our big landing, with bands playing and people singing. Now, some barge operator is again trying to swamp us.

"Those buildings on the west side. They are off limits since nine-eleven." It is obvious we were nowhere near or headed toward them before being pulled off the river. They are well over a mile from where we were canoeing. Our course is clearly on the east side of the river. Finally I find my billfold and offer my driver's license. The policeman in charge takes it and relaxes.

"Sorry. The barge captain described you guys as much darker… Arab features and in army garb. Said your packs were bulging with what might be explosives. He claimed you were headed dead on for the Corps headquarters. Here's your license. Enjoy your trip." The others now take their hands off their pistols.

Enjoy the trip. Right! Where are the city fathers with a pat on the back and a friendly, "Well done?" Is this to be our welcome to New Orleans? Neither of us speaks until we are well out of earshot. "Can you believe that?" I ask Darrin softly.

The first rush of adrenaline, the one that comes when being pulled over by the police, diminished long ago. We are now both feeling anger and hurt. Again a barge operator has messed with our minds and lives. What do they have against canoeists? There can't be that many of us on the river.

Is it the Red Lake Indian and St. Mary's Catholic Mission logos? I doubt we will ever know. Does it even matter? The only good coming from this final act is more than enough evidence to show that some towboat operators are purposeful in harassing. Terrorists! Ha! What a laugh. Well at least it is another good story to tell the grandchildren.

Jackson Square is anti-climactic. Although there are lots of people walking the levee's promenade, none are interested in us. They seem distant and distracted. A canoe coming in is no big deal. No one points or waves or asks us where we have come from. Even that isn't too bad. I mean, we are dirty, sweaty, and sporting a couple days' growth. We are hidden under broad-rimmed hats and dark glasses. Besides, it is hot and humid. There is no reason to get excited and sweaty over a canoe landing.

Upon landing we are immediately greeted by a group of unkempt, strung out, homeless youth. They are eager to help us unload and carry things up the embankment. My bias envisions gear disappearing into the milling throng in Jackson Square and the Café de Monde just over the levee. "We're going to leave the gear in the canoe until our ride comes."

"Hey, man, I'll stay here and watch your stuff. You guys get a taxi."

Right! Do I look like I just stepped off the boat? "Thanks man, but my son is going to stay with the canoe while I find my brother." Darrin gets out of the canoe. His 6 foot 3 inches military look is enough to dissuade any further offers. We do, however, ask a favor. "Will you take our picture?"

"Sure, man."

Darrin stands nearest the shore while I move into the river. "It'll look good you towering over me. People will see an old, bald-headed guy and say, 'My God, if that old fart can do it, so can I'."

At the information booth next to the Café de Monde, I ask, "Can you tell me where I can find a telephone?"

"See the front corner of the Café de Monde…"

"Perhaps I can be of assistance." I turn to see Pete coming around the corner, eyes gleaming with delight. He has been sitting in the shade of the information booth. Recognizing my voice, he came out into full sun. His friendly, warm smile and excitement are heartwarming. "You actually did it! God, you look good…you lost some weight." There is genuine appreciation in his voice. It feels good.

His willingness to travel from Denver to New Orleans and back to Minneapolis, just to be of assistance, is a gift of no small proportions. For the first time I feel a real sense of pride for Darrin and me. Pete has completely let go of his own ego and is turning every second of energy and attention to our accomplishment. It is rewarding and comforting. How rare it is for this sibling to feel humbled by the genuine appreciation of an older brother. All the toil, anger, sadness, and a thousand other negatives I experienced melt away. I feel only his unspoken gift of respect. It is a true bonus.

POST SCRIPT

After six months, I'm just beginning to realize what I learned.

- Personally—I have a deeper understanding of how God's goodness sustains me.
- Bottleman—Neither he nor his daughter ever returned my calls. I pray the worst didn't happen.
- The final exploits of James and Huck and Tom are unknown to me. I never met up with them again. I found no internet-related articles. I suspect James was successful and Huck and Tom were not. I did find Dan Steinbeck's article on our trip.
- Partners—Make sure their spouses or girlfriends don't have too much pride of ownership in them.
- Barge Surfing—We did try it twice. Both times we paddled hard just to stay in the wake. It worked as long as we could paddle a hundred strokes per minute. It does not give the push ocean waves do surf boards.
- No inappropriate boating behaviors were ever reported to the Corps or sheriff's offices. At the time we saw no benefit in it. We also believed that one day this book would be published.
- My middle three fingers and right arm have most of their feelings back. I will have no Red Badge of Courage. My post-trip physical included a neck and back MRI. Some degenerative disc spacing, calcified herniation and right-sided foraminal stenosis on discs C6 and C7, coupled with poor canoeing posture, caused pinched nerves. The resulting stabbing pains and loss of arm and hand use

were temporary. A little more physical therapy and muscle strengthening is needed.

- The second night off the river, halfway through dinner, I realized my lack of exercise did not warrant the meal portion. I will need to change eating habits or face the sorry consequences.
- The mud between Baton Rouge and New Orleans is a booby trap. For the first two months off the river, my ankles and feet drove me crazy. I went to three drug stores that first night, purchasing every conceivable anti-itch medication. Nothing worked. A terrible rash, a swimmers itch of sorts, all red and bumpy, arose. Ankle high down, my feet became polka-dotted, brown socks. It felt so good to scratch them; they were soon dyed red. Whenever water touched it, the rash multiplied faster than Gremlins.
- Father Pat and the Red Lake Mission School have yet to reach their endowment goal.
- My appreciation of Darrin's physical ability and leadership has found new highs. Our marriages are intact and thriving. Our father/son relationship is still ironing out the bumps.
- Life is a bit surreal. Going farther and farther away from family, job, and stability, arguing over the dumbest things, all seemed the norm. It was a great escape. It was easy to trade my wife's lovely flower garden for the Mississippi River Valley. My thoughts constantly drift back to getting on the river.
- Next summer I will take the church youth group on the Miss. Some will grumble about covering fifteen to twenty miles a day. It is then I will take them jumping off the forty-foot high soft, sand cliffs south of Wabasha, allowing them to land knee-deep in granular sand. We will swim in the clean waters and fish like Huck and Tom. I will have them hooked. This story will never end!

GLOSSARY

Barge—a long, non-motorized, flat-bottomed boat used to carry cargo on rivers. On the Mississippi they are connected together in sets of two to twenty-four. Their function is comparable to train boxcars.

Bow—The front of the canoe.

Crashing—Portaging canoes and back packs from point "A" to "B" in a forest by following a compass reading, breaking a new trail rather than following an established path.

Dredging Barges—These are equipped with either a large digging arm, a dredge line and bucket, or a vacuum pipe that brings silt from the river bottom to a land site.

Gunwales—The top right and left-hand sides or rails of the canoe.

Indian Time—This means an activity starts when the people and moment are appropriate rather than an artificially set time. An activity could start anywhere from an hour to two hours or more from when people began gathering.

John Boats—Small, flat-bottomed boats used mainly for river fishing. The bow is squared off and thrust forward at a forty-five-degree angle.

Lock—A set-aside portion of the river, enclosed with cement walls and gates, where the water level can be raised or lowered to easily allow craft to move to the top or bottom of a dam.

Rez—An Indian Reservation.

Smudging—A blessing or cleansing ritual of sweet-grass or sage smoke. It is wafted via an eagle's feather over individuals or objects during Native American prayer and ceremonial events.

Tacking—Changing the direction of the canoe so as to allow the wind to hit it somewhat broadside, similar to filling a sail, thus aiding the movement of the canoe across the water.

Towboat—A one-, two-, or three-engine, square-bowed boat, similar in size to a tugboat and used for pushing barges up and downstream.

Trembling Sod—When a marsh dries up and leaves a layer of sod, six to twelve inches thick, suspended in air between rocks, etc., the earth will move when walked upon.

Stern—The back of the canoe.

Thwart—A bracing bar between the gunwales; it is used to provide rigidity to the canoe's shape.

Watertight Pack—These are special lightweight rubber or plastic bags. When sealed properly, they float without ever becoming water logged.

Wing-dams—Small dams jutting out, thirty to one hundred yards and perpendicular to the shore. They are used to re-direct large amounts of side water into the main river channel. This helps maintain the water depth needed for commercial traffic.